Praise for
STRINGS ATTACHED

"*Strings Attached* is a riveting tale of operatic proportions. Love, betrayal, death and redemption!"

—**Deborah Birnbaum, international opera singer and vocal coach**

"Trauma is a universal theme, and Laurinel Owen digs deep to find meaning in the twenty-seven years she spent with a narcissistic, bigamist psychopath and how her upbringing contributed to her less-than-wise choices.

"Perhaps what is not a universal theme is Ms. Owen's life as a talented and celebrated musician. The reader is swept into a world of musical notes that are more than slightly off key. It takes great courage to share one's descent into hell while being paralyzed to change the circumstances. But redemption, while a long time coming, is why readers will not want put the book down.

"Owen's story, of not only survival but also of endurance and finally healing, maps out her perilous journey—one that is ongoing as the author embraces a new way of living."

—**Donna Keel Armer, author of *Solo in Salento: A Memoir*, the *Cat Gabbiano Mystery Series*, and a series of travel anthologies on London, Rome, and Paris**

"Laurinel Owen's poignant memoir, *Strings Attached: A Memoir of Betrayal, Bigamy, and Self-Discovery*, vividly portrays the disturbing, real story of a young American cellist who innocently begins her career in apartheid South Africa. A tale of romance, deception, and sordid political secrets, her life begins to unravel, and she finds herself in financial ruin until, finally, she turns to the power of music and meditation in her search for acceptance and understanding. Laurinel relates this electrifying story with candor, courage, and humility."

—**Nancy Rosenfeld, literary agent, co-author of *New Hope for People with Bipolar Disorder, Revised 2nd Edition: Your Friendly, Authoritative Guide to the Latest in Traditional and Complementary Solutions***

"An evocative tale of love, bigamy, and betrayal that is set in a vivid context—a South African family mired in the secrets of a Nazi past."

—**Annalyn Swan, co-author of *Francis Bacon: Revelations*, Times of London Art Book of the Year, and *de Kooning: An American Master*, the 2005 Pulitzer Prize winner in Biography**

"In *Strings Attached*, author and professional cellist Laurinel Owen recounts in brisk prose and breathtaking detail the romantic conflicts and tribulations encountered by a twenty-something who, after decades of self-reflection in a variety of stimulating settings, ultimately finds inner peace."

—**Carol A. Hess, musicologist, author of *Aaron Copland in Latin America: Music and Cultural Politics*, Distinguished Professor of Music, University of California, Davis**

"Laurinel Owen has shared an amazing story in this memoir. Listening to this international cellist play so beautifully and commandingly in concert, one wouldn't know the life she's had professionally and personally. . . As the story unfolds, [she discovers] that her marriage was a lie. A lie that affected her

emotional, financial. and professional life. [In] the aftermath [she tries] to reclaim her self-confidence, identity, and financial security. From her modest Texas family upbringing to arriving in South Africa to perform in the orchestra to meeting her physicist 'husband' and moving to Long Island where they created a life together, she crafts a tale of intrigue and deception—and a heartfelt journey to resolution. A real page-turner."
   —**Tricia Foley, author of *A Summer Place: Entertaining by the Sea*, *Summer Place: Living by the Sea*, and *Marry L. Booth: The Story of an Extraordinary 19th Century Woman***

"Owen has written a thriller of a memoir that sweeps through several continents and four decades of love and betrayal. Her writing is graceful and vivid, and we are caught up in her passion for music and life. She nevertheless turns a dispassionate eye on herself and the price of self-deception. We're with her on her journey through bitterness and regret, lawsuits and despair, to healing through various forms of therapy, including psychotherapy, hypnotherapy, and the saving power of friendship."
 —**Amy Birnbaum, CBS news producer 1990–2022**

"One reads *Strings Attached* with the page-to-page anticipation of a great mystery tale. Only this tale was all too true as our heroine/writer experiences deception of every kind, playing out through several continents by her bigamist husband with his particular brand of poison tainting . . . his wives, children, inheritances, financial investments, and more. [In the] meantime, our heroine/writer, a successful cellist, is sharing her musical magic with appreciative audiences around the world.

"This is also a story of courage. Laurinel, heartbroken and confused by the lies, works constantly to support their household while she experiences one unbelievable shock after another, drawing upon a strength and determination that took her to multiple resources in search of the truth, both to unravel the events and then to understand herself, a quest in which she recovers the power she had given freely to audiences and to others but [which] had eluded her in her personal life since childhood.

"It is a story of transformation sought through body disciplines such as Tai Chi, acupuncture, and chiropractic to psychological therapies to discover and claim the fullness of her spirit. The more she sought the truths behind the experiences that taught her about herself, the more she also attracted help in unraveling the complex tangle of documents covering three continents.

"All of this is told with her artist's eye for details both physical and emotional so that the reader is invited to feel and see many layers in the story's settings.

"I will be encouraging people to read this unique, entertaining, and thought-provoking book. with confidence that it will enrich their understanding of the strength of the human spirit while it provides an extraordinary literary experience."

—Gloria D. Karpinski, spiritual director, teacher, author of *Midnight Rainbows: A Memoir, Barefoot on Holy Ground*, and *Where Two Worlds Touch*

Strings Attached :
A Memoir of Betrayal, Bigamy, and Self-Discovery
by Laurinel Owen

© Copyright 2024 Laurinel Owen

ISBN 979-8-88824-394-7

NON-FICTION
All rights reserved. No part of this publication may be reproduced, stored in a retrieval system, or transmitted in any form or by any means—electronic, mechanical, photocopy, recording, or any other—except for brief quotations in printed reviews, without the prior written permission of the author.

Published by

◄köehlerbooks™

3705 Shore Drive
Virginia Beach, VA 23455
800-435-4811
www.koehlerbooks.com

STRINGS ATTACHED

A Memoir of Betrayal,
Bigamy, and Self-Discovery

LAURINEL OWEN

VIRGINIA BEACH
CAPE CHARLES

For the woman who brought me into this world,
my mother.

And for the woman who guided me through this world,
Carol Denicker.

TABLE OF CONTENTS

Prelude..10
Overture in South Africa, 1980.................12
The National Symphony Orchestra..........20
Dynamics of Romance..............................34
Christmas *Crescendo*.................................51
Major and Minor Chords........................59
Accelerando...70
Modulation..74
Development..79
Dissonance...87
Counter Rhythms.................................... 90
Introit..102
Here Comes the Bride............................112
Second Theme.......................................119
Recapitulation.......................................132
Finale..141
Dies Kyrie...149
Misterioso... 165
sf—Subito forte...................................... 168
Retrograde... 177
Requiem...182
Interpretation..190
A German Requiem............................... 198
Pianoforte... 203
Stringendo.. 208
Dal Signo.. 216
Sturm und Drang.................................. 223
Sotto voce... 230

Pesante.. *234*
Da Capo al Fine....................................... *239*
Agitato... *245*
Diminution... *249*
Deciso... *258*
Fugue... *265*
Variations on a Theme...........................*275*
Da Capo.. *281*
Con Mistero..*288*
Bravura...*292*
Parlante..*297*
Tremolo... *316*
Sotto Voce...*321*
Suspension...*326*
Ruhig...*332*
Postlude : Funeral................................... 337

Author's Note

This is a work of nonfiction but is a reconstitution of my memories, most notably conversations. I have changed many names for reasons that will be obvious to the reader.

PRELUDE

The police caught me flying downhill just short of liftoff. No escape. I pulled to the left, rolled down my window, and faced a teenager sporting pimples and a holstered gun.

"Officer, this looks dangerous. Cars coming over the hill can't stop in time—"

The words were barely out of my mouth when we heard screeching tires. Wham, bam, shazam: four vehicles crashed into the car that had barely missed me. The youngster shakily handed me the violation.

Back at home, I wrote a letter to the court explaining that I had been followed by a persistent tailgater and was speeding for "safety's sake." I sent it off, then tacked the ticket to the corkboard above the kitchen's midget-sized fridge. There was no reply from the court, so on the Friday due date, I drove to the nearest police station to pay the fine.

"I owe you some money." I handed the ticket to the hawk-nosed, barrel-chested officer sitting at the steel desk.

He was temporarily shaken out of his stupor. "Lady, this is a court summons." His accent marked him as Afrikaans. "Today at 9 a.m. you were summoned to appear before the judge to plead your case."

I became the damsel in distress.

"Monday morning, go to the courthouse. Your number will be called again. Plead your case. He'll rule and determine the penalty."

Three days later, I walked up the forbidding stone steps to the Johannesburg courthouse. The granite entrance was festooned with statues of elephants and lions, obviously upholding the righteousness of apartheid justice.

I found my courtroom and snuck in. It was a cattle call. Most of the seats were occupied by African males: some in tribal robes, others in blue overalls. The majority wore mismatched, ragged hand-me-downs.

The judge, wearing a heavy black gown, reigned at the far end of the hall, seated high above us on a dais. Perched precariously on his balding pate was a small, stiff, white wig tied into a short ponytail with a black ribbon. Mounted behind him, the orange, white, and blue flag of South Africa seemed to crown his austere and formidable authority. As each presumed-guilty party approached the bench, the languages switched from Zulu to Xhosa to Afrikaans, with the occasional sprinkling of English.

After a dozen cases, I noted a pattern. If the accused pleaded, "Not guilty," the gavel would fall with thunderous finality. No mercy.

At last I heard my name and case number called. I stood, stepped into a small, gated enclosure, and lifted my head heavenward to the white-wigged god. I heard my crime announced for all to hear—speeding and contempt of court.

The voice questioned menacingly: "How does the accused plead?"

I wiped my palms down my skirt and choked out, "Guilty."

"Do you have anything to say for yourself?"

I launched into my story. While driving home from church, I was forced to speed to avoid a tailgating car. I became more and more nervous as I spoke. *What is the title I'm supposed to use to address a judge?* I asked myself. My mind scrambled for the word. Suddenly, I remembered and with authority proclaimed, "Your Highness . . ."

CHAPTER 1
OVERTURE IN SOUTH AFRICA, 1980

The limo picked me up on Christmas Eve in Hartford as a blizzard moved up the East Coast. Saying goodbye to Anne, my "adopted mother," was poignant—promises and a quick hug and jostling of suitcase and cello. Seated behind the driver, I watched the flakes turn from tiny crystals into swirling dervishes. Traffic stopped as we neared New York City's JFK International Airport.

Miraculously, I caught South African Airlines flight 100 and landed on Christmas Day at Johannesburg's Jan Smuts International Airport. I unbuckled the seatbelt, then released "Mr. Cello" from the window seat, folding and pocketing his red carbon-copy ticket.

"Be aware of shifting luggage in overhead compartments," a guttural voice admonished in both English and a language I assumed was Afrikaans.

I grappled toward the front of the aircraft in my fedora and long, black wool coat, which I felt gave me an air of mystery and accentuated my long blond hair. Shouldering my cello and bag, I struggled through the plane's narrow door in anticipation of my future as a self-supporting, employed adult and stepped out onto the other side of the world. A wall of dry heat hit me. My first breath of thin, mile-high air singed my lungs.

As the line of passengers swept toward Immigration, hints of reality penetrated my sleep-deprived brain. I stepped forward. Behind a Formica desk stood a whiskered officer in white shorts, knee socks, shoulder epaulets, and a peaked cap. *Is he military?* I wondered. Or maybe he was a clone of Sir Edward Elgar, Queen Victoria's court composer. I gratefully unburdened myself of my cello and handed over my passport and the newly issued "life book," the South African equivalent to the US green card, which was my permanent-residence permit and license to work.

"You're a bit far from home, lady." He squinted at my documents. "We don't have the opportunity to welcome many visitors from the States. I calculate that you are about twenty-four years old."

"Yes sir, I am," I replied, studiously polite.

"No husband?"

"No sir." I was getting really hot and sweaty in my coat and hat.

"I'm sure a pretty girl like you will easily snare a worthy bloke here."

Shopping for a guy was the last thing on my mind. I'd been taking cello lessons for so long; now it was time to see the world and earn a living by following my calling.

He pointed to my instrument. "Guitar?"

"No sir, it's a cello."

"I see." He produced a handkerchief from his pocket and swiped it across his sweaty forehead. "And what, may I ask, are you doing with that thing here in South Africa on Christmas afternoon?"

"I'll be playing in the South African Broadcasting Corporation's National Symphony Orchestra." I had waited months for South African documents. Christmas just felt like another day on the calendar—a hot and exciting one.

He tugged his whiskers, lifted his cap, then whacked my passport with his stamp. "You are going to love it here. *Next*."

Having successfully passed through Immigration, I gratefully shed the winter wool and followed the thinning stream of White passengers to the baggage claim, where two Black men in blue coveralls lifted luggage off wagons. They had lugged the load from our aircraft by hand and were now lining the suitcases in a neat row. I spotted my two matching dark-blue suitcases, college graduation gifts from my parents a few years before. Stuffed with music, each weighed at least a ton. I corralled a trolley and haphazardly piled it with all my worldly possessions.

The arrivals hall was large but nearly empty; the two or three curio shops—a coffee house and a kiosk selling cigarettes and newspapers—were closed. I scanned the area for my contact. Suddenly he found me, though George and I had never met; the cello in its ruby-red case was probably my giveaway. He was the stepfather of a cardiologist in whose home I had performed as a student. When the kind doctor learned I would be working in her homeland, she organized for her parents to take me in for a few weeks until I found my bearings.

We shook hands. I gauged his height at five feet four inches—two inches taller than me. He carried a distinguished paunch and wore platform shoes, his quick smile framed by a trimmed, devilish salt-and-pepper beard.

George eyed my luggage. "Let's get home. We're having the couple next door for Christmas dinner, and Ev is waiting on us to serve the pudding." Gallantly, he picked up both suitcases, the bigger one hovering only a couple of inches off the ground. He shepherded the cello and me through the gleaming glass doors toward the parking lot and his little white Ford.

While George juggled my luggage into the "boot," I drifted to the right side of the car. He glanced my way. "Are you driving?" I immediately recognized my mistake and with some embarrassment circled back to what in America would be the driver's side.

He deftly negotiated the exit, then asked, "How was the flight? Where did you stop to refuel?"

"Ilha do Sal off the coast of Angola, which was pretty grim," I responded.

My first hazy impression was that Johannesburg seemed similar to Dallas, where I had grown up: the highway skirted steely, modern downtown buildings flanked by scrubby vegetation, bright sun, and open sky. Twenty minutes later, as we headed toward Emerentia, the R24 dissolved into lush suburbia. Peeling blue gum trees lined the avenues. Yards were immaculately groomed. *This must be a rich country*, I thought.

We turned right into a brilliant, sunlit garden boasting blooming birds of paradise, agapanthus, and fiery red-hot pokers. Brightly shimmering ruby flowers studded trees that resembled gargantuan clones of the puny potted plants sold in grocery stores to decorate tables back home for Christmas. Here the poinsettias were magnificent monarchs as tall as the houses.

"Here we are," announced George as he cranked the hand brake.

My bleary gaze fell on the house, a single story of beige brick with a terracotta roof. Other homes in the neighborhood featured high fences around their entire properties, but the Kallmans' stood open to the street. Behind the flowering plants, though, the windows had iron grates.

We wrestled my luggage past the armored front door. Christmas dinner was in progress—three people. My cello safely poised in a corner on the polished tile floor, I surveyed the scene through North American eyes: a sweaty Black servant squeezed into a white jacket, his chest slashed by a burgundy sash, his white-gloved hands removing the remains of a silver platter of ham. He bowed with a "Yes, madam" and removed the scraps of the feast.

Greetings bounced around. My head spun, not only from the thirty hours of traveling door-to-door with no sleep but also at a scene that seemed absurd to my limited experience. I had yet to fully see in action the apartheid system where the 10 percent White population kept the other 90 percent in ignorance, servitude, and poverty.

The image screamed of a system built on servility, much like the South of my youth, where the Civil War was still being fought through proxy battles. In the 1960s and '70s, my Texas public schooling was segregated, and my Texan maternal grandmother once used the N-word in our home.

My father, a "dammed Yankee," had retorted, "Elsie, never use that word in my home again!"

She batted back, "I'll call them nigger because that's what they are."

I had a momentary flash: *Get me out of here!* Then my mother's training in Southern politeness kicked in. I had just arrived. *Give them a chance.* George indicated my seat, and we joined the tableau.

"How on earth did you find your way to Johannesburg?" Ev seemed to speak for everyone. She appeared to be older than her husband and was certainly taller. Her face was wrinkled (from the sun? cigarettes?) beneath cropped white hair.

"Well." I stalled to collect my thoughts, my history, and my spirit of adventure. "After conservatory, I got a job in an orchestra in Mexico City but realized I still needed more training, so I moved to London to study with William Pleeth. You probably haven't heard of him, but he's one of the best."

I was afraid I was bragging but didn't want them to think I was a lightweight, either. I got the sense that I was a fresh distraction from the habitual loop of local gossip.

The servant theatrically brought in the flaming plum finale. He bowed and placed the dessert (which they called "pudding") before Madam. There was a lot of oohing and aahing as the alcohol burned off and the flames died. Then Ev sliced and served while the whipped cream was passed around.

We settled into the sweet, and the conversation circled back to me.

"You were living in London?" Ev prompted.

"Yes." I shook off my fatigue and lifted the spoon. "I'd blown through my savings and had to get a job but didn't want to return to the States and fall into the traditional routine of my fellow students: graduate school. I took auditions with orchestras in France, Holland, Scotland, London."

George piped up. "What made you choose those orchestras?"

I turned my palms skyward. "The train tickets were the cheapest."

I explained that I had been offered two positions and accepted both. The first was in Edinburgh as a solo cellist with the Scottish Baroque Ensemble. I loved performing in the historic castles and was eager to stay, but the contract hinged on approval by the British government as a permanent resident, which required proof that no Briton was capable of fulfilling the job requirements.

My second opportunity came when I answered an ad in London's *Daily Telegraph* for the South African Broadcasting Corporation. Originally, I took the audition to gain experience playing under pressure. Among other pieces, I had to perform a movement of the Schumann concerto, an insanely difficult work written late in the composer's life when he was in a mental institution, hospitalized because of syphilis. The melody is disjointed and jumps all over the fingerboard.

"It must have gone okay," I said, "because here I am."

"You said yes to both offers?" asked Athol, the sunburned, balding neighbor, with a tinge of incredulity in his voice. "How did that work out?"

"I figured at least one job would fall through," I replied. And I had been correct. Even with solid contacts, my application for a work permit in the UK was denied. My student visa expired, and I was forced to return to the US to wait on approval for South African permanent residence.

"It all sounds very brave," commented Ev. "What did your parents think about you coming to the other side of the world, especially to a country with such a poor reputation as we have here?"

"I didn't ask what they thought," I said. "I've been paying my own way for several years. I decide for myself and am independent. Sometimes it's scary, but good." There was no reason to speak of my authoritarian father, who used money as a weapon of control. If he paid, I would have to do it his way. That was a condition I couldn't accept since our opinions about my future rarely aligned. My mother took his side to keep the peace and show a united front. And because they both worked long hours, teaching strings in public school, followed by private lessons at home and rehearsing with their string quartet, I learned to become self-sufficient.

George spoke up. "Then what did you think about experiencing our political nightmare?"

I experienced a moment of confusion. I had just arrived an hour before, yet I was expected to speak on current events on a foreign continent? I scrambled for an answer.

"First of all, I needed a job, and this was the offer I got. The last ten years or so, I've been sealed in a practice room four to six hours a day. My interest has been cello sonatas and chamber music. I'm a blank slate."

After dinner and a shower, I cantilevered the bedroom window open. There was no screen, so I stuck my nose out into the still-hot African air. A new job, new culture and language, new accommodation, transportation—the other side of the world! I listened. Birds faintly squabbled, and the sweet scent of frangipane drifted on a barely perceptible breeze. I breathed in Africa and my unimaginable future. Exciting, yet how could I not be apprehensive?

CHAPTER 2
THE NATIONAL SYMPHONY ORCHESTRA

The concert season began on January 12, giving me a couple of weeks to acclimatize. Without public transportation, I needed a car to get to work. George was the car maven. Together we scoured the classified ads in the back pages of Johannesburg's daily paper, *The Star*. His initial advice was to get a *bakkie* (a little pickup truck) so I could "throw the cello in the back." I countered, "And rain and sun?"

The search continued. All the money I had saved from playing three summers with the Filarmónica de las Américas in Mexico City had evaporated in rent and lessons in London. My yearly starting salary was R10,000 (South African rands: about $12,500 in 1980 dollars). Without a penny in my pocket, this seemed like a fortune, especially since I could count on a check every month.

On a handshake, George offered a short-term loan of R1,700. This generosity enabled the purchase of a 1976 sunbaked-brown Ford Cortina, a four-door coupé with lightly worn, tan, plastic bucket seats. The three-speed gearshift was no problem since I had learned to operate a manual transmission in a Sears parking lot in the family's greenish mid-'60s Rambler when I was fifteen—while my younger brother, Darrel, whooped with laughter at my initial ineptitude. At thirteen, he'd already learned to hot-wire the car.

I practiced shifting from first gear into second with my "wrong" hand, right elbow resting on the doorframe. After a few turns into oncoming traffic, I got the hang of driving on the left side of the road.

As I found my bearings, I observed that almost every property had guard dogs: rottweilers, German shepherds, pit bulls, and especially Rhodesian ridgebacks—African-bred lion killers. Crime seemed to be a systemic concern. Open windows were a temptation. Thieves would thrust fishing poles into an unprotected room and snag whatever was within hooking distance.

After a week or so, I found gorgeous accommodations in Northcliff, several kilometers away from George and Ev. I shared the kitchen with the owner, Michaela, whose husband spent more time in Germany than in Jo'burg with her. My side of the house was entirely private. Its sunken living room allowed me to position my new stereo system to sonic perfection so I could blast my Beethoven, Brahms, and Shostakovich LPs (my collection from the US had finally arrived!) to skin-tingling highs. The bathroom's sliding glass door opened to a huge avocado tree whose fruit I ate every day for breakfast, sliced on whole grain bread from a local bakery. All this for R200 a month, which I could just afford.

I was still finding my way around, so George kindly gave me a ride on my first day of work and dropped me off in the parking lot of the South African Broadcasting Corporation's Auckland Park high-rise office tower. In the gathering summer heat, I stepped through the automatic doors into air-conditioning and first-day jitters: new job, new colleagues, new repertoire. Would I fit in professionally, make friends, and be accepted? Would my playing be good enough?

A uniformed security guard checked me in, and my photo was taken for the required ID; both the building and the employees were potential targets for terrorism. The SABC was the state-owned vehicle for disseminating apartheid propaganda and a monopoly that controlled the only three TV channels—one each for English, Afrikaans, and Bantu (a general term for the hundreds of African languages, primarily Zulu and Xhosa)—as well as several radio stations. The guard escorted me through a labyrinth and down to a lower level, where I was handed over to the orchestra's manager, Tony.

Tony's cigarette smoldered in a green holder. Was it jade? Whatever the material, it was the exact color of his suit, which featured stylishly wide lapels. His brightly patterned tie was also broad. He transferred his cigarette to the other hand as he extended his right. "Welcome. Let me show you where to unpack."

He ushered me into a smallish, wood-paneled auditorium. The stage was at entry level and set up for a ninety-piece orchestra. About 250 to 300 seats fanned up toward a glass-walled recording booth. I set my case on the cello side (to the right, facing the conductor's podium). Tony indicated my assigned position in front of the double basses: last chair of the cello section.

I had no idea of the programming for the first concert. As Tony turned to take another drag on his cigarette, I went to the music stand at my appointed seat and opened the folder. Bedřich Smetana: Overture to *The Bartered Bride* (irreverently called "The Battered Broad"), a late Mozart piano concerto, and Brahms's First Symphony. Glancing through the Smetana, I hoped the tempo, *vivacissimo*, wasn't as fast as I feared—running eighth notes in cut time. Well, I'd find out soon enough. I returned to my cello and released it from the garrote holding its neck in place.

As I unsnapped my bow from the case, other musicians were also unpacking, tightening and rosining their bows, tuning, and greeting one another. A smiling, tanned woman with frizzy hair set her cello beside mine. She was a few inches taller than I and wore perfectly fitting slacks. The blue scarf around her neck contrasted with a yellow silk T-shirt. Though I was focused on the upcoming rehearsal, it felt good to be acknowledged. With a smile and a heavily accented voice, she said, "Happy New Year. I'm Irit. Obviously you're new."

We had only a few moments for introductions. It was 10 a.m. Tony reemerged with a fresh cigarette clenched between his teeth, clapping his hands to indicate showtime. Everyone found their seats. I had no stand partner and sat alone. The rest of the section sat two to a stand. The concertmaster, who sat in the first chair of the first violin section and led the orchestra, stood and pointed his bow toward the middle of the ensemble.

The principal oboe sucked on a reed. On cue, he pushed the carved sliver into the ebony, silver-keyed barrel. His face ballooned and turned red, and a beautiful, clear A (442 Hz) announced the pitch. Our leader matched the A with a gentle stroke of his bow. Next, the concertmaster invited the winds, brass, and finally the strings to tune, a necessary ritual observed by every orchestra around the world.

An anticipatory hush fell. Our conductor swooped in and jumped onto the podium.

"Smetana."

There was a general jumble of page turning and fumbling. He tapped the stand with the baton, raised his right hand, scanned the group to make sure all eyes were on him, then gave the upbeat, downbeat, and we were launched.

My worst fears were realized at warp speed. Everyone else seemed to be in perfect unison. I wasn't even playing by the seat of my pants. The syncopation, ties, and offbeats were way beyond my sight-reading abilities.

We finished bashing through the entire overture, and while the conductor had his back to us as he rehearsed the violins, I took the chance to mime the notes on my cello's fingerboard in a desperate bid not to make a fool of myself on the first day. Thankfully, I was sitting in the back. There was no doubt what I would be doing that evening.

We turned to the Brahms symphony, which I had played in college. When we reached the last movement and the entire string section soared together, I was transported back to high school. Our orchestra conductor had chosen it for our school's pride song, which we sang at Friday-afternoon pep rallies to cheer on the football team.

An hour and a half into the three-hour morning rehearsal, Tony returned and clapped to announce, "Teatime." Most of the musicians put away their instruments, though a few remained in the hall for individual practice.

I rose from my chair to stretch, and Irit graciously introduced me to a few players. The cello section, nine members strong, was led by Hilda, a sun-dried South African whose cigarette dangled via a long, Marlene Dietrich–style ebony holder. Her wraparound Indian skirt spoke of a Bohemian proclivity, and she advertised, to whomever would listen, her gambling prowess at the roulette tables in Swaziland, where betting was legal.

Johnny was the born-again Mormon principal percussionist.

"Look out for this one," Irit warned. "He has an unerring eye for the pretty ladies."

At this, Johnny grinned, licked his lips, and playfully slapped her backside. Irit pointed out a few other string players who were also South African nationals, but most of the ninety musicians were imported from Europe. "I'll introduce you to Bob, first trombone, and Mike, second. They're the only other Americans."

"And you?" I asked Irit. "I can't place your accent."

"I'm from Tel Aviv. I came here eight years ago with the guy over there, second flute." She gestured dismissively past the viola section to a man polishing the head joint of his instrument. "But we're divorced now."

"And the conductor?" I inquired.

"He's imported from Switzerland. We don't have a permanent conductor. It's a rotating roster, mostly from Europe: the UK, Germany, Italy, Scandinavia, occasionally the States."

"I can't believe his energy. The guy is dancing around like a marionette."

"Just wait," Irit laughed. "He'll be near collapse by tomorrow. The high altitude takes a while to get used to. And coming here from Europe is a real schlepp since the planes have to fly around the western bulge of Africa."

* * *

A few weeks into the job, I found my rhythm with rehearsals, performances, and recording sessions and felt more at ease. In addition to our live concerts, which were recorded for radio broadcast, we occasionally filmed programs in the studio. The SABC also ran television programming from 6 p.m. to midnight with a few imported shows from the States and Europe. Saturday afternoons featured White athletes playing cricket or rugby—colonial games.

During the concert season, we practiced six hours a day at the broadcasting tower, which was tiring, especially when the orchestra rehearsed Haydn, Mozart, or Verdi with their simple baseline cello parts. I preferred more challenging music. On Thursday lunch hours and Friday and Saturday evenings, we moved downtown to perform on the stage at city hall. The musicians entered through the stage door rather than the main President Street entrance, whose grandiose Ionic columns and half dome were flanked by massive palm trees.

The orchestra also met at city hall for dress rehearsals. The resonance of the vast, open space filled my heart and imagination with an inner vibrancy, an anticipatory electricity. Cases and bags were scattered throughout the auditorium's thousand or so vacant chairs, and though we played only for ourselves, the hall felt charged with energy, and so did I.

Often, the conductor was already on the podium, leafing through the score and considering a few gnarly passages that remained scattered or needed intonation work. Excepting disasters during a previous rehearsal or specific passages needing review, we ran the program in performance order. This gave me a chance to learn the repertoire, as I had little experience.

Generally, at the dress rehearsals, after we'd rehearsed the first two selections and before running the large-scale work, such as a romantic symphony, Tony returned and announced, "Teatime." The entire orchestra charged down two city blocks to the Brazilian, a long, narrow Italian coffeehouse with bar stools positioned along a Formica counter on which a conveyor belt ran. We shouted our orders as we entered and crowded together, trying to get the first espresso, cappuccino, or toasted mortadella-and-mozzarella panini that sailed out of the kitchen past our eager noses. Dirty cups and plates went on the upper deck of the belt for their return to the kitchen. We had twenty minutes to drink, eat, pay, then rush back onstage for the second half of the rehearsal, now caffeinated and satisfied.

For concerts, we dressed in long, formal black gowns for the women and white ties and tails for the men. The auditorium sparkled under the illumination of enormous crystal chandeliers. Our audience comprised the elite, all well-dressed couples—women decked out in their jewelry and cocktail dresses, men in elegant suits and ties. Like the orchestra, everyone in the audience was White.

That was no surprise. "Native" Africans couldn't afford the tickets, nor could they legally sit with the White audience, and they would never have made it back to their townships before their 9 p.m. curfew. "Coloureds"—Indians and Malays—were an in-between ethnicity also segregated and excluded from concerts. They lived in prescribed areas. (My Dutch friend Pim Broere, the impresario, told me his ex-wife, who was German, was once barred from the hall for wearing an Indian skirt because the guards thought she was Coloured.) Rather than considering the gross inequalities, I concentrated on learning the symphonic repertoire. My calling was music, not politics.

There I was, buried in the back of the cello section, last chair. But within a couple of weeks, I was asked to reaudition. Our cello section's second chair, "principal B," was vacant—a position directly under the conductor's nose: more interesting, more responsibility, more challenging, more money. I badly coveted that spot. Even though I was contracted as a full member of the symphony, the leaders of each section had yet to gauge my playing ability and level. I felt confident with the Concerto in B minor, Opus 104, by Antonin Dvořák.

We met in a wood-paneled room across the hall from our usual rehearsal space. I sat facing the principal players of the string, wind, brass, and percussion sections, who were fanned out in front of me while I performed from memory. My accompanist pounded out the orchestral reduction on a seven-foot Steinway grand piano.

The concerto opens with eighty-six bars of full orchestra—strings, winds, and brass. It feels like the exposition to a symphony. In this mini performance, my accompanist cut the introduction until the piano diminuendoed into a hushed tremolo. I attacked the first B with all my weight, my right arm sinking into the bow, pulling it fast to follow with the two quick notes at the tip, the weak part of the bow. The motive developed, resolving into forceful chords. The work is powerful and both physically and emotionally demanding for the solo cellist. I was well prepared and confident since I had performed the concerto in competitions and auditions over the last several years.

Then the concertmaster placed several excerpts from the standard orchestral repertoire on my stand. It was the Finale of Tchaikovsky's Fourth Symphony. He pointed to the middle of the page—running sixteenth notes ("semiquavers" in British parlance, which was used)—and indicated the tempo and that I was to read the music "at sight," with no preparation. All said, I played well. I was still young enough to think that enthusiasm and determination compensated for experience.

Over the following weeks, I waited patiently but received no feedback regarding my audition, which was frustrating. Was the committee looking for something I didn't have? Or was the admin dragging their feet so they wouldn't have to pay me more? I didn't feel comfortable asking my colleagues, thinking that would sound arrogant.

Two months after the trial, the orchestra was scheduled to play *Scheherazade*, a dramatic tone poem by Nikolai Rimsky-Korsakov that symphonically portrays the tales of the *Arabian Nights*. For this performance of the Russian masterpiece, our conductor was a young, dynamic, muscular, full-haired Persian, Ali Rahbari, who had recently escaped Iran and the persecution associated with allegiance to the shah.

Unfortunately, during our second rehearsal, when the orchestra's climax diminished, sensually inviting the entrance of the contemplative cello solo (undulating arpeggios and ornamented melodies, often in duet with the violin), it became apparent that first cellist Hilda's technique was not up to the challenge. Her sound petered out as her bow ricocheted across the strings like a Mexican jumping bean. Her fingers were not merely out of tune; they found notes from an entirely different piece—an atonal one.

It was only two days before the first performance, and there was a total breakdown. Conductor Rahbari cut off the orchestra, slashing the air with a wild gesture, and violently threw the baton down on the podium, where it bounced and landed in front of Hilda's endpin.

Our concertmaster/leader, whose role was to represent the musicians, was an intense Lebanese violinist named Omar. His luminous tone, passion for the music, and in-depth knowledge of the repertoire commanded my respect. Now he stood, his wavy, graying hair falling over his brow. He tucked his violin under his armpit and slapped the music closed.

"Completely unacceptable!" Omar's voice was shrill. "We cannot continue under this ridiculous circumstance." In a fit of spit-squirting theatrics, he stormed out of the rehearsal. For a few seconds, the entire orchestra froze.

The conductor flattened his hand over his heart and bowed while gently indicating to Hilda that she should follow him into the hallway. She set her cello on its side and the bow on the stand. Her already slight frame seemed to crumple. As Hilda exited the auditorium, her tiny feet barely kept her ballerina-like slippers from slipping off.

The door closed behind her. Cacophony erupted. What was happening? The first bassoonist stood and theatrically lit up a cigarette. The principal second placed his violin on the chair and walked to his case to dry-swallow a little pill. Johnny rolled the snare drum. I overheard a violist say, "About time."

The notes before me swam across the staff as I imagined how Hilda must feel: humiliated, embarrassed, crushed. All this on top of the residual nerves of playing a big solo for which she was unprepared. The orchestra had responded like a pit of vipers ready to devour one of its own.

Ten minutes later, the hallway door opened. Tony charged into the rehearsal hall and motioned for me to step out of the auditorium. At first, I was unsure he was gesturing to me. I laid my instrument down with the neck slanted across the chair and carefully set the bow on the stand. The entire ensemble watched me walk across the auditorium. I hadn't the slightest idea what was happening, but the tempo of the gathering drama was *allegro* (lively).

Omar was pacing the corridor, his violin still tucked under his arm like a rifle. He swung around and gulped in a dramatic slurp of air: "You'll move up to first chair and play the solos." It was an order.

The conductor spoke in a suave *sostenuto,* his words prolonged and fingers expanding through the hair on his temple. "I've heard so much about your musicianship, my dear. Now we will give you the opportunity to express it."

In one dizzying moment, I took over the leadership of the cello section. *Is this really happening?* Amid a cloud of excitement laced with anxiety, I returned to the hall and removed my handbag and instrument from the last chair. Another cellist packed away Hilda's cello and stored it in Tony's office. I sat down and somewhat shakily greeted my new stand partner, Maureen, a rosy-cheeked lass from somewhere near Wales. Her wide-eyed look asked, *"What is this all about?"* But I needed every second of the five minutes I was granted to prepare the solos. As I stabbed a hole in the floor with my endpin (an atavistic habit I've since abandoned now that I respect floors), I glanced up and saw Rahbari's arm encircle the concertmaster's shoulder. The gesture encouragingly said, *"We have solved the problem."*

He jumped on the podium, eyes scanning from left to right across the orchestra, then back to the trombones. The baton lifted and dropped into the downbeat. The brass section introduced the scene in commanding unison. An ocean of sound transported us as the upper strings played the melody and the cellos described the waves in rocking triplets. The brass *fortissimo* ebbed. The strings relaxed with a decrescendo, and Scheherazade's tale was taken up by the solo violin. I positioned my fingers simultaneously on four notes and pulled my bow from the C string up to the A to produce the rippling arpeggios that represented the undulating sea. The two voices, violin and cello, intertwined.

At 4 p.m., the rehearsal concluded. I had survived. Although it had not been my best playing, I longed for a pat on the back. The only buzz was from the other musicians wondering what happened to Hilda and if she was coming back. We later learned she had been given the week off. She returned as a member of the cello section, relieved of her leadership responsibilities, which she seemed to prefer. The pressure of performing alone had likely become too demanding, and nerves had defeated her.

I practiced like a demon for three days before the first performance, experimenting with the speed of my vibrato, deciding on which note to change the bow direction, timing the shifts, exacting intonation, and working to perfect a warm, sensual, projecting tone that could penetrate the far reaches of the city hall auditorium. Not only was I committed to expressing the music's essence, but I also wanted to establish my ability to lead. It was my chance to prove my worth.

On the evening of my debut, I was still warming up backstage when the manager announced the curtain call with clapping hands. Mingling with the other black-robed players, I walked onstage and, with superficial confidence, took my new seat at the head of the section. I was psyched and prepared, but string players' anxiety shows in the bow stroke. Any jitters result in a bouncing bow rather than smooth, supple *legato*. I gazed out into the audience and saw, in her usual fourth-row aisle seat, the critic from *The Star*. She was flaunting her white notepad. I thought, *I'll show her what it means to play the cello.*

We performed the first half of the program. After the applause, the audience dispersed during the "interval," and the orchestra exited the stage. Twenty minutes later, the hall lights dimmed. We returned to the stage and quietly retuned. I heard the throbbing harp arpeggios, saw the baton's wave that signaled the cue for my solo entrance, and inhaled. My bow sank into the D string; my fingers and arm vibrated to their maximum. The solo violin and I interlaced melody and accompaniment to reframe the fable. There were moments when the rapture of the harmonies supporting the melodies brought tears to my eyes and the notes on the page were in jeopardy of swimming away. I desperately tried to stay focused over the thirty minutes of the tone poem. When the brass trumpeted their final fanfare, the orchestra rose together to gratefully accept a standing ovation.

Surrounded by the decibels of ninety musicians expressing what words could not, I felt a profound sense of privilege at being able to serve the music and share in its interpretation. How was it possible for these tunes, rhythms, and textures to be formed in someone's head, notated on paper, and then recreated by a huge and varied ensemble of instrumentalists? This feeling of awe was especially powerful during the first performance.

The next morning, I read a review in *The Citizen*: "The new young lady leading the cellos is an artist." The praise was inspiring. I privately celebrated and doubly committed.

Now the real work began. I had to learn the repertoire: symphonies, concertos, and overtures by Beethoven, Mozart, Haydn, Brahms, Schubert, Schumann, Tchaikovsky, Mendelssohn, Prokofiev, and Shostakovich. The counterpoints, harmonies, and sheer volume of musical vibrations that had inspired me mostly through records and miscellaneous live performances up until now were motivating. So was the pressure of my new responsibilities.

My duties included coordinating the cello score with the concertmaster's bowings (the direction the bow moves). The section leaders received copies of the first violin part, which we had to follow when our melodies coincided. The librarian would then transfer any changes into the other players' copies.

My bowings, such as where to change bow direction during a *legato* passage or how many notes to put in a slur, often produced grumbles from my colleagues, who were used to playing a Sibelius symphony, for example, the same way they had for years. Sometimes the conductor would stop us and request a different bowing. Then from the desk behind me I'd feel a tap on my shoulder or a bow poking my back, and a colleague would request a "rubber" to erase the old bowings. It got old real fast.

Lack of experience and knowledge of the repertoire motivated me to listen to recordings, study scores, and endlessly bash away at awkward passages with the metronome. I was only a few months into my new life, riding a professional high tempered by my inner critic saying I wasn't up to the job. I could hear my father yelling from the other side of the house while I practiced: "Do it again. You keep missing that shift. Slow it down and do it right. Can't you hear it?" His love and praise seemed to depend on what chair I got after an audition.

I tried to balance my insecurity by putting in more time and working harder.

CHAPTER 3
DYNAMICS OF ROMANCE

Warming up onstage before each concert, just before the heavy crystal chandeliers dimmed, my stand partner and I had a perfect view of the audience. We soon began recognizing subscribers and would acknowledge familiar faces with a subtle wave from behind our cellos.

"I love that ancient couple in the first-row aisle seats," Maureen said one Thursday night. "She is gorgeous. He is like a statue. So imposing. I bet he's a surgeon."

We dug into the next rhythmic passage, independently reviewing our parts until another page turn.

"Do you see that guy in the seventh row?" I pointed, pretending to indicate an instruction but instead admiring the man's deep tan, luscious hair, broad shoulders, and intense focus. "The one sitting alone between two empty seats? He's been here every Thursday for weeks."

Maureen casually glanced over her cello's scroll and faked tuning her C string. "The guy in a striped shirt and tan pants? I'd say he is at least a hunk and a half."

"What do you think he's looking at?"

"You, of course." With a nod, she found the subsequent exposed passage, and we continued our last-minute drilling before the conductor jumped on the podium, gave the downbeat, and we rocketed into another concert.

* * *

Six months after my arrival in South Africa, I turned twenty-five. I invited my friends from the orchestra to a party. Turkey was not indigenous to South Africa, but I found a frozen specimen imported from Israel that I managed to defrost and roast. I sliced fresh bread, opened jars of mustard and mayonnaise, set out beer and wine, then cranked up the volume: Bee Gees, Billy Joel, Barbra Streisand, Donna Summer, and Diana Ross. It was winter and cold at the end of June, so we danced in my living room and stood in the kitchen around the buffet, filling one another in about our pasts and how we ended up at the bottom of the world.

My Israeli colleague, Irit, and I were tightening bonds: coffee on days off, followed by wandering through the cosmetic aisles of Stuttaford's department store in Rosebank, testing perfume and eyeing the knockoff designer handbags.

We discussed everything. Irit had just married her next-door neighbor, David, an attorney, after leaving her flutist husband several years earlier. I had separated from a German violinmaker boyfriend in London. Her parents had escaped Hitler's Germany. My family moved seven times before I was thirteen. Irit was dedicated to family. I was escaping mine. She became the older sister I never had.

Despite sanctions, Johannesburg was vibrantly alive. Theater, cinema, music, lectures, dance, opera, and art were varied and creatively fertile. The deadwood was television. At work I was constantly teased because the hot TV serial of the 1980s was *Dallas*, with its titillating intrigue of greed, corruption, and unholy liaisons.

I didn't have a television and only saw our concerts on the studio monitor, but friends told me that the news from the SABC detailed Black-on-Black violence in the townships, armed robberies, and White women being raped by native assailants. This kept the White minority vigilant and suspicious. Though I went to school in the segregated South, where there was plenty of prejudice, I saw that the Black faces who surrounded me were human, kind, and caring on both continents.

As winter turned into spring and the jacaranda trees blossomed, I decided to move. I loved my accommodations, but the landlady had moved to the Cape Province, and I now shared the kitchen with her son, who decided on a whim to double the rent.

I answered a classified ad in *The Star* and signed a lease to rent a little yellow brick house about two miles from the SABC with Julie, the ex-wife of the orchestra's principal oboist. She was Welsh and had custody of their two-year-old son, Christopher, an exact miniature of his towheaded dad.

The Afrikaans neighborhood surrounding No. 14A Glasgow Road in Westdene was dotted with tiny cookie-cutter houses, one-car garages, and minuscule gardens cordoned off by fences and protected by the usual guard dogs. The three-bedroom house Julie and I shared was distinguished by spectacular ruby-red bougainvillea twirling around the wrought iron fence near the front gate.

To help with the housekeeping, Julie hired Victoria, a member of the Xhosa tribe. It seemed all women domestics were named after English monarchs; at least, that was how they introduced themselves to their White employers. Elizabeth was the other common choice. Victoria wore the traditional attire—a hand-printed, loose-fitting, floor-length dress and turban headdress of gold, orange, and black. Her hands were dry and raw from hours of washing clothes and dishes without gloves, and her bare feet were callused and split, but her face, with its high, round cheekbones, radiated joy, especially when her lips parted in a broad smile.

Victoria cared for Christopher, mopped the floors, scrubbed the bathroom, washed the dishes and clothes, and ironed sheets, jeans, and even underwear. We had a washing machine, though no dryer. A clothesline extended from just outside the back door and across the cement patio. Starting on one side of the line, she pinned wet clothes that waved like colorful Tibetan prayer flags and were bone dry by the time the last sock was positioned at the far end. Then Victoria could go back, clear the line, and start ironing.

Employing Victoria was a luxury for which I felt some guilt. We provided a tiny one-room lean-to composed of cinder blocks and a corrugated tin roof behind our modest brick home. She had a toilet and sink but no shower. The single window was seven feet off the ground and faced south, away from the sun. Her accommodations had no heat or air-conditioning, though neither did ours. My conflict swiveled between guilt at the exploitation of such cheap labor and solace that she was employed rather than starving in the oppressive slum conditions of the segregated townships. I saw what I wanted to see and justified my decision.

When I tried to discuss my concerns with South African friends, the response was invariably "Yes, you're right. We should have followed the example you set in the States and slaughtered the natives." I had no reply. I was in a foreign country, could not change the system, and, as a guest, had to live on their terms—or leave. My small consolation (delusion?) was that I treated Victoria with respect and paid the going rate for a full-time, live-in servant (a fraction of what I earned, which was not extravagant).

⁎ ⁎ ⁎

Soon after we moved in, I went to my mailbox and found a light-blue airmail envelope with a twenty-five-cent US stamp. It was from Gary, a former beau. With a frisson of unanticipated pleasure, I tore open the fragile paper.

We had first met three years before in a Stop and Shop parking lot in Hartford, Connecticut, the Wednesday before Thanksgiving. It was late afternoon but already dark and cold. My car had died. Gary gallantly offered to jump the dead battery. While it charged, we exchanged a little background. I was a cello performance major at the Hartt School of Music, and he was finishing a degree in economics at Trinity College. He started the car and asked me out for dinner.

I thought I was in love. His thick, sandy-blond hair, lean, muscular frame, and interest in global travel and business appealed to my inexperienced, open mind and heart. We spent the spring semester together as a couple but planned our futures in opposite geographical directions. We were twenty-two years old and not ready to commit.

I read Gary's letter. He was traveling the world after earning an MBA in international affairs and wanted to make South Africa one of his stops. His goal was to invest in or start a business. South Africa might be a possibility. Could we meet up? I was wary because the way he had ended our relationship had not seemed honest, but I wrote that yes, he could come.

I fell under his spell for the second time as soon as he stepped through the sliding glass door. We spent his two weeks in South Africa enjoying dinners out and walks around the pond down the street. He attended symphony concerts, and again we ended up in bed. He was attentive, interested, and loving. What young woman wouldn't be seduced by the arrival of an athletic, rich, gorgeous young man coming all the way to Southern Africa to woo her?

Gary left with promises to return. And he did, after spending time with gorillas in Rwanda, touring the pyramids of Giza, and exploring the Forbidden City in Beijing. He brought back an ivory bracelet (poor elephant), an ounce of Beluga caviar, a bottle of Georgian sparkling wine, and a beautiful, small, green-jade statue of a Chinese dragon. He and baby Christopher bonded, he came to all my concerts, and he became a fixture on Glasgow Road.

As Gary and I grew closer, his jealousy reared its ugly head if I even casually spoke with another man. His response was either stone-cold silence or, as he discovered my insecurities, cruel and hurtful putdowns.

Four months after Gary's arrival, the principal bassoonist and I had lunch together in one of the restaurants at the SABC (rather than our usual canteen dining). Patrick was an Irishman engaged to a gorgeous Jewish woman, for whom he was converting. Over lunch, he regaled me with the tale of his required circumcision. The number of stitches he endured increased with every telling.

When I recounted the story to Gary, thinking he'd find it funny, he went ballistic. "I can't believe you'd have an intimate lunch with that guy and allow him to talk about that!"

"What do you mean?" This was absurd. "It's like fishermen and their stories about the big one. Patrick is totally harmless. This wasn't a confidence. He brags to everyone."

"I won't put up with your flirtations." His rage was mounting, and he slammed his fist on the tabletop, shaking the plates.

I backed down and apologized, promising to distance myself from further contact. I still wanted to please him, but the list of prohibitions was lengthening. He said I was fat and didn't exercise enough, my concerts were mind-numbingly dull, and I practiced too much and didn't understand him. His specialty was icy silence. Unfortunately, our relationship was, as before, tumultuous.

I was attempting to dance around my supposed misdemeanors one afternoon when I answered the phone. The voice was baritone and German accented. I sat cross-legged on my African rug, facing a book-lined wall with the receiver crammed between my ear and shoulder as I scanned the shelf for a misplaced Russian novel.

The caller gave his name, but it was way too long and foreign to catch, let alone remember. He got right to the point. He was a professor at the University of the Witwatersrand, would be traveling to the UK to give a lecture at Oxford University, and wanted to buy a cello for his son while he was there. He had read in a concert program that I had spent time in England.

"Could you possibly give me some advice?" he asked.

I gave the caller the contact details for several of my British cellist friends while my finger edged across book spines. Casually making my recommendations for where to shop, I quickly wrapped up, stood, and tilted Turgenev's *Fathers and Sons* off the shelf as the conversation ended.

Just before I hung up, I offered, "If you ever attend a National Symphony concert, come backstage and say hello."

In the meantime, my relationship with Gary continued to deteriorate. I loved our discussions of literature (we were both reading the Russian classics) and future dreams, running together on the university track, and his quick wit. But if I unwittingly provoked him, his anger would detonate.

I was used to criticism from my childhood, when my father rarely praised my brother or me. We were told what to do and how to do it. And so I used every technique in my limited twenty-five-year-old's arsenal to mold myself into the image Gary desired, but still he complained I spent too much time with my friends and didn't pay enough attention to him. It didn't matter that I had a job and he didn't. He insisted he should come first.

After nine months, our relationship imploded. It was October, which in South Africa, on the mile-high escarpment, was heavenly. The clean, bright spring air and perfect-temperature days were intoxicating. That evening, all the windows in my house were open, and the little white sparks in the centers of the scarlet bougainvillea blooms seemed to reflect the stars. I was preparing stuffed trout with roasted new potatoes and a fresh green salad when I heard his car door slam shut. He entered through the sliding glass door with an aura of anger pulsating around him.

My reaction was to soothe and appease. I joyously opened my arms for an embrace. He was stiff and obviously aggrieved. *What is it now?*

"You make me sick," he said. "No way can I eat that poison. You and your food are disgusting."

He torpedoed along the six-foot parquet hallway to the bedroom. I heard him collide with the bed and scanned my mind, searching for a possible crime. Nothing.

That was it. *Enough*. I couldn't play the rag doll any longer.

My mind in turmoil, I scraped the food into the garbage, then silently slid open the front door. His car was parked behind mine in the driveway. I unlatched the gate and walked down the street, guided by the moonlight. Continuing two miles through the park around Westdene Dam to the SABC tower in Auckland Park, I showed my ID, and the guard let me in after hours.

I phoned Irit. Luckily, she answered. She was just putting her baby son to bed. Her husband would pick me up, and I could stay overnight at their house. Thirty minutes later, my savior screeched into the parking lot in his tiny green Italian sports car.

The next morning, Irit dropped me back home so I could pick up my cello and change before our rehearsal. I didn't know what to expect. Would Gary still be there? His car wasn't in the driveway. Would the house be trashed? Retracing my steps from the previous night through the front gate and up to the sliding glass door, I found a mountain of cut flowers wilting on the front step in the early-morning heat. What a relief to find him gone. Though I was confused and agitated, I had to attend rehearsal and focus on the score. I'd have to fake it.

I brushed my teeth, changed my blouse, grabbed my cello and music, then raced off to work. While we rehearsed Schubert's Unfinished Symphony, the previous evening spun like a top through my head. I had to walk away—no, run away—from his insanity. Did that mean I hadn't tried hard enough?

When I returned home that afternoon, I found a message on the answering machine. Gary apologized and was so sorry. It would never happen again. But I held firm. I was done. His jealous rages and stormy silences tipped the balance, and I had fallen off the scale.

I had put a lot of effort, time, and emotion into that relationship. Admitting I was wrong about him threw me into a dark, deep hole. I lost thirty pounds and my self-confidence, which was so powerful professionally and yet so lacking when it came to love. Soon after our split, the orchestra's second bassoonist told me she was dating him and that he'd found a South African company to invest in. I was happy to let her have him.

Some weeks later, after a lunch-hour concert, I was chatting backstage with another musician when our conversation was interrupted by the approach of a tall, bronzed man wearing a blue-and-white-striped raw-silk shirt and tan slacks. His thick hair was silver at the temples, his gaze intense. I took a breath and tried not to stare. There stood the man from row seven whom I'd ogled for weeks. We turned to include him, and introductions were made.

"I've just returned from the UK," he said in a German accent, his focus on me. "Thanks to your suggestions, I found a beautiful eighteenth-century Banks School cello for my son at Hills & Sons."

My colleague and I exchanged glances. "Congratulations," I replied. "You went directly to the top: the world's premier violin shop."

That's a powerful connection, I thought, then let it go. His vibe felt too aggressive, but he sure was hitting all the buttons from the attraction angle.

A week later, I received a postcard depicting a Turner seascape from London's Tate Museum. It was signed KLAUS VON ÖSTERBERG. (No wonder I didn't get his name the first time on the telephone.) He asked if I would like to see the cello he'd bought. I wasn't so interested in the instrument as I was in him, but the breakup with Gary was still an ache, so I let the thought dissolve. However, Klaus was persistent and called again. We set a date.

Spring was past its prime. The lavender blooms of the jacaranda trees lining the streets fell like dancing snow and filmed the roads. A faint aroma of honey hung in the air as Klaus pulled up to the house in his ancient Ford Escort. I slid open the glass door. The cello entered first.

The man was unstylishly dressed in a once white undershirt and tan chinos held up by a thinning black leather belt, accessorizing the ensemble with black rubber flip-flops. He could have been wearing either a tux or bathrobe and I would still have been dumbstruck. He was movie-star handsome but not trying to impress. I looked for a wedding ring. None. *He must be divorced.*

I assumed a natural, interested-but-aloof persona; after all, he was seeking my expertise. As I tightened and rosined the bow, I asked what subject he taught. He explained that he was a physicist in charge of the nuclear accelerator at the University of the Witwatersrand (Wits), where he designed and carried out experiments with subatomic particles to unearth the mysteries of matter and expand the field of physics. He headed the particle accelerator laboratory and taught physics and mathematics to medical students. He outlined his two PhDs in nuclear and particle physics from Oxford University, where he had recently lectured on his theories of time reversal. *Wow! Brains and beauty. Is this guy for real?* I thought but kept my focus on the task at hand—the cello.

"I want to uncover a unified theory of the universe," he concluded.

"I guess that means you went to college for a long time." I sat down and plucked the cello's strings, preparing to tune. He seemed not to understand my irony (or was he nervous?).

I stroked the open strings, played a few scales to gauge the instrument's balance, then tested its response with a snippet of Bach.

"Your son is lucky to have such a glorious instrument." I gave my blessing, loosened the bow, and returned it and the cello to its battered case. Outside, I walked my guest the few feet to the curb, where we shook hands.

Our encounter a month later surprised me. I performed in a chamber music concert for flute, harpsichord, and cello in an art gallery. After the reception, Klaus reintroduced himself and offered to carry my cello to the car.

As we walked to the garage, I asked if he liked Baroque music, since that was all the ensemble had presented the entire evening.

"Of course." His answer was confident and immediate. "Bach was a genius. I could listen every day to his cello suites, English and French suites for clavier, and preludes and fugues." His knowledge of classical music impressed me, and his sincere interest in my passion was disarming and intoxicating.

Soon he was regularly coming for dinner, albeit often arriving late. I would call his office, and the phone would ring and ring. He always had a ready excuse about an experiment in the accelerator that ran overtime. His work clearly took priority.

Then, finally, he would arrive, excited to explain his cutting-edge experiments that would prove his theories and win him a Nobel Prize. He prided himself on his ability to elucidate these ideas in a language accessible to nonscientists. It was flattering that he seemed to think I was smart enough to understand. Soon I found myself bragging to others about his accomplishments and dreams, as if I were the moon reflecting the sun's bright intensity.

He openly and lovingly talked of his kids: Karl, a high school freshman who attended a private boys' school on a singing scholarship and studied cello privately, and Alexandra, who at eight was already swimming competitively. His paternal sensitivity made him the antithesis of my own father, whose regard seemed to be only for himself.

In turn, I detailed the joys and challenges of learning a Dvořák or Mahler symphony while combating orchestra politics, such as cello colleagues protesting my bowings or mutiny in the wind section. Everyone took exception to the conductor's phrasing or technique. There were complaints about rehearsal style and endless repetition. All agreed that we, the musicians, could play the symphony better without the clown on the podium. Since Klaus came to the concerts, he seemed to enjoy my insider knowledge and valued my love and enthusiasm for music and my need to communicate my art.

I usually cooked, but occasionally we splurged and ate out. We loved Papa Dante's in Hillbrow, the cool, late-night, happening part of the city. Papa made the best *fettuccine fra diavolo*, a spicy, tomatoey seafood sauce piled high on homemade pasta, as well as Klaus's favorite, veal piccata. "Our" table was next to the window where we could people watch and keep an eye on the activities in the kitchen. Had I been so inclined, I could have reached out and stirred the pot bubbling on the stove.

This was the scene where, several months after we had been regularly seeing each other, I coaxed Klaus to reveal his personal history.

"Please tell me about your childhood," I asked. I was frustrated by his seeming avoidance of the topic. So far, he'd revealed almost nothing about his family, and I wanted to know him.

His hand trembled as he splashed an inch of the shiraz into my wineglass. He was reluctant, but I remained silent and expectant.

"My father died under mysterious circumstances in a taxi on his way from Zürich to Germany. I was barely two." He took a ragged breath, and his face paled beneath his bronzed complexion.

"What was he doing in Germany?" My breath caught with his in unison. "I thought you grew up in Switzerland."

He explained that his parents were German and had met in New York City, where his father owned a bank. Shortly after Klaus was born, they moved because his father, Friedrich, felt that with the outbreak of the war, Switzerland offered the best prospects for his business.

"So, you have an American passport?" I queried.

"I do. I was born in Brooklyn," he replied. "And I inherited my father's title, Freiherr. 'Baron' in English."

After his father's sudden death, his mother scrambled to pull together the scattered fortune, which was difficult because of the war. Because she was often away, Klaus was brought up by a series of nannies in elegant, multistarred Swiss hotels.

"Don't look so concerned." He brushed off my empathy for that abandoned little boy. "My childhood was full of adventures. I was left alone with my imagination and grew up free of pampering."

"How did you get to South Africa?" I asked.

"My mother fell in love and married a German doctor, who painted professionally," he explained. "They couldn't stay in Switzerland, and few countries would accept German immigrants. They first landed in German Southwest Africa [now Namibia] and finally settled in Pretoria."

I gathered he hesitated to share information about his German parents because of how people might judge him, even thirty-some years after the war. He also appeared resentful toward his mother, perhaps feeling she was negligent. With this new information, a better picture of Klaus came into view: he was an innocent intellectual who buried himself in work to escape pain and to keep from feeling. With his love of nature, art, and music, he was sensitive and insightful, but in relationships there emerged a calibrated distance.

When the steaming plates of delicious distraction arrived, the conversation reverted to a more neutral topic and one of our favorites: books. That segued to our next stop after dinner.

Exclusive Books was a three-minute walk from the restaurant and felt intimate even amid the screeching tires and honking horns of downtown traffic. Although sanctions were in full effect, the shop's shelves were jammed with classic literature, new releases, art, science, history, and magazines from the UK, US, and Australia. Noticeably excluded were anti-apartheid White South African authors such as Nadine Gordimer, J. M. Coetzee, Andre Brink, and Athol Fugard.

We made our purchases, then drifted around the corner for a coffee and discussion about what we had bought and planned to read first. I was plowing through the classics and had found three paperback novels by Charles Dickens for R0.95 each, and Klaus splurged on the *Reader's Digest Encyclopaedia of Garden Plants and Flowers* and a small volume by M. I. Finley, *The Ancient Greeks*. How wonderful to find someone as ardent about ideas and as curious as I was.

Klaus held open the door to the coffee shop, took my jacket, and hung it up, then pulled out a chair for me.

"Why did you choose this?" I asked when the waitress had left to place our order. He was fingering the encyclopedia, almost caressing a photo of *Digitalis purpurea*.

"I grew foxglove in my garden outside of Oxford." His demeanor became soft and nostalgic as he flipped through the pages. "Nature and mathematics hold the secrets of the universe. They are both supremely beautiful."

The waitress set down my cappuccino and Klaus's chocolate cake.

"Would you like a bite?" He picked up the fork and speared a piece.

"No, thank you. You were talking about nature."

"A few years ago, I was in Namaqualand, which is eight hundred kilometers north of Cape Town on the border of Namibia on the Atlantic coast. It was early spring and had just rained. Normally the region is exceedingly arid, but flowers were blooming everywhere. I sat on the ground and counted over forty varieties within arm's reach. I'd like to show you."

* * *

During the several months after my audition, subsequent promotion, and the fated lunch-hour concert, Klaus and I had become closer through our after-concert debriefings, dinners, movies, picnics, gardening, paging through art books, listening to records, and walking through parks. He was respectful and sensitive, but I wondered at his diffidence. Perhaps he was overly concerned about our seventeen-year age difference, which I found glamorous. Perhaps he had been hurt and wanted to go slow. I was too polite to pry. We held hands, walked arm in arm, and kissed good night—until one evening when we ended up on my new sofa after dinner. Dishes were piled high in the sink for Victoria to wash in the morning. The house was now all mine after Julie and little Christopher had moved in with her new beau.

The couch had only recently arrived—a special order piece covered in whitish, knobbly-textured Indian cotton. I loved its position against the wall opposite the speakers. Above it hung a handwoven mohair tapestry in earth, mustard, and ocher colors, depicting primitive South African cave paintings; I had commissioned it after seeing the artist's work at a gallery.

Klaus's musical passion was the Russian Romantics. I chose Mussorgsky's *Pictures at an Exhibition* to paint the scene. After the brass "Promenade," the wind section blew "The Gnome" into the frame. Klaus's arm fell from the sofa's back onto my shoulder. The dynamic dropped to a *pianissimo*. The orchestra filtered into transparency, a spiderweb of gossamer textures depicting gardens of "The Tuileries." My palm rested inside his upper thigh. The hand on my shoulder carefully, sensitively encircled my face. He drew my lips to his. I tasted the coffee. I felt the stirrings of pent-up desire.

Our bodies, at first primly upright, now elongated. His caresses seemed respectful, thoughtful, even shy. His fingers splayed under my arms and down my ribs. I squirmed. Too ticklish. It felt like I was leading, the seductress. He had always been meticulously respectful, but I wanted more.

"Are you sure?" His voice was raspy yet lyrical as his breath misted my ear.

My index finger breezed across his mustached lips to silence him. His hands freed my tucked-in blouse, then ever so slowly crept between fabric and skin, drawing up from my waist and along my chest. I felt the roughness of his raw-silk shirt, the buttons pressing into my flesh. His fingers ran harshly through my hair, his teeth gently pulling my earlobe, lips brushing down my neck while his hands found and supported my hips. I wrapped my arms around his shoulders. Holding me tight, he rolled us over.

"The Great Gates of Kiev" closed. The record silently spun on the turntable. Neither of us moved.

"Lauri, I've fallen in love with you," he whispered in my ear. "Marry me. I want to be with you forever."

I couldn't think. I was happy, and we had moved into a new stage—a relationship. Was this love or just words? I didn't care. I felt great.

CHAPTER 4
CHRISTMAS *CRESCENDO*

The following morning, the sun reflected Granny Smith–apple green off the kitchen walls. A hand-painted Chinese umbrella hung from the ceiling in a corner across from the windows, which were curtained in my home-made calico drapes. The room felt cozier. We sat beside each other at the round breakfast table. Klaus talked openly about our lovemaking and how meaningful and important it was for him, whereas I found the subject difficult. In embarrassment, I kept my attention on spreading marmalade on the toast. I didn't know how to talk about sex. Was that a subject one discussed?

I wanted to marry Klaus and had said yes. I had never felt this way—so connected, in harmony, and in sync. I was in a state of completeness and surrender, committed yet in no rush.

His expressive green eyes locked onto mine. "Tomorrow I'm driving to the Indian Ocean for the Christmas holidays and will be away for a couple of weeks. Why don't you join me? My children, Kurt and Alexandra, will be there. I really want them to meet you so you can develop a relationship. It's important for me and for us."

I was startled. I'd never asked to meet his children, and he had never offered, but now the dynamics had changed.

"I'd love to, but my mother is coming from Texas." I was already scheming how to orchestrate the visit with my mother so I could go to Nature's Valley. "What do you have in mind?"

"We are usually only the family," he continued, his eyes soft and alluring. "Probably just my mother and one or both of my brothers with their wives and kids."

He suggested that I drive with my mother to Cape Town, spend a few days seeing the sights, then put her on a plane back to Jo'burg rather than driving back together.

"The house was built by my stepfather right within the nature preserve," he persuaded. "It's on the coastal road from the Cape and stunningly beautiful. I want everyone to meet you. Please say yes."

Last night's proposal had seemed in the moment, perhaps inspired by our lovemaking. This sounded heartfelt.

My mother's visit, however, was not the only complication. Before meeting Klaus, I had connected with an English dentist I met when the orchestra played for a convention in Durban. Paul and I maintained a flirtatious communication after he returned to Southampton. He had worked in Cape Town for several years and planned to stay with friends there over the Christmas holidays. Meeting up could be fun, and I had committed before getting involved with Klaus. It felt too late to back out.

I concocted a loose plan to juggle my mother and two suitors. I would show my mother Johannesburg, then drive 900 miles to Cape Town, where we would meet Paul and stay with his friends. We could check out Table Mountain, explore the Cape of Good Hope, where the Atlantic and Indian Oceans collide, and visit wine country. Then I would send my mother on her merry way and be free to meet my love in Nature's Valley.

In anticipation of my mother's visit and in light of Klaus's proposal, I considered my parents' marriage. They had met in 1951 when my mother was a student at a Baptist women's college in central Texas. Her grandmother, who as a child had traveled by covered wagon from Tennessee to Texas, paid the tuition fees by selling eggs from her farm. My father was her music professor, a violinist and graduate of the Juilliard School in NYC. He proposed on April Fool's Day, 1952, and they married two months later, never having been on a date. She was nineteen, and he was thirty-three.

My father had grown up in a Detroit suburb and was the youngest of three sons, all two years apart. His father was a successful pharmacist and drugstore owner. His mother had dropped out of school in eighth grade to take care of her younger siblings when their mother died. The unruly brothers grew up out of control on the streets, but music lessons were mandatory.

In contrast to my father's relative wealth, my mother's family was dirt poor. Her father was a Texas cotton farmer. Though the farm had no running water, they had the dubious luxury of a "two-seater" (outhouse) and used the Sears catalog as toilet paper. She traveled to the three-room schoolhouse (first through eighth grades) in a horse-drawn buggy. The week's thrill was their Baptist preacher coming for a dinner of fried chicken, stewed okra, and grits after the Sunday sermon. Her mother prepared the dinners from scratch: raised the bird, wrung its neck, then plucked, gutted, chopped, and fried it. The Depression was catastrophic for my mother's family. Three of her four grandparents killed themselves—two because they couldn't pay their debts and one who suffered from cancer.

She was dominated by an authoritarian, uncompromising mother, who controlled every thought and action of her three daughters and son. Combined with a passive, submissive father, my mother developed into a timid, introverted, naive young woman.

Her new husband swept her off her feet and into a fairy tale. She must have been overawed by his authority, musicianship, knowledge, and high energy. He opened possibilities for escape and entrée into a musical world of creativity and collaboration. At his suggestion, she took up the cello so they could play chamber music together.

Our father was strict, uncompromising, and domineering. He instilled and demanded strict discipline. There was little affection, only anger, irritation, and judgment. My brother and I were raised on rules: up at 6:30, practice for an hour, eat breakfast, walk to school, do the chores, get straight As, make first chair in youth orchestras, enter and win concerto competitions, no listening to pop music (only classical), and five-minute timed phone conversations. No sports, because of the cost—only free activities with friends, haircuts by Mom, and homemade clothes.

As my brother and I became adolescents, our father's rules became harsher. Perhaps he felt he was losing control of us. He set a stopwatch for our practice regimen. Two minutes of silence added two minutes to the clock. Darrel didn't comb his hair, so when he was fourteen and the style was shoulder-length hair, it was shaved off. I once left a drawer open, and the entire contents of the closet and bureau were emptied onto the floor.

Most embarrassing was that Dad would interrupt my rehearsals with a trio I had formed with two high school friends and find an excuse to show off and start tickling them. His behavior was inappropriate and humiliating for both my mother and me. If I complained and asked him not to intrude, he would respond that I had an attitude.

I found a way around the laws and dicta: shut up, shut down, and stop communicating. I maneuvered and contorted myself to be the perfect daughter, yearning for acceptance and the cessation of criticism. In this police state, emotions were not allowed. Suppressing feelings made it easier to get along in our volatile and unpredictable world. It was safer to do precisely as expected.

My brother took the opposite approach and refused to cooperate, which inevitably led to punishment. He lied about skipping school. He jumped out the window at night to smoke and drink in the field across the street. At thirteen he would disconnect the odometer and "borrow" the car.

As punishment for disobedience, Dad designed a paddle that Darrel had to make in tenth-grade Woodshop. Because it was too long, he was instructed to shorten it and add holes for quicker, harder delivery. Our father would order, "Assume the angle," meaning "Grab your ankles." Darrel reported that our father's wallops were twice as hard as that of the school's vice principal. Dad hit my brother almost every day, which has left a mark on me.

To escape and find independence meant earning my way. That was what I was doing in South Africa, and I didn't need my mother's advice or what I perceived as criticism. I had received enough.

It had been seven years since I'd lived under my parents' roof, and the bond with my mother was rocky. Though she was loving, she was submissive and hadn't protected us. I resented her complicity in my father's cruelty. Every move I made after high school—Cincinnati, Hartford, Mexico City, London, Edinburgh, Johannesburg—took me geographically farther and farther away from home, and now an ocean and a hemisphere separated us both physically and emotionally.

I anticipated the visit as an imposition and threat to my freedom.

But the plans were set: Paul was coming from England, my mother from Dallas, and we would make the trip to Cape Town. I didn't have the guts or the integrity to call it off and hurt feelings.

I enjoyed seeing Paul again. He was tall and slim with blond, curly hair setting off tanzanite-blue eyes. His smile was genuine, his accent posh. He dressed comfortably but with style. Now that Klaus had proposed, I was too in love to allow myself a diversion and still too carefree about the potential consequences of my decisions and actions. So, the connection with Paul was merely amiable on my side, though he seemed more serious. He had sought out an eighteenth-century text, *The Elements of Musick Display'd*, had it rebound in burgundy leather and gold leaf, and gave it to me on Christmas Day.

The three of us cabled to the top of Table Mountain, toured the incomparable Kirstenbosch Botanical Garden with its exotic plants, wandering flocks of guinea fowl, rocky waterfalls, and life-size stone Shona sculptures, and drove west to visit the Cape Dutch vineyards of Stellenbosch. Paul made natural and unrushed overtures: taking my hand, casually draping an arm across my shoulder, delivering good-night kisses. I tried to be warm, congenial, and empathetic, but it was a hollow and inauthentic show.

Just after Christmas, my mother and I went downtown to shop the sales. She wanted to take a gift back to Dad. We strolled along, peering into shop windows, and she paused at a display of handbags.

"I'm not happy with your behavior toward Paul and his friends." She wasn't looking at me, but I saw her reflection.

"Yes . . . and?" My breath deepened. I was ready for a fight and prepared to go from zero to sixty.

"I'm concerned about your lack of gratitude for Paul and his friends' hospitality." She started walking away, forcing me to follow.

"Don't tell me what to do!" I exploded. "I'm not a child. You can no longer control me through your checkbook." I wanted to smash the shop window.

"I'm merely expressing what I see, and it isn't pretty," she countered. She stormed down Oystercatcher Road, her plastic handbag swinging on her left elbow. I caught up to her as her jaw tightened.

"I don't care what you think. This is my business, not yours." Dragon fire was flaming from my mouth. "Maybe it's better you go home so that you don't have to see."

She stopped, tears in her eyes. Likely her motivation to visit was to reach across and strengthen a tottering, if not broken, bridge. "Is that what you want?"

I ignored her pain. "Absolutely, yes."

A cellist friend offered to host my mother overnight in Johannesburg. I put her on a plane in Cape Town, made a lame excuse to Paul, expressing how nice our time together had been, then thanked our hosts for their generosity, threw my suitcase in the car's boot, and turned up the stereo's volume.

The freedom! The release! The excitement! The small detail that I would arrive ahead of schedule in Nature's Valley with no way to inform Klaus—whose family's house, like most in Africa, had no telephone—did not worry me in the slightest. He wanted me, and I was expected. A day early would be even better.

I drove the 350 miles from Cape Town to Nature's Valley in one shot. The curvy two-lane road wound along the cliffs, opulent with tropical flora and accented by crashing ocean waters far below. At the Cape of Good Hope, the brown Indian Ocean mixed with the blue Atlantic in an eternal jousting match. As the narrow highway coiled through some of the most spectacular landscape in the country, I popped one cassette tape after another into the player: French jazz violinist Stéphane Grappelli, the Belgian singer Jacques Brel, and chanteuse Édith Piaf. With every mile, I shed the conflicts of the past few days: my guilt at misleading Paul, misusing his friends' hospitality, and my ill treatment of my mother. The Cortina's windows were rolled down, and my mental and emotional doors firmly closed on the week's events as I drove toward my glorious future.

CHAPTER 5
MAJOR AND MINOR CHORDS

I arrived in Nature's Valley eight hours later and had little trouble finding the residence. The nearly threadbare tires crunched along a driveway of seashells and sand. I cranked the parking brake. Unsticking my sweaty thighs from the tan plastic upholstery, I fumbled for my comb and angled the rearview mirror to assess the damage from the salt-laden wind that had torn through the open windows.

The car door creaked. I barely took time to stretch, left my suitcase in the car, and hurried up the path to the bungalow's front door. After two weeks away from my soulmate and lover, I was more than ready to be welcomed into his family, whom I knew I could charm.

I confidently knocked. Almost immediately, a slim, short-haired, blond woman of about forty greeted me. *She must be the wife of one of Klaus's half brothers*, I thought. That meant she should have the same surname as Klaus's stepfather.

"Mrs. Richter?" I was friendly, if not chirpy.

"No, Mrs. von Österberg."

I tried to hide my uncertainty. *Is this another relative Klaus hasn't mentioned?* "I'm a friend of Klaus's. Is he here? I'm . . . expected."

"He is down at the lagoon, windsurfing with our children. He should be back in an hour or so. Would you like to come inside and wait?" She was matter of fact and unperturbed. Obviously, she had no idea who I was.

"Thank you." I could barely speak, almost choking. "But if you could point me toward the beach, I need to get out and walk. I drove nonstop from Cape Town, so . . ."

She gestured, and I stumbled down the two shallow steps in confusion as the door quietly closed behind me. My mind raced through the possibilities. With the name von Österberg, she couldn't be Klaus's sister-in-law. *And why would he vacation with an ex-wife?* There was only one explanation: Klaus was still married and had invited me on the family vacation with his wife.

With unsure steps, I trudged the path toward the water. I found Klaus sitting alone on a beach towel, his eyes scanning the blue, still expanse of the Groot River estuary. The ethereal scene of water gently lapping on pearlescent sand and sunlight reflecting off the breeze-rippled water did nothing to quiet my pounding heart.

His eyes lifted, and he faced me with a somewhat dazed expression. He had been lost in thought.

"Lauri, my love, I can't believe you're here. You came early."

His hand touched my bare calf.

"You are *married*."

Klaus slowly stood and grabbed my arms, almost pinning them to my sides. His eyes narrowed and hardened. He glanced away from me and seemed to focus over my shoulder on the far-off windsurfers, who pirouetted like exotically colored parakeets. He turned back and gazed into my reddening eyes. Tears of sad realization trickled down my face.

"I love you so much. I thought I would lose you and will do anything to keep you."

"You said you want to marry me. How can you? You're already married." I wanted the earth to open and swallow me so I wouldn't have to deal with the abominable revelation that he had lied and betrayed my trust.

"I don't love her. I love *you*. I'll get a divorce. We will be together, I promise."

His arms wrapped around me, his skin hot from the sun.

"No." I pushed back from his embrace. "Not telling me is the same as lying. I trusted you and . . ." My voice was becoming shrill. "Complete insanity. You invited me on your *family vacation* to meet your wife." I gulped for air. Forget fight or flight. I was frozen. "I'm going home." My confidence escalated as I spoke. "It isn't only about me. What about her? What about your children?"

Again, he pulled close, soothing my insecurities and anger, breathing into my ear, and I felt him harden through his skimpy Speedo. Did he love and desire me, or was he inflamed by this scenario of confrontation and conflict? I was desperate to be loved and needed.

"Ute will leave tomorrow with her sister, and we will be alone," he said, earnest and beseeching.

It was the first time I had heard her name. I stood like a statue in his arms, unresponsive, trapped. *How can he be so casual and so assured?* After the past few days of conflict with my mother and the convoluted situation I had created with Paul, I suddenly felt helpless and didn't have the strength to drive hundreds of miles across Africa back home to Johannesburg. Was there also a vague undercurrent of insecurity hinting that I might be nothing without him?

"What will you tell them, your family?" My voice quavered. "Won't they see how in love we are?"

"I'll tell them you're distressed with the departure of your mother, and I said I'd support and help you cope." He spoke easily, his lips feathering the top of my head. "Don't worry. It will be okay. I promise."

"How can you be so sure? Am I even expected? I don't understand how you can be so dispassionate and cool. You don't seem the least bit concerned."

"I can handle this. Trust me." His voice now carried an edge, maybe even a coldness.

"Who will you say I am? How do we know each other?"

"We met at a symphony concert after you gave me contacts to look for Kurt's cello in London, and we became friends. Ute doesn't care what I do as long as I can pay the bills and do the chores. Don't waste your energy on her."

With this statement, I assumed he was saying the marriage was dead, and the proof seemed to be in all those hours we'd spent together.

The children were nowhere to be seen, apparently happily windsurfing in the shallow lagoon. So together we walked back to my car, the beach towel slung over his shoulder, his flip-flops squelching on the sand. My mind was numb with white noise, a sensation I was familiar with when under pressure. *How can I prepare for one of the most significant performances of my life when I can't think straight?* I wondered.

We entered the empty lounge and heard murmuring in the kitchen. Klaus dropped my suitcase next to a 1970s-style sofa and left me in the living room as he went to concoct explanations.

I was roaming the room, distractedly studying the paintings, when the front door opened and banged shut. Two excited voices halted midchatter. I turned to see an adolescent boy several inches taller than I with a pleasant, open face. I assumed this was Kurt. Although his hair was wet, I saw he wore it shorter than his father's, probably the private school's required cut.

Just behind him stood a skinny little girl wrapped in a red-and-yellow beach towel. *This must be Alexandra. Did*

Klaus say she was eight? Which would make Kurt fourteen? Her sun-bleached hair clung to sun-pinked cheeks beneath the swimming goggles perched on her forehead. She stared at me with startlingly light-blue eyes. Her expression asked, *"Who are you?"*

I held out my hand to Kurt, who shifted his flippers under his other arm to take mine.

"Hello," I said. "You must be Kurt. I'm Lauri, a friend of your dad's."

"Are you American?" This seemed to interest him.

"I am. And I know you play the cello. We have that in common." I wanted to make them feel comfortable around me.

I turned to Alexandra. "Hello, Alexandra. Wow! Looks like you've been enjoying a good swim." She gave me a shy smile but said nothing. In the ensuing silence, drips plopped on the floor from wet suits. I traced little sandy footprints back to the front door.

Klaus came back dressed in a T-shirt and khaki pants. "Did you introduce yourselves?" he asked the kids, his manner brusque. "Good, then go shower and change for dinner. We'll be eating just now."

I only had a few minutes with the children. A typhoon whirled through my head, but I was left with a vague impression that they seemed wholesome and well brought up. I wanted to like them and for them to like me.

A woman with an authoritative presence entered the room—commanding, regal, confident, and strikingly beautiful. She was followed by Ute, who was wiping her hands on a dish towel. The energy shifted. Klaus stiffened, almost soldierlike. His mother's formal bearing left me feeling miserably underdressed in my white shorts, tank top, and sandals. I was expecting to meet Klaus's mother, since this was her home, but her density and ostentation left me speechless and threw me into greater self-doubt.

"I understand you are in distress." Her speech resonated deep in her throat. She did not extend her hand or introduce herself. "We have made room for you at our dinner table."

Klaus finally stepped forward. "This is my mother, Marie Gabrielle Heinrich."

I was almost inspired to bow and click my heels, I was so intimidated. I was utterly out of my depth.

"And this is Ute, who I believe you already met." We shook hands, and she turned away from me toward her husband, eyebrows furrowed together. Her hand was icy cold. *Is she used to Klaus bringing younger women home to meet her?*

That evening, Klaus's family and I sat around the oblong dinner table. Ute asked who would like wine.

"Yes, please," I replied. She opened a bottle of summer-temperature Chenin blanc. She and I were the only takers. The meal was bleak: white fish, white potatoes, white bread on white plates.

An opaque silence prevailed as we chased sole and potatoes around our dishes, keeping our eyes on our plates. No one made an effort to ease what I felt as growing tension. The silence was awkward. My discomfort intensified, and I sank into a cage of bewilderment, a small and unworthy animal. *Why is Klaus silent and not coming to our rescue?*

Through the open windows, I smelled the salty air and felt the sea spray dampening my skin. Klaus remained uncommunicative, like a primordial, megalithic rock on Easter Island. Waiting—the observer. As a guest and interloper, I couldn't begin to understand the dynamics of this ensemble: mother and son, husband and wife, parents and children, mother-in-law.

Mrs. Heinrich sat across the table from me, the silver hair twisted over her forehead accentuating her steely, pewter-toned eyes. She appeared the most at ease of our glum group.

Kurt and Alexandra, napkins in laps, elbows to their sides, quietly and quickly pushed the food onto their forks with their knives. Their gay chatter had dissipated with the solemnity of the adults. I sympathized with their confusion—not knowing who I was or why the family was acting so grim. I wanted to ask about their windsurfing, shell collecting, or friends, but it wasn't my party or my job to start the conversation. Who were these youngsters that Klaus had spoken so fondly of—Kurt with his mathematical prowess and Alexandra with her love of animals and urge to protect them?

I contemplated what Ute must be thinking. *Does she know about and consent to her husband's infidelity, as Klaus indicated?* No, the atmosphere was too strained to signal acceptance. *But does she suspect? Is she trying to figure out what is going on?* Maybe that was it. I found it difficult to get a sense of her. She was silent, probably straitjacketed by her own uncertainty or, more probably, anger, while I sat exposed as "the other woman."

Then it hit me. I was in love with another woman's husband; she was sitting across from me, a polite little girl from Texas in an adulterous relationship, and we were sharing food. *How can I allow this? Is this my fault?* But Klaus had wooed me under false pretenses. *Or if Ute were a better wife, maybe he wouldn't have strayed.*

I was chasing a boiled potato around the plate when Frau Heinrich's throaty German accent reverberated across the silence as if from the depths of a cave. The echo seemed directed toward me. "I'm wondering. What are you reading?"

The earth stopped shifting. This was firm ground. Since studying with my beloved Russian cello professor and mentor, Raya Garbousova, I had devoured many of her country's classics. I launched into a list of books I had recently finished by Alexander Solzhenitsyn, the Russian dissident. Coincidentally, Mrs. Heinrich was reading him as well. Though the dinner table was round, the conversation ricocheted between the two of us, our discussion animated and excluding everyone else. My confidence rose. I cautiously congratulated myself for holding my own with such a powerful and dominating personality.

After dinner, a bed was made for me on the floor in the lounge. My head rested on a pillow facing the stone fireplace. Above the mantel hung a portrait of the matriarch, Marie Gabrielle, painted by her deceased husband, Hans. Klaus's stepfather, one of South Africa's most celebrated portraitists, had painted the members of the South African Cabinet of 1961, the year South Africa became a republic. The surrounding walls were adorned with figure drawings and oil still lifes of flowers, primarily feathery pink-and-white cosmos.

The house was asleep, as were the birds and frogs. The lagoon's gentle waves were barely discernible. I had driven most of the day, learned my lover was married, and just met his wife. Sleep was an impossible dream. I turned over for the thousandth time, trying to assemble a puzzle despite its missing pieces. Suddenly, silently as a cat, Klaus slipped in beside me. The warmth of his body touching mine was alarming and electric yet deliciously familiar.

His breath purred into my ear: "You were wonderful tonight. I haven't seen my mother so engaged since we arrived. In a few hours we will be alone, my lovely Lauri."

After the drama and antagonism of the past two weeks—the again-broken relationship with my mother, the days of driving, the shock of the truth—I nonetheless felt myself yielding to his urgency and praise.

"I've missed you almost beyond endurance. It's been miserable here without you. You can't imagine the torment I've suffered being away from you for so long. My only solace has been cold showers. Darling. Oh, Lauri. I need you."

Klaus's lips were on mine, his tongue stopping my speech. Tears pooled in my eyes and spilled down my face. *This isn't right. Why is he doing this? Who does he think I am?* I turned my head and with flattened palms shoved against his bare body.

"I can't," I gasped. "Your wife is *upstairs*!" He'd pushed too far. I twisted away, and his arms loosened. Reluctantly, he rolled away from me. Then his lips brushed mine one final time, and he was gone.

The night was long. The pull to Klaus was so strong, and I wanted to get to know his children. But I sought the courage to do the right thing and leave as soon as possible. First thing tomorrow, I would say my thank-yous and drive back to Johannesburg.

By the time I got up the next morning, most of the household had already ventured to the beach. I showered and was repacking my clothes when Frau Heinrich entered the lounge for a private conference. Two sets of nearly identical eyes seemed to pulse with intensity: those of her portrait and those of its subject, who sat imperiously before me. While her hair in the painting was dark with only a few delicate wisps of gray, in life it was nearly white. Still, the likeness was striking.

"Please be seated. We have a very serious situation here."

I obeyed and sat across from her on the edge of the nearest chair. Instinctively, I said nothing, poised for execution.

She didn't bother with niceties. "You will leave immediately. You are no longer welcome in my home. You are destroying a marriage and a family. I have two other sons that I can offer you, but not Klaus."

I felt blindsided. Her words stung, especially after our seeming connection at dinner. Through my hurt, I also felt a flame of anger. I hadn't even known until a few hours ago that there was a marriage to destroy. *Is this situation my responsibility? Is it hers to fix?* And how could she offer me her other sons, who were also married and had families? I had never been spoken to like this and didn't know how to respond. I never talked back or confronted elders. I wished Klaus were there to guide and support me.

I took a shallow breath. "I'll find your son and tell him I'm leaving."

The chair I sat on had become molten; I stood just before the threat of incineration, opened the door, and quietly walked out with my suitcase.

Klaus stood outside the front door, his thumb directing the spray from a green hose onto the roses. Had he been aware of the consequences of his invitation?

He looked up. "What was that all about?"

"Your mother just threw me out. I have to evacuate. I'm leaving."

His finger pulled away from the hose, and water sprayed his flip-flops. His mustache drew under his lower lip. "*Bullshit.* That is total bullshit." He dropped the hose and jerked off the spigot. "I'm taking you. The bitch. She has no business interfering with my life."

I froze, still numb as his tirade continued. *What is he saying? Is he choosing me or fighting his mother?* I wondered what had prompted Marie's decision—whether she had experienced a similar situation in her own marriage. *Did Ute speak to her?*

"You will not drive alone. I'm responsible and will protect you from this bullshit."

Within minutes, Klaus had hurled my suitcase into the boot, and we were in the car. He slammed the driver's seat back and violently threw himself behind the wheel. There were no goodbyes. Hot wind whipped our hair as seashells sprayed from beneath the nearly bald tires. Relief flooded me. I was no longer alone. Klaus was in charge.

He maneuvered through the sandy streets toward the highway that crossed the arid, drought-stricken Karoo. The four-cylinder engine whined, finally maxing out at 120 kilometers per hour, taking us toward an unknown destiny.

CHAPTER 6
ACCELERANDO

From the passenger seat, I angled my body and studied Klaus's profile highlighted against the *kopjes*—little flat-topped hills—that followed us along the veld. He was darkly tanned from hours in the direct African sun, with just-silvering hair, thick and slightly wavy, falling over a prominent forehead. His full black mustache gave his cheeks an added angularity, punctuated by a strong, straight nose.

How could I be so drawn to this man who had deceived me, lied to his wife, abandoned his kids, and disrespected his mother? (And yet I had done the same only the day before.) His sheer beauty eclipsed my concerns. *Is he protecting me? Proving his independence?* My thoughts jammed against one another in confusion. He was breaking all taboos to be with me in this 180-degree turn in his life. He had planted his flag in my soil.

We hurtled through the dry, barren Highveld and into the Great Escarpment. I breathed in the parched heat of the Karoo. The first kilometers were strewn with expletives until the lava flow of Klaus's volcanic emotions had ceased. His reaction shored up my shaky belief that love was more important than honesty.

His death grip on the steering wheel eased as his hand found security on my open thigh. I needed space to decipher my reactions to the last eighteen hours. But I couldn't yet call him out on his actions.

I rummaged through the shoebox of cassette tapes, searching for something to give order to the turmoil. The insistent rhythm of Beethoven's early string quartet, op. 18 no. 4 in C minor, developed from a churning gesture into intricate layers of complexity and nuance that accompanied us until the mood subsided and the fumes of conflict dispersed.

"Tell me the story. How did you meet Ute? What is she like?"

I braced myself. This might be hard to hear, since I already sensed she was the enemy, but I needed to know why he had married her. *Does he often fall in and out of love? Is he looking for someone to take care of him? Was it passion?*

Before answering, he covered my hand with his. "I swear I never loved her. I settled." His eyes were trained ahead on the unending horizon. His jaw tightened, and his words became measured as he continued.

He had been a student at Oxford when he met an American violist with whom he fell deeply in love. When she left him for someone else, he was devastated. Taking advantage of the moment, his mother sent Ute to England from South Africa for "comfort." She came from a good German family, and he had known her from his days swimming at the pool in Pretoria, where his family had immigrated after leaving Switzerland.

"I married her because it seemed expedient, and I wanted children." His voice was flat. "I blame my mother for pushing me into it. Our relationship is based on me slaving to pay the bills and her demands that I do chores. We live completely separate lives."

That coincided with the little I knew of his situation, but I didn't understand how his wife could accept his absences.

"How can Ute put up with you never being at home?"

"Like I said, we have no relationship."

"Haven't you been terribly lonely? How have you been able to survive all these years in a loveless marriage?" I was desperate for more confirmation of love, more reassurance.

"My passion for physics," he answered quickly. "My work has been my salvation, until I met you, my dear, sweet Lauri."

I could relate to that sentiment. And I certainly understood the rigors of discipline as a basis and starting point for inspiration. Music had often provided me with an escape, a distraction from the pressures and demands that life threw in my path. Technique and expression offered a means of centering and focus. For several years while I was in college, I would play Bach's Cello Suites in order each week—the first, in G major, on Monday, followed by the D minor on Tuesday, concluding on Saturday with the D major, and, finally, resting on Sunday. The habit became almost prayerful.

"But what will you tell Kurt and Alexandra about why you left today?" I asked, suddenly thinking about his innocent children and how they might be affected by their dad leaving with an unknown lady.

He squeezed and released my hand. "Don't worry. I'll make it okay with them."

I finally asked the central question. "How did you envisage it working out with me meeting your wife?"

"I thought she'd be gone when you arrived."

"Weren't you playing it pretty close? I mean, look what happened. I wish I had known from the beginning that you were married."

"Yes, but I am going to fix it." His voice regained a stern and fierce edge. "I fell for you the first time I saw you on the stage at city hall. You were so fresh and beautiful. I was afraid you wouldn't give me the time of day."

The time of day, maybe, but he was essentially correct; I wouldn't have allowed myself to fall in love. Silence fell as the road rolled ahead like an unending tape measure. The tires sang their constant, one-pitched song. No cars approached or followed. Evening came quickly, revealing the sky's star-spangled immensity.

I inhaled the scorching air and sensed the desert's ancient mystery. Buried memories from childhood appeared like the wavy mirages preceding us on the highway: a family trip across America from Pennsylvania to the Grand Canyon; another to Florida, where my brother and I both contracted chicken pox. Then, as now, we were trapped in a car for hours, desiring freedom from captivity.

My eyes scanned the moon-shadowed cacti and ghostly tumbleweeds dotting the landscape. The baked air dried my lips as we drove from sea level to Johannesburg, 5,751 feet higher. The tires had devoured hundreds of miles while time and space seemed suspended.

Fifteen hours and 750 miles later, with only a quick stop in Bloemfontein for food and petrol, we pulled into my driveway. My bare legs were glued to the seat, my T-shirt and shorts soaked through. My toes found the forgotten sandals as I pried myself out of the car. I stretched and imagined the ensuing days of blissful vacation, alone with Klaus, building the foundation of our future together.

CHAPTER 7
MODULATION

We awoke to a hot late-December morning. The bedroom windows were wide open behind the ubiquitous burglar bars, but neither sunlight nor breeze penetrated the room through the lined curtains.

After toast and coffee, Klaus suggested we cool off with a swim. The university pool was Olympic sized and surrounded by golf-course-green grass. We spread our towels to stake out our patch, then dove in. I quickly tired, and while Klaus swam lap after lap, showing off his impressive butterfly stroke, I took refuge on my terry-cloth retreat. Hugging my knees, I surveyed the other bikinied and barely clad guests, all the while keeping a keen eye on Klaus. Were other women eyeing him too?

A professorial-looking swimmer wearing a bathing cap and goggles exited the changing room. She placed a wicker basket shaped like a diver's bell on the grass near the shallow end of the pool. Opening the carrier to a hesitant British Blue, she cooed, "Come, kitty." The woman dove into the pool. The reluctant feline cowered out of her cage, then, with a lowered belly, rushed to the pool's edge, plopped into the water, and paddled hysterically after her mistress.

Klaus and I took our first tentative steps toward buying groceries together. The expedition felt shy and new. I wanted to please him, feeling like I was in competition with Ute. At the butcher's station I self-consciously asked, "What would you like, chicken or steak?" We continued through the aisles as I selected items in deference to his preferences. At the checkout, I paid. I didn't want him to take money away from his family for me. I saw the way he dressed and the car he drove and remembered comments he'd made about having to scrimp.

A day later, Klaus insisted on taking me to his family's home. "I want you to know who I really am, my love, and show you how I've lived."

Before, when I'd asked, he explained that he had accommodations at the university lab, where the accelerator ran twenty-four hours a day. Now subtle alarm bells rang. I was reluctant to go. This felt like a breach of privacy—trespassing. Why was this important to him?

Greenwood was an older and more established neighborhood than mine, the trees bigger, the fences higher, the dogs fiercer. First, we toured the garden. Pointing to blossoming vines, ornamental trees, and exotic flowers, Klaus proudly and fluently rattled off Latin names, which I would learn was one of his passions.

Gloom cloaked the house's interior. With the curtains drawn, light virtually was eliminated. As we progressed through each room, Klaus remarked on the paintings by his stepfather, whose style I recognized from those on the walls of the Nature's Valley bungalow. I stopped before a portrait of a seated nude woman: a lacy white drape over her lap contrasted with the dark, forest-green background.

"She was my stepfather's secretary and model." Klaus also lingered. "Here, she is idealized. In real life she was fat."

I thought that rather unkind.

We continued our tour. Klaus pointed proudly to the furniture he had made: a dining room table, a bookcase, a coffee table. A scorpion sting of discomfort writhed up my back. *Shouldn't this be off limits?* This was my married lover's home. This was where he really lived with his wife and children.

Thankfully, we didn't venture to the bedrooms. Was he trying to be honest and candid or to goad me into a reaction? I sensed a disguised motive beneath his enthusiasm, which I was unable to penetrate. The entire experience was beyond my lexicon, another layer smeared across the burden of way-too-fresh revelations. I squirmed but wanted to share in his evident pride, so I squelched mine.

Aside from this trip to Klaus's house, the hours seemed so idyllic that I was mesmerized into thinking this could last forever. I am reminded of Shakespeare's words in *The Merchant of Venice*: "But love is blind, and lovers cannot see."

I made excuses to myself by reframing the disastrous Christmas scene into something I could deal with: he had chosen me over his wife, and I was so important to him that he stood against his mother to protect me. My heart was desperate for love and the need for someone who cared about me and for whom I could reciprocate that love; I assumed our problems would evaporate. Klaus would fulfill my needs as I would his.

On the third day, we sat at the small, round pine table in my neon-lime kitchen. The sun was well on the way to its apex when the wholemeal bread popped out of the toaster. Coarse orange marmalade accompanied the bacon and eggs. The coffee was as strong and hot as the sun.

As I ground pepper on my egg, I asked, "What shall we do today? There is an outdoor art exhibition at Zoo Lake. I could pack a picnic."

Klaus carefully placed his knife on the edge of his plate. His hand reached for mine. "I have to drive to Nature's Valley to pick up my family and bring them back home."

"You do?" My heart pounded faster. "When? We have two more days of vacation."

"You met Kurt and Alexandra. They depend on me, and my duty is to protect them. I'll have hell to pay with my mother and even more with Ute. I promise that the second I'm back, I'll come to you."

"And divorce?" Insecurity bubbled up. Yes, the kids needed him, but so did I.

"Of course, my love." His eyes were sincere. "I'll make this right."

I drove him back to Greenwood, where he picked up his other car, having left one in Nature's Valley. We stood in the driveway. He crushed me to his chest with his lips pressed on top of my head, his mustache prickling my scalp. Then he took my face firmly between his palms and tilted my chin so I gazed directly into his eyes.

"I love you and want you desperately. Leaving is torture. Please wait." His mouth was on mine. I tasted the wet saltiness of my tears mixed with his mint toothpaste and coffee. Then he was gone.

Time is so elusive. When one is layered in doubt, when the ego feels neglected and alone and the body unfulfilled, the hours languish. In a state of equilibrium and joy, there never seems to be enough time, but when one is suffering, time stops so the pain can take the heart in its cruel fist and squeeze. My body craved his. Yet my mind understood his responsibilities, which I registered as more important than my needs, so I talked myself into admiring his decision.

While I was trapped in uncertainty over the following days, my cello helped pass the time. I worked through technical passages and edited parts. A big Beethoven concert was scheduled for the start of the new season in mid-January, and though the Fifth Symphony is probably the most played of the entire orchestral repertoire, the slow movement, with its variations in the devilish key of A-flat major, is a cellist's intonation nightmare.

The symphony is generally based in C minor and has four movements. The opening motif—*da-da-da dah*—is echoed, expanded, and overlaid with the textures of winds and strings. It conveys tension, a pent-up explosion. Minor keys with a lowered third step often express sorrow, grief, and anger.

The first melodic theme—birdlike, soaring, and relaxed—quickly erupts into a demanding question and answer. I jotted in a couple of bowings. Was Beethoven reading my mind? I focused on executing even string crossings so the rhythm wouldn't sound bumpy, and I worked out fingerings. Beethoven went deaf and couldn't hear the music he composed, performed, and conducted. Maybe I was experiencing emotional deafness. I returned to a passage with awkward long slurs—many notes on one bow stroke.

I tried to concentrate. The third-movement fugue, a theme layered and spinning one on top of another in imitation, was aggressive yet mysterious. How conniving the mind is. I conjured in my head the full score with piccolo, contrabassoon, trumpet, trombone, and timpani. A hazily formed happily-ever-after image emerged. The rhythm became heroic—the famous scientist and the concertizing cellist. The last forty bars repeated the cadence in triumphal C major. Neither Beethoven nor I would give up.

CHAPTER 8
DEVELOPMENT

In the New Year, Klaus returned as promised. He said little about how he had (or had not) resolved the conflict with his mother or Ute, merely assuring me everything would be okay. He had explained to Ute that he wanted a divorce but gave no details, and as usual, I didn't pry. For me privacy was sacred and asking personal questions taboo.

Our routine continued much as before, except I was now haunted by the niggling reminder of his duplicity. On my left shoulder sat the devil of distrust and on the right the angel of adoration.

I saw how hard Klaus worked: long hours conducting experiments at the lab and writing pages of mathematics. Combined with the internal and persistent voice of my father—"You can do more. You can be better; it's still not enough"—I pushed my own agenda forward. I gathered promotional material, supplementing it with a demo tape of several solo radio performances. This led to recitals in Durban and the Eastern Transvaal. I also booked performances in Bulawayo and Salisbury, Rhodesia (now Harare, Zimbabwe). In Salisbury, the country's capital, I soloed with the National Symphony Orchestra, comprised of the remaining colonialists still hanging on after the civil war.

Robert Mugabe had recently been elected prime minister of the newly established Black government. As White South Africans were unwelcome, my US passport was an advantage, ensuring that my work in the apartheid country was not advertised.

I stayed with an American family from Boston; the wife played second clarinet and her husband trumpet. The weekend I arrived, they swept me off to play softball with US Marines attached to the American embassy. Coiffured with crewcuts, the Marines' muscles bulged. I struck out. Nonetheless, an embassy official offered, and I accepted, a second passport so I could travel through Africa without officials seeing my comings and goings from South Africa.

Several days later, we performed Saint-Saëns's Cello Concerto. Toward the end of the first movement, the wind section got lost and, instead of executing an alternating imitation of the cello line like beautifully choreographed dominoes falling one after another, the parts dissonantly paralleled. I was left swimming—no, drowning. Where was the orchestra? Where was the beat? From my podium just in front of the concertmaster and facing the audience, I looked up at the conductor. His baton flapped violently up and down in an ineffective attempt to reestablish the beat. Like the orchestra, he seemed confused. My only chance of survival was to stick to my part and not jump around or try to adjust. The orchestra tossed triplets across the stage and through the audience like a deck of cards flung into a hurricane.

When the newspaper's reviewer complained that my sound was small as the soloist, I wasn't surprised. For some time, I had felt my cello was holding me back. Since I often performed in large venues that required my tone to cut through dense instrumentation or compete with a huge nine-foot Steinway piano, I became frustrated with my instrument's limited power, response, and quality of nuance. Imagine competing in a car race using a motor outfitted with a hamster wheel.

Also, it was a larger Strad model. (For 300 or so years, the designs of Antonio Stradivari's instruments have been copied and replicated because of their superior tone.) The distance between notes on the fingerboard is critical for intonation, and I am petite, my fingers short.

Technique combined with imagination can create a palette of colors. Like an actor's voice, no matter how subtle the innuendo and nuance of emotion, there must still be projection. My cello was not up to the job; it was weak, with a muffled tone and pinched nasal quality that lacked resonance and power.

On my return from this concert tour, I shared these frustrations with Klaus.

He had his own news: his mother's elder sister, his beloved aunt Trudi, had died, and he was the executor of her will. He planned to fly to Bremen to settle her estate and would be gone for ten days. Because his grandfather had been the concertmaster of the Metropolitan Opera Orchestra in New York City, his aunt had several of his violins, which he would bring back from Germany.

The day he returned was, as usual, brilliant, the air bone dry, the sky cloudless. I stood on the faded yellow-and-red flowered carpet of my glassed-in porch. My heart quickened as his grungy Ford scraped the curb in front of the house. I walked the few steps to the street. Our greeting was almost formal. As usual, he wore khakis held up by a worn-out black belt and a white undershirt accessorized by flip-flops.

I helped carry in the violins, which we lined up on the floor in front of the LP records. Then his arms were around me. Pressed against his chest, I realized he felt different. There was less of him. He looked rakish with his hair falling across his forehead and his belt a notch tighter.

"For a week, I only ate apples," he murmured, his mustache feathering the top of my head.

We turned our attention to the hidden treasures.

"Let's start with the best." Dragon-like scales rippled across the case's top. The violin seemed to be embedded in the belly of an alligator.

With difficulty, we snapped back the latch and eased the lid open on disused, creaking hinges. I caught my breath and gently lifted the violin from its sarcophagus. Beneath the deep-orange-brown varnish, the maple back glowed with a rich, shimmering patina. The scroll was obviously carved by a master's hand, and the instrument's overall character was of power, strength, and masculinity.

"Magnificent," I whispered, thumbing each string to gauge the ring. "Do you know its history?"

Klaus fished around in his briefcase. "The papers are here somewhere. Yes, here it is. Does the name Wurlitzer mean anything to you?"

"Of course. That was a famous violin shop in New York City back in my father's day."

"I gather that my grandfather bought this in the 1920s after immigrating to New York and then brought it back to Germany when the war started. When he died, my aunt put it in a vault, where it has been for twenty or thirty years. Now you are holding it."

"Any idea of its attribution?" I wanted to know the country of origin and maker.

"Let's see." From a folder, Klaus pulled an embossed certificate. Curlicues and swirls danced around the edges, ending with an ornate signature at the bottom of the page.

His finger underlined the Italian name. "Tomoso Balistrieri 1770, Milano."

I took the proffered certificate. "It looks like he paid five thousand dollars in the 1920s. That was big money. But not as much as now. What do you want to do with it? Do you have a plan?"

He put the document back into the folder. "It's not up to me. My aunt's will has put it in my custody until Alexandra is eighteen. At that point, if she passes the Royal College exams at the highest level, it will go to her."

"Well, she's a beginner now and only eight years old. You can't just leave it in a vault for another ten years. It needs to be played. As it is, the instrument is probably dead asleep and desperate to be used. When did your grandfather die?"

"Decades ago."

I thought for a moment and proposed, "Would you consider loaning it to an artist? The violin would be played, and you could require insurance. That would serve three purposes: a chance for the instrument to open up, a needy musician could use a beautiful violin, and you wouldn't have to pay the insurance."

The other three instruments ranged from student quality to one that looked rather interesting. We tossed around several scenarios, and after a few discussions, he and I hatched a plan to take a trip to Europe and the States to pull together some capital. We would sell my cello and his violins, then with the proceeds buy a better instrument for me, since I was becoming increasingly frustrated with my American-crafted 1860s George Gemünder cello.

He agreed to all my suggestions. Evidently he valued me if he was willing to put his inheritance toward my passion. No one had ever cared about what was most important to me.

I asked Klaus if he could get away from work and his family responsibilities.

"You know the marriage is dead."

"You've spoken with her about a divorce?"

His expression became pained yet soft. "Yes, of course. We are at a point where my family life is only about doing chores. I am the proverbial cart horse pulling a huge load. If I make a false move, she takes her revenge on the children, knowing that I will not permit it. I can't allow them to suffer."

"But she knows you want out?" I needed more assurance.

"I'm here with you right now, aren't I?"

I swallowed my frustration. There was no tangible proof of his legal separation, even though he'd dangled the carrot of spending so much money on me.

Over the next few months, I wrote letters to dealers in England, Holland, Germany, Switzerland, France, and the US to set up appointments for our trip and get a sense of their inventory and prices.

As the departure day approached, I realized that checking my cello into the baggage hold, even protected by a hard case, was risky. I couldn't afford to buy "Mr. Cello" a seat, and flight cases were unavailable in South Africa. I got creative and fashioned a foam coffin with a corduroy cover to fit my hard case. With the six-inch padding and burgundy fabric, it looked like I was traveling with a large sofa.

Our flight to Amsterdam flew around the bulge of Africa and stopped in Monrovia, Liberia, where the plane refueled. When we arrived the following morning at the Schiphol airport, I anxiously waited at baggage claim for my whale-sized luggage to emerge from the chute onto the conveyor belt. It finally materialized, but upon inspection, the "sofa" seemed to have been slashed with a machete. The baggage handlers in Monrovia had clearly attempted to hunt down anything of value but were thwarted by the fiberglass shell. Fortunately, there was no real harm to the instrument, except several pegs had popped out, and the strings were loose. With this evidence of damage, Klaus talked the airline company into two free tickets from Amsterdam to London. He was wily.

While in Amsterdam, we visited a world-class dealer, Max Möller, and then wound through Germany to Munich, on to Zürich and Basel, and back north to Paris. Our time together was a dream: the excitement of the chase and discussions that led to decisions, the hours traveling across Europe in our micro rental car, the days planned around appointments in shops where I handled and played tens of thousands of dollars' worth of glorious instruments and bows.

By the time we arrived in London, I had auditioned dozens of cellos. There I fell in love with a cello made in 1740 in Piacenza by the Italian master J. B. Guadagnini; its tone was rich, full, balanced, and sensual. I also appreciated its smaller size. The body was a bit shorter and so were the strings, which meant I didn't need to extend my fingers like a contortionist to play in tune.

Klaus and I had the two fiddles assessed and showed the "interesting" violin to nearly a dozen dealers, hoping to learn something about its origins. Each expert suggested a different country, ranging from Bohemia to the Netherlands and Spain. Finally, Charles Beare, considered the world expert on violin authentication, chuckled and in his posh British accent said, "Find the dealer who says it is Italian and get him to sell it for you." (Italian string instruments are the most sought after and command the highest prices.)

We could get the best price for my American-made instrument in the US, so on Beare's advice we decided to make a quick trip from London to New York, where we consigned my cello and the mystery violin to an expert who certified the violin as made in the late 1800s by the Neapolitan maker Vincenzo Postiglione.

Pulling together the money was a juggling act. Finally, after shuffling around funds and a loan, we puzzled the financial pieces together. We were now £45,000 (about $75,000 in 1984) poorer, and the Guadagnini was mine.

Jet-setting between Africa, Europe, North America, and back kept our adrenaline on full throttle. Most of the destinations were new to me, and sharing this experience with someone equally curious and passionate made our bond even closer. Klaus's inheritance paid for a nice chunk, which made me feel cared for, proud, and indebted. The three of us returned to Johannesburg, and for the next thirty years, that fabulous cello became my trusted voice and inspiration.

Imagine cocreating with an instrument constructed at the time Bach was composing his Cello Suites (1742), sixteen years before Mozart was born. In its seventy-fifth year (1815), Beethoven penned his last cello sonata, and the cello was over a century old by the time Dvořák finished his Opus 104 masterpiece, the Concerto in B minor. I later learned that at the turn of the twentieth century, Saint-Saëns wrote his Cello Concerto No. 2 for a former owner. Simply drawing the bow across the strings gave me a shiver of pleasure as I imagined the other hands that had made music with this magical box.

Over the subsequent months, I recorded solo works with piano as well as trios with violin and piano for the SABC. I also performed the Haydn, Milhaud, and Dvořák cello concertos with my orchestra. And it was Klaus who made the purchase of this precious instrument possible.

CHAPTER 9
DISSONANCE

One day in April, as fall approached (in the Southern Hemisphere), Klaus arrived with a cold edge to his voice. "Ute threw me out. I went back to the house to pick up the children, and all my clothes and books were strewn down the driveway and flung all over the front garden."

He explained that when he opened his car door to climb out and see what was going on, Ute had torn out of the house, screaming, "Get out! You'll never see your children again!"

"What about the kids?" I asked. "How do they feel? It's got to be hard."

"I will make it up to them somehow." Klaus's jaw and fists were tense. "But you see what she's capable of."

I felt some selfish satisfaction. My position seemed to be getting stronger. We bought a massive desk and armoire, and he became a permanent resident. However, my inner gloating was short lived when, a week later, I received a letter from Ute threatening to sue me for "alienation of affection," along with a photocopy of the law she'd taken from a *Reader's Digest* compendium. She claimed that I had directly contributed to the breakup of her marriage. South African law seemed to implicate me as a third party who had stolen her husband, and she was entitled to take me to court and fine me tens of thousands of rands.

"Look what I received in the mail today." I handed the paper with a scrawled sentence in aggressive ballpoint pen to Klaus.

He was dismissive. "This is just a scare tactic in hopes that you'll kick me out."

"Well, it's working." I was shaken. "What should we do?"

"We'll clean out the garage, and I'll park in there."

"What about concerts?" I envisaged spies and tattletales.

"Yes. I see your point. Until this blows over, we should be careful when we go out."

We decided that the only course of action was never to be seen together. Though Klaus was still living with me, he came late at night, parked in the garage, and told his wife that he slept at the lab. I left my car out on the street, where it was stolen for the first time. Even with these precautions, I didn't feel relief. Soon I experienced her wrath firsthand.

One evening, the orchestra performed a "runout" concert in Roodeport, a thirty-minute drive east of the SABC. The first half of the program was Mozart's *Don Giovanni* Overture followed by the evocatively romantic First Piano Concerto in E minor by Frédéric Chopin. During the "interval" (intermission), I left my cello backstage and entered the foyer with several other musicians to mingle with guests and meet friends. A sophisticated-looking elderly couple I had never met approached me. We were discussing the pianist's artistry and interpretation when, out of the contained smoking and drinking crowd, a crazed shriek shattered the subdued cacophony.

"That whore stole my husband!" It was Ute. She was screaming over and over, pointing with a quivering, outstretched arm.

Concertgoers scattered. Conversation stopped. Heads turned. Mouths opened. As her tirade mounted, I shook, wreathed in embarrassment and shame. The ranting seemed endless as I reversed course and retreated to relative security. I attempted to pull myself together before the downbeat of Beethoven's *Eroica* symphony. Why couldn't she give him up? Did she really want him back? When I told Klaus, his reaction was not one of sympathy but rather of fed-up anger.

Not long after, one winter night around 1 a.m., Klaus and I were just falling asleep when we heard pounding on the sliding glass front door. The hammering grew louder and more insistent.

"I know you're in there, you bastard!" It was Ute. She pounded and pounded, the stress mounting. I wondered if she had left the children alone. *Is this her reaction to Klaus asking for a divorce?*

Fortunately, the windows were closed against the chill, and Klaus's car was safely hidden. The entire neighborhood's four-legged community erupted along with our Old English sheepdogs, Cookie and Thurber. All of Johannesburg must have heard. Then, undeterred by the rosebushes, she moved from the front door to the bedroom window. An hour passed with no letup.

Cuddled in bed, I whispered in Klaus's ear, "How long can this continue?"

"Indefinitely." He sounded exasperated. "She has infinite endurance."

We dragged the mattress off the bed and into my practice room at the back of the house. Dogs yelped interminably.

The next morning, despite the burglar bars, the front door was cracked, the bedroom window had shattered, and a brick had dented the bedroom floor. I was also starting to shatter.

CHAPTER 10
COUNTER RHYTHMS

"Truth is like a lizard; it leaves its tail in your fingers and runs away knowing full well that it will grow another one in a twinkling."
— Ivan Turgenev to Leo Tolstoy (1856)

Klaus bought glass and putty and fixed the window. Fixing me was harder. Although he continually promised we would leave South Africa together and immigrate back to the United States as soon as he divorced, the threats and attacks from Ute made me feel more anxious, threatened, and precarious. Klaus's famous refrain was "We are almost there. Hang in with me just a little bit longer."

And I did. There were enough good times to keep me on the hook. We took up cycling. Klaus had spoken of his days as a near-professional bike racer. With the help of a pro shop, we designed (and I bought) two beautiful, custom-made French racing bikes. We pumped up and cruised down the hills in Johannesburg, and my thighs got so tight and sore that I would massage them behind my cello while counting rests during orchestra rehearsals. My feet became numb from the shoes clipped into the pedals. My wrists tingled from the angled handlebar grip. I was getting in excellent shape, and we connected without fear of reprisals.

Klaus was his family's breadwinner, and he had no money to spare. Though I wanted Klaus for myself, my heart and pocketbook allowed his responsibilities to come before my needs. The ground rules were set. Klaus made me feel desirable, accomplished, worthy of attention, and capable. I wanted to return that gift. I hadn't received support from my father, and maybe paying Klaus's way would ensure I had his. So, I paid the rent, groceries, and for the bikes.

One long weekend, Klaus managed to escape his grueling hours at the lab, and we drove 250 miles southeast from Johannesburg to the Drakensberg Mountains. The "Dragon" mountains are a 600-mile range dividing the lower coastal region of southern Africa from the high escarpment where Johannesburg's gold and diamond mines are located.

We hiked, catching our breath on outcrops displaying vistas of mountains whose peaks pierced the clouds. The panorama revealed sharp, pointed summits over 11,000 feet high and other mountains that looked sawed off as if the dragon had been wounded while fiercely defending his empire. Even when the trail became treacherous, Klaus stopped to point out delicate flowers or obscure plants peeking from between the rocks. He cited their Latin names and tenderly noted their leaf structures and growing habits, which sparked my curiosity and opened a world of flora hitherto unexplored.

But back in Johannesburg, I was suffocating. The unjust, bigoted apartheid government had led to international sanctions against the country. The laws forced "natives" to live miles from their work in slum townships like Soweto and Alexandria, without running water or electricity. Husbands who sweated their lives away in the gold and diamond mines far from their families could barely support themselves, while big businesses like the diamond monopoly De Beers became gorged with cash. Black nannies raised White babies only to be ostracized from the host family for the slightest infraction.

When I auditioned in London for the position, I hadn't even known South Africa was a country. Five years later, through my observations, conversations, and experiences, my eyes had opened to the workings of the police state and the brutality of the government toward those deemed racially inferior—anyone not of the purest "European" blood. The crime, racism, and geographical isolation of South Africa became oppressive, and I could no longer ignore the violence. I wanted out.

Considering that my car had been stolen three times, the need for electric gates and fences, the police roadblocks, and the newspaper censorship, I knew the time had come to return to America while I was still young enough, at twenty-nine, to build a career, maybe as a freelance musician, a member of a chamber ensemble, or a teacher.

My professional life had begun with joyous intensity; however, after years playing a predictable rotation of "war horses" (Beethoven, Brahms, Mozart, Haydn, Tchaikovsky, etc.), my initial enthusiasm was dulled by the sensation of being a small cog in an encumbered machine. The orchestra's atmosphere was hostile. I felt confined by the arrogance of the conductors, the relentless schedule, the repertoire, and the internal battles. Orchestra politics created a snake pit that attracted pessimism and frustration. I yearned for more independence and autonomy.

Klaus felt likewise stifled at the university, where his brilliance and insights weren't recognized. He was convinced he could win a Nobel Prize if he were not stuck at the bottom of the world. He even composed and recited his acceptance speech, which I saw as a fun game of dreaming big.

In 1985, we traveled to the States. Klaus interviewed at several nuclear labs: Los Alamos, in New Mexico, SLAC at Stanford University, Cal Tech in Pasadena, and Argonne National Lab outside of Chicago. I planned to apply for a graduate degree in cello performance wherever we ended up so that I could establish connections, having never worked in the US.

My disenchantment with the job and South African policies increased upon our return.

Irit, my best friend, was sick of my Klaus stories and distancing herself from me. She had long ago given up believing his grandiose claims, and I felt alone in my frustration. I still had professional goals and wanted to continue my musical development. Returning to the US seemed like the best course of action.

Klaus and I agreed to leave South Africa and establish a life together in the States. I submitted my three-month notice to the SABC orchestra. The letter was short and gave no explanation for my defection, nor did I show my hand to my colleagues before playing my last concert with the National Symphony.

During those final months of fulfilling my professional obligations, I organized storage and boxed up the little house. After months of discussing the transition to America, Klaus delayed. There always seemed to be a big experiment, the result of which would clinch his reputation as a leading scientist. Therefore, he had no time to pack or help find a good home for the two sheepdogs. His response was always "Ask me tomorrow." Translation: "You do it; this is not my priority."

In April, I took the dogs for a last walk around Westdene Dam at the end of Glasgow Road, where just months ago, running off leash, Cookie had scrounged what looked (and smelled) like a half-rotten hand from the murky shore. She wouldn't drop it, insisting it was hers—*"Go find your own,"* she seemed to say to me.

After this final romp, they happily jumped into the back seat of the Cortina, oblivious to their future in an Old English sheepdog rescue shelter. *At least they're together*, I told myself. I couldn't afford to airfreight such large dogs around the world. Taffy the Scottish terrier and Yo-Yo the Himalayan cat were sedated and caged, then flown off to Dallas via Frankfurt. Anxious to have me back in the States, my parents agreed to take them.

The winter morning when the moving company was scheduled to pack my belongings and put them into storage was typically brilliant, the sky crystal clear and the air miraculously clean. The crimson bougainvillea I had planted three years before had spread to cover the iron spindles on the front garden fence; their butterfly faces splendidly intertwined with the white roses. The huge blue-and-orange moving truck stopped in front of my house right on time.

Nearly a dozen overall-clad men swarmed in like a militia of black ants. They filed through the front door in a silent stream. As crockery, books, LP records, the brass bed, and a few treasured pieces of African art were wrapped and boxed, I saw the last five years of my life dissolve. I was advancing with my plans, yet I sat alone on the front step, weeping. My unknown future lodged like a question mark in my heart. Where would we settle? How would my professional life develop? When would Klaus follow through on his promises of commitment? The decision to leave would undoubtedly change the course of my life.

The truck pulled away from the empty house, and I was left with one suitcase, my bicycle, and my cello. Klaus was vague, but it became clear that he still had more work to complete and wasn't ready to leave. I had quit my job, sold my car, and was homeless. In desperation, I contacted an agency and signed up to be a house sitter, which meant free accommodation.

For another three months, I clung to my South African life and floated, subbing with the opera orchestra in Pretoria, practicing, and gradually realizing my boundaries were nonexistent and I'd given away my power. Yet moving back to the other side of the world alone felt very scary. I had never worked in the US and had lived abroad for over seven years. I had no contacts in the States, no money to tide me over, and was uncertain if and when I could get a job. The thought of flying from one city to another to audition was overwhelming and financially impossible.

I moaned for the hundredth time, "I'm totally frustrated hanging around waiting for you. I packed up the house, sold my car, sent Cookie and Thurber to the shelter and Yo-Yo and Taffy to Dallas. Why can't you pull the trigger? I've got nothing here, and I never see you."

"I'll say it for the last time." Klaus's voice sounded as strained as mine. "I haven't found a position in America, and the work I'm doing now is vitally important for our future. My divorce hasn't come through since my attorney is dragging his feet. You know I am doing everything humanly possible to get us out of here."

"But why is it taking so long?" My voice ratcheted up. "I followed your instructions to the letter, and you're not following through."

"Like I just said."

He was a brick wall and wasn't budging. Klaus's reasons for delay seemed so valid: an important experiment, not enough money, no solid job prospects. He had an unerring way of leading me to believe that even after so many disappointments, something fabulous awaited us right around the corner (and indeed, we had already had some wonderful adventures). His promises often came true, albeit not on the initial timeline. Like a gambler feeding quarters into a slot machine, hoping for the jackpot, I stuck around for the payoff.

In August 1986, I was house-sitting in a home with no telephone and a seriously depressed little black dog and had hardly seen Klaus in two weeks. I thought we were a team sharing the same vision, but his actions didn't support my expectations. It was time to regain my power. The broken record of his excuses had stopped working for me. Enough. I drew a line in the sand.

He came two hours later than agreed. We sat across from each other at our favorite Italian hole-in-the-wall restaurant in Hillbrow, Papa Dante.

"I bought my ticket to Dallas today," I announced calmly while spearing a calamari tentacle.

Klaus's face was blank, even cold. It was an expression I knew. He did not need anyone. Here was a man who would never be lonely. His life was his work, and I was a diversion that supplied a bit of refreshment when he was occasionally thirsty.

"You can't wait another week? We are near the finish line. I told you I'm going to divorce court next week, and now you're collapsing."

"How many times have you said that?" I tried to keep the accusation out of my voice.

"I've explained the challenges I face." He started ticking off points with his fingers, finishing up with "And I'm still trying to nail down a settlement with Ute, who is playing hardball. I know my freedom and success are just around the corner. Can't you support me this once?" His voice was now edgy.

My heart headed toward lockdown. Something told me to stand up and take action. I had become dependent and needed to find freedom by creating my own scaffolding, both professionally and emotionally.

"You know where I'll be. I'll support you from Dallas. Come find me when you're divorced. If that's next week, like you promised, then we'll be apart for only a few days." My heart seemed to stop as my words evaporated into the garlic-filled steam from the kitchen.

+++

Two weeks later, Klaus drove me to the airport, and we shared a tearful goodbye. Nipping into one of the curio shops at the last moment, he bought me a two-ton wooden salad bowl. (He loved big, solid pieces of wood.) At the gate, his arms wrapped around me, his lips pressing against my crown. Again he promised to come as soon as he finished a government-sponsored experiment, something secret he couldn't talk about involving national security. As usual, his explanations were enveloped in mystery.

To finance the trip, I first went to London to sell several bows I had purchased in Europe and from various South African sources. Although I made a good salary by South African standards, I had spent most of my money on Klaus: I paid the rent on our house and for our dinners out, groceries, and treats, though it didn't feel like a sacrifice. He was his family's breadwinner and had no money to spare.

I spent a week in London, then moved back in with my parents after thirteen years of independence. I had no car, no job, very little money, and lived on unrealistic expectations. I practiced, read chamber music with friends from high school, played a few gigs, and constantly thought and worried about Klaus's arrival. I tried to keep my concerns to myself and put on a brave face when speaking with my parents. But I was torn between feeling abandoned and being sure that Klaus was the man I wanted to spend my life with. Though I had times of doubt, I told myself he would eventually come.

A wisp of consolation came from my bike. My muscles gained strength, and my body stayed taut. After the high elevation of

Johannesburg and its hilly terrain, I felt fit enough to challenge Lance Armstrong in the flat, low-lying Texas environs.

A couple of months after my departure, Klaus informed me that a position had opened at the Argonne National Laboratory outside of Chicago. He had been offered a job and would have the contract posted to me. Finally, some good news on which I could act. On that cue, I applied and was accepted into a graduate program in cello performance at Northwestern University. I mailed in the deposit. Every day for several weeks, I expected the contract from the lab to arrive in the mailbox. Every day, I was disappointed.

What was going on? I obtained the lab's general telephone number from directory assistance and quickly got through to the head of the physics department.

I used my professional voice. "I am calling for Klaus von Österberg."

"Yes. What is this about?" He seemed preoccupied, his response dry.

I remained neutral. "Dr. von Österberg is in Johannesburg and asked me to find out what has happened to his contract."

"There must be a misunderstanding. Dr. von Österberg has not been offered a position." The scientist sounded somewhat annoyed, almost defensive.

"So, there is no contract?" I kept my tone in check.

"Yes, that is correct." He disconnected.

I tried to reach Klaus at the Johannesburg lab. The seven-hour time difference between Dallas and South Africa was challenging. When we finally connected, Klaus insisted that the job fell through because the lead physicist committed suicide when funding was denied.

"I am trying to work on cutting-edge physics, discovering how the universe works, and I have to deal with fundraising." He sounded exhausted.

He had often mentioned the insecurity of relying on government support of science, especially fundamental research that in the public's eye had no immediate payoff.

"Can't you understand the complexity of our situation?" He sounded not only frustrated but angry. "I'm as disappointed as you that the job fell through."

Though I'd paid the fees, I canceled my spot at Northwestern, which didn't feel like a sacrifice because I didn't know much about the program. I had studied chamber music at a weeklong seminar with the cello professor while I was in college, and the school had a good reputation and a strong music department, but I didn't feel an emotional pull to return to the classroom and play in a student orchestra.

Then Klaus again delayed. This time, he intimated there was a scientific collaboration between South Africa and Israel. The assignment was "top secret" (insinuating it was a nuclear bomb), and he would be under "house arrest" after his return from Israel, living at the university lab and unable to leave the country until he completed the experiments. The work would pay a fee of $10,000, which he would send from outside South Africa (which had stringent currency-exchange prohibitions). The good news was that he was divorced and would have his attorney send copies of the papers to me.

The divorce papers never came. We concluded that the documents must have been lost or stolen. Considering the African mail system, this seemed probable. Eventually, the promised sum was transferred to my bank account to tide me over until he could come. *He must be out of the country*, I reasoned, though in my heart I had vague doubts.

In May 1987, after nine months of worry and anxiety about his true intentions, Klaus arrived. He had successfully finished his work for the government as well as a crucial experiment he felt confident was so impressive that he would most certainly receive a job offer on its merit.

In a state of nervous excitement, I drove to the Dallas–Fort Worth airport to meet his flight. When I spotted him, he looked haggard but gorgeous. His six-foot-two frame had been crammed in coach from Jo'burg to NYC, then to Dallas. As I intertwined with him, hot tears of gratitude ringed my eyes. My heart throbbed with joy; my psyche sang in relief. The misgivings and insecurities that had engulfed me suddenly seemed ungrounded.

He tossed his battered red suitcase into the trunk, gently placing the silver French racing bike across it. We buckled up, and I exited onto the LBJ freeway. As soon as I felt comfortable knowing where I was going and was safely in a lane that allowed the cowboy drivers to roar past, we began reconnecting. I'd booked a B and B so we'd have more privacy than if staying with my parents.

Our lovemaking was tender, lacking any need for desperation or urgency. He was a sensitive lover, bone tired yet needy and reciprocal.

As we lay together, he on his back and I folded next to him, past years of frustration surfaced. I was torn between expressing accusations of his seeming negligence and being elated to see him. Togetherness felt so good, yet I had many questions.

"I wouldn't have come if I wasn't divorced." His tone was weary, fatigued, and exasperated. "I will only tell you once. This subject is too painful, so don't ever ask again." The German autocrat was speaking. "I had to agree to give Ute everything—the house and my pension. I even gave up the right to see my children. I've only escaped wearing my underpants."

"You aren't serious?" I asked and elbowed up to gaze into his eyes. "You agreed to never see Kurt and Alexandra again? Is that the best outcome for them and you?"

"I had to do it to be with you." He turned to his side to hold me. "If I have any contact with them, Ute will retaliate by making their lives intolerable. I simply can't allow that. Maybe one day they will be able to see the truth."

I looked into his eyes and felt the constriction in his heart. I had firsthand experience of her rage. *How painful for him to leave his kids.* On top of that, because of the "classified" work he did, the government had forbidden him to return to South Africa.

This sounded insane, yet I knew South Africa was a land of inequality, injustice, and outrageous laws. *He must really love me to accept these draconian consequences.*

In my heart of hearts, though, I felt this situation had worked in my favor. I couldn't imagine his kids coming 10,000 miles to stay with us and invade our private utopia; they might harbor anger toward me, the witch who stole their father. Moreover, I saw Ute as a nightmare from the past to be permanently banished from our lives.

The next day, we got down to the serious business of finding a landing place. I typed the results of his experiment for publication on my mother's IBM typewriter. The paper was accepted in *Physical Review Letters*, a prestigious physics journal. With this accolade and Klaus's contacts from years before at Harwell Atomic Energy Research Establishment in England, he secured a summer residency at Brookhaven National Laboratory in eastern Long Island, and we planned the move.

Again, I found myself in his vortex of happening, expectation, and action. With this decision, the trajectory of my life changed.

CHAPTER 11
INTROIT

We stayed at my brother's house after the B and B and for a week scanned the ads in *The Dallas Morning News*, then bought an enormous, high-mileage, navy-blue 1982 Lincoln Continental with a powder-blue leather interior using $7,600 of the money Klaus had sent. The futon we bought to sleep on barely fit rolled up on the behemoth's back seat. Between it and the roof, we packed our clothes until a mere squint of visibility out the back window was all that remained. That little gap, however, was often obliterated by a kitty hunkered on the back of the front seat. Our bikes were strapped onto a rack behind the trunk.

The monster V-8 engine took us northeast through Arkansas, Tennessee, Kentucky, Indiana, Ohio, Pennsylvania, New Jersey, then over the George Washington Bridge just north of New York City and, finally, into Long Island. I was still so entranced and starstruck with Klaus's return that I couldn't visualize what our future here would be like. I simply knew it would be magical because we were finally together and could support one another.

Brookhaven National Laboratory, founded in 1947, was built on the ex-Army base of Camp Upton, a (rarely advertised) Japanese internment prison during WWII. Since its inception, their physicists have conducted revolutionary experiments on particle accelerators, reactors, the Relativistic Heavy Ion Collider, and the National Synchrotron Light Source-II. More recently the focus has broadened to encompass chemistry and biology research.

The admin assigned us to a mobile trailer on the lab campus. A dozen or so of these "homes" were clustered in rows and used as temporary housing for guest scientists. Cinder block steps led to the entrance. The "living room" featured a flimsy, threadbare sofa beside a toothpick-like chair. The chair's vaguely orange polyester fabric covered a foam cushion that was at its best forty years before, when the lab first opened its doors. A few feet away was the kitchen, with a two-burner electric stove, minute oven, and half-size fridge; and in the back was the bathroom and bedroom, its two single beds separated by a rickety nightstand. A gooseneck lamp provided a skirt of illumination.

Notwithstanding, the environs were glorious. Unspoiled Christmas tree forests were inhabited by foxes, groundhogs, wild turkeys, deer, a busy bird life, and (we suspected) coyotes.

I had been so uncertain about Klaus's arrival that my spirit now expanded with gladness at again becoming a free agent away from the parental home. I was like a caged animal released back into nature, eager to begin a life unencumbered by threats, authoritarian expectations, and the insecurity of waiting.

That summer, Klaus settled into long work hours that extended late into the night. I was alone with my cello, thoughts, and empty days. In Johannesburg, I had been a big planet whirling through a small universe. Now I was in a black hole—no career, no contacts, little communication with the outside world. In that small caravan, I questioned my purpose. I had realized my dream, but I was alone in it.

In a concerted effort to expand my marketability and broaden my knowledge of Renaissance improvisation and

Baroque performance practice, I decided to learn the viola da gamba (forerunner of the violin). I needed more to do, and this was a possible creative outlet. I rented a six-string instrument with a swan-head bow, then signed up for lessons with one of the foremost gambists in New York City.

The bass gamba has almost the same range as the cello. The tuning is different (similar intervals as a six-string guitar), but the frets make intonation much easier. There is no endpin, so the instrument is held between the knees; the calves form a sort of shelf on which the gamba is balanced. That wasn't so difficult, but the bow grip required a trickier adjustment. Instead of the hand positioned above the frog as on a cello bow, the palm is underneath and faces upward.

Soon I was proficient enough to sub for my teacher at Saint John the Divine on Manhattan's Upper West Side in front of an audience of several hundred. I performed the continuo part (the bass line) of the Bach Violin Sonatas with Nina Beilina, the virtuoso playing Klaus's violin. Only three of us were on the stage: the violinist, harpsichordist, and me. It was scary. Just keeping those unwound gutstrings in tune was a nightmare. Any slight change of temperature or humidity, and I'd have to retune. (I shouldn't complain. I had only six strings to worry about, whereas the harpsichordist had double strings on two manuals/keyboards, which needed constant attention.) Performing with master musicians kept the fire blazing in my belly.

※ ※ ※

One day, as I penciled in a fingering, the phone rang. The voice was huskily female, the accent thick German. Every nerve and cell of my body went on high alert.

"This is Frau Heinrich. Please put my son on the line." There were no greetings or niceties.

Overdrive took over. The last time we had spoken, she blamed me for causing a rift in Klaus's marriage and evicted me from her home in Nature's Valley. Heart pounding, bow arm and knees quivering, I willed my voice to remain steady.

"I'm sorry. He's at work," I answered.

"His secretary said he was at home with his wife." Ten thousand miles of telephone wires vibrated with imperious stiffness. "But his wife is here in South Africa."

Repeating myself seemed the safest option. "I'm sorry. Klaus is not here."

Shakily, I returned the receiver to its base. Klaus and I had only been back together for a few months. Head spinning, I spent the day conjuring scenarios, imagining connections, envisioning departures, telling myself stories. He said he was divorced. *But is he really? What does his mother want?* I worried he would feel compelled to return to South Africa.

That evening, Klaus innocently opened the flimsy door and dropped his briefcase on the curling linoleum floor. I pounced.

"Your mother called this afternoon." I was worked up into a lather. "She wanted to speak to you."

Klaus was unperturbed. "Okay, obviously I was unavailable."

"She said your wife is in Johannesburg." All my fears that he was still connected with Ute had returned and amplified.

"My mother is a senile old lady with nothing to do but pry into business that doesn't concern her and where she's not welcome." He was both adamant and incensed, radiating frustration. "She is a prying bitch and talks bullshit. How could you take her seriously? You know what she's like. You met her."

"But you swore that you are divorced." I was shaking. "Doesn't she know? Why did she say your wife is in Johannesburg?"

"She's got nothing to do but cause trouble and stir things up. Don't waste our time on this. You are getting aggravated for nothing."

He was right. His mother had accused me of ruining a marriage I didn't know existed and then offered me her two other married sons. Klaus was so dismissive of the call that I convinced myself my panic was unwarranted. The intrusion meant nothing to him; I was turning a mere puff of smoke into a forest fire.

∴

In the fall of 1987, after Klaus's preliminary trial of three months, Brookhaven National Lab offered him a contract. The ground under our feet solidified, and with an income stream, I could make plans to stay in Long Island. My contacts with wives of the lab scientists led to a real residence. That January, we moved out of the trailer and rented a small three-bedroom house on Long Island's south shore from a Danish physicist who was relocating to Waxahachie, Texas, to work on the Superconducting Super Collider (which was canceled in 1993, having already cost $2 billion).

This was the era of the Cold War leading up to the fall of the Iron Curtain. Klaus was assigned to work for the Strategic Defense Initiative, dubbed "Star Wars." Instigated by Ronald Reagan, Star Wars was a national commission to construct space stations armed with antimissiles to defend the US from Soviet rockets. Klaus was selected to lead an experimental team at BNL to discover "the position of a neutralized particle beam by using a non-interfering method called laser resonance fluorescence."[1*]

He became consumed with designing an experiment around the few hours the team was allotted on the accelerator. There were so many competing groups that Klaus's had to take the "dog" shift, and though he often worked through the night, he

---

1 [*] *Brookhaven Bulletin*, June 8, 1990.

was on fire with the challenge. I struggled. Not only was he away from home most of the time, but when we were together, he was totally drained.

One day, just after I'd finished washing lunch dishes, there was a knock on the door. A man in a brown suit with closely shorn hair and a serious expression pulled a badge from his inside jacket pocket: Federal Bureau of Investigation. My first thought was that something must have happened to Klaus. Why else would he be here? I hadn't done anything wrong.

"May I come in?" Though he was burly, his voice was tenor.

"Yes, please. How can I help you?" Warily, I stepped aside.

"I am doing a background check on Klaus von Österberg." He pocketed the ID. "His work requires security clearance. A secretary at Brookhaven National Lab said he had a wife at home."

"We live together but aren't married." I briefly described our situation and how we had ended up in Long Island. He took a few notes, but his questions were innocuous, and it must have been evident that I knew nothing about his work.

"May I now ask you a question?" I decided to take a chance and ask if he had access to South African divorce records. "We have talked about getting married for some time now. Do you know if he is divorced from his wife in South Africa?"

"I'm sorry. I'm not authorized to share any information with you. You must work that out with him."

I supposed his job was not to sort out my personal life. He simply needed to assess whether Klaus was a government security risk. We shook hands, and then the man was gone, leaving me dazed and feeling a bit dirty, as if I were an inconsequential bit on the side and not a real player in the drama of Klaus's life.

It was dinnertime when Klaus came home, carrying the black handmade leather briefcase I had given him last Christmas.

When I told him about the guy from the FBI and his questions, he was soothing.

"I understand that you are upset." His tone was perfunctory as he set the satchel in front of the closet. "You can't imagine the hassles I faced today with deadlines, incompetent secretaries, union guys who can't get off their backsides to put our equipment in place because it's lunchtime, suppliers that don't deliver, phones ringing, reports due yesterday. Now you're worried about a goon bureaucrat. Please don't spend another nanosecond thinking about him."

※ ※ ※

Nina the Russian virtuoso had left Moscow in the 1970s when Stalin allowed a limited number of Jewish musicians out of the Soviet Union; they were subsequently granted political asylum in the US. When Nina escaped the USSR, she took only a worthless piece of junk more closely resembling a cigar box than a violin.

In the fall of 1989, she invited me on a concert tour of South America as solo cellist with a small chamber orchestra. When Klaus drove me to the airport to catch the flight to Santiago, Chile, he dropped a bomb.

"I'm going to South Africa tomorrow." His eyes remained fixed on the highway.

"What? You told me that you could never go back to South Africa." My eyes swung from the road's mesmerizing broken white stripe to Klaus's impenetrable profile. "You said that you are persona non grata."

"My mother is critically ill with a heart condition. Her financial situation is dire, and apparently my two brothers are too busy to take care of her." He showed no emotion other than to grip the steering wheel tighter. "I have no choice. I have to go."

"How is it that the government gave you a visa? I don't get it." I was about to embark on a transcontinental tour, and he was throwing this at me.

"I've arranged special dispensation and will be accompanied to and from all locations. I'm staying in Pretoria with my mother and will only have contact with her, her physicians, and the art gallery in Johannesburg where I hope to sell one of my stepfather's paintings because she needs the money."

My flight was leaving in two hours. I couldn't think. *How could he make so many arrangements and not tell me sooner? Should I be mad that he wants to help his mother? Will he contact Ute?* I feared I would never see him again. He gave me a telephone number to reach him, but that didn't assuage my anxiety.

And sure enough, I tried calling him from Chile, Argentina, Uruguay, Brazil, and Paraguay to no avail. Even on the stage of Buenos Aires's famed Teatro Colón, one of the world's great opera houses, while accompanying Nina in an Argentinian tango duet surrounded by hundreds of people, I felt deserted, insecure, and worried that Klaus had changed his mind and was leaving me. I grieved in anticipation of my loss.

Finally, at the Iguaçu Falls, which divide Argentina and Brazil, with toucans flying overhead, orchids decorating the limbs of trees, and the thundering spray of the water, I was distracted and reminded of how small my problem was in the overall magnitude of the earth's majesty. The grandeur and power of nature reminded me of Africa's Victoria Falls, though without the hippos, crocodiles, or elephants.

The concert tour was a fabulous success, yet I came back to New York a wreck. I had convinced myself that Klaus would not return to the US and I would be left stranded. Despite the pesos and reais spent on phone calls, I could not connect, and my mind roiled with memories of broken promises.

I took the AirTrain from JFK to Jamaica, Queens, then the Long Island Railroad to Patchogue and a taxi home. My cello weighed heavily on my shoulder as I dragged my suitcase to the front door, twisted the key, and entered our dark, empty house. Instead of remembering the triumph and glorious concerts, sharing in the celebration of Vivaldi's *Four Seasons*, marveling at the wonders and magnificence of the Iguaçu Falls, flying over the Andes at sunset, and absorbing the resonance of famed concert halls, my mind and spirit were tortured: *Will Klaus return? Will I be left alone? How will I manage?*

Two days later, he reappeared, just as he said he would. He dropped his red vinyl suitcase by the door. Then his arms were around me. My tears stained his sweaty shirt, and his mustache gently prickled my head. Though relieved and comforted by his return, I couldn't erase my feelings of abandonment and demanded answers. Why couldn't I reach him? Didn't his mother have a phone?

His explanation was typically reassuring. I must have had the wrong number; if not, the connection between Montevideo, for example, to Pretoria was sketchy.

I wondered if this was true.

But thanks to his ministrations, his mother's health had improved, and she was no longer in the danger zone. He was able to sell a painting to the Johannesburg Art Gallery, the proceeds of which could support her for several years.

"Thank goodness I went. My brothers, Josi and Petre, had completely abandoned her, and her situation was acute." His stance sounded heroic.

"Did you see Kurt and Alexandra?" I asked.

"Of course not." His brow tightened. "I wouldn't dare. How can you even ask?"

His answer left me torn between being glad he'd had no contact with Ute and feeling empathy for his children, who must have been desperate to be with their father.

* * *

Though Klaus and I both worked backbreaking hours, it seemed we were always broke and had to watch every penny. The most critical period was when we returned from a lecture tour Klaus gave in Italy. In anticipation of the substantial fee he was promised by the universities in Bologna and Trieste, we racked up a beefy credit card bill that included hotels, restaurants, and a rental car. The promised fee never arrived. Klaus chalked it up to the flaky, incompetent Italian education system. I was stuck with the payments, which took four years to pay off.

Every time I asked Klaus why we were so strapped, he had a ready excuse.

"You know I had to give Ute my pension. I'm putting every penny into my retirement account. I'm way behind and have to catch up. I'm saving for us—our future. I don't want to be a burden on you in my old age."

I did my bit, comparing the price of tomatoes, finding the cheapest gas stations, and keeping the house temperature at a chilly sixty degrees in winter. I directed all my earnings toward the credit card debt. No meals out, no movies, no vacations, no new clothes, and no treats. I turned into a machine as Klaus pushed me to take on more work and earn more.

CHAPTER 12
HERE COMES THE BRIDE

Klaus and I had discussed getting married many times before leaving South Africa. He always asserted that it was important to declare to the world our love and devotion to one another. In Johannesburg, a jeweler had made us matching wedding rings (that I paid for), which had been sitting in a drawer for five years. When the subject arose after moving to the States, Klaus protested that the experience of the divorce and losing his children was still too painful. This was also his reaction to my requests to see the divorce papers. I would have to take his word. He couldn't risk that kind of hurt again.

I didn't understand: Klaus had committed to Ute, so why couldn't he commit to me? I cajoled. What if we could marry without the hassles of blood tests and divorce papers that New York State required? Yes, he said, that would make it more palatable.

I went to the library and did a little research. The Commonwealth of Virginia said it all: "Virginia Is for Lovers." Unlike New York, Virginia didn't require proof of a divorce decree for marriage. We could drive down to Washington, DC, get married by swearing on the Bible, celebrate with an extravagant meal, enjoy the National Gallery of Art, and visit my dear friend Anne Koscielny, my "adopted mother," who was now a piano professor at the University of Maryland. Klaus agreed. We scheduled the nuptials with a justice of the peace.

On a Thursday in May, we escaped work and drove south. Our wedding with the justice of the peace was set for the following morning in Alexandria. We checked into a hotel in Georgetown that offered reasonable rates and a central location. After the drama we had endured for five years in South Africa and another five in the US, I felt like a helium balloon joyously floating to even more elevated levels of bliss.

We battled the New Jersey Turnpike, I-95, and the insane Washington Beltway traffic, then checked into the hotel and decided on an early night. I luxuriated in a steamy shower while Klaus lay in bed, channel surfing. All aglow and ready to explode into song from exultant expectation, I burst from the bathroom door, toweling my wet hair.

Klaus's face was ashen. The TV was muted.

"Something's wrong? Are you okay?" My mood plummeted as I went into caretaker mode.

"I can't. I can't do it. I have to call it off." He was sputtering.

I dropped the towel and walked around the bed to sit beside him, tucking one hand under his neck while the other searched for his hand. "Can't do what? What do you mean, my love?"

"I have to call it off," he repeated in a whisper.

"Call what off?" My heart stopped. "What do you mean? What are you talking about?"

"I can't do it," he said again. His eyes remained on the silent television.

All the blood drained into a throbbing pain in my chest. "I don't understand. We've worked ten years for this moment."

"My first marriage was so bad," he rasped. "I can't do it again."

"But I am not Ute. You promised so many times."

His voice was a whisper. "You have to honor my feelings."

"And my feelings?"

The next day, we drove back to New York in silence. All arrangements were canceled. The entire situation was beyond my understanding: so much emotion, so many trials, so many expectations dashed.

I shut down amid the anguish of disappointment and rejection. I was so hurt that I couldn't communicate my feelings.

Hurtling north on the New Jersey Parkway toward home, he finally spoke.

"I know you feel hurt. What can I do to make it better?"

I didn't know the answer. Part of me wanted to tell him this was the last straw, but I couldn't envision a life without him. I loved Klaus—his sensitivity to nature, his humor, and certainly his intellect and passion for my music. I wanted to be with him.

In acute confusion, I considered the situation when we returned to New York. My career was progressing with concerts as I met other musicians. My intellectual life was deeply satisfying; my dear friend from South Africa, Raymond, had immigrated to New York City, and his partner, Pim, my impresario buddy, regularly traveled back and forth from Johannesburg. The four of us were bonding ever tighter. Klaus and I had a lovely home, garden, and two sheepdogs.

The thought of jumping ship ten years into the relationship was too scary to contemplate. And what would be the point? I had never wanted children, so there was no pressing need to marry. We loved one another, and I knew he wanted to commit. Maybe the timing wasn't right yet.

***

Four months later, we reenacted the previously aborted marriage scenario: a hotel in Washington, DC, next-day appointment at a justice of the peace in Alexandria, Virginia, fancy dinner, art museum, and visit to Anne. The date was set for September 11, 1992.

I'd meticulously ironed a navy-blue linen jacket and skirt a friend had passed down. Klaus's suit was slate gray with a white pinstripe. The fit was tight. His stepfather's medical tie clip with the caduceus secured a dark-blue, white-polka-dotted silk tie. His striped dress shirt was rumpled because he refused to "waste time" ironing and its placement in the suitcase had been haphazard.

I envisaged, dreaded, and expected that at any moment he would bail again and call off the marriage. This was not the joyous occasion I had dreamed of. We arrived as scheduled at the justice of the peace's office on a quaint, cobblestoned street. A somberly dressed secretary ushered us into a low-ceilinged office with a worn, beige carpet, an institutional steel desk, and a huge Bible on a rickety lectern. (Perhaps the low-priced service fee should have warned me.)

The justice's smile was that of the Cheshire Cat's—ear to ear. His teeth were capped and dental-school perfect. Both hands extended to envelop my cold right palm. He was so gratified to be able to unite this happy couple. But first, we had to fill in a couple of forms.

Klaus and I each took a pen and bent over the desk. We filled in our names, ages, parents' races, birth dates, marriage statuses, nationalities. I checked off SINGLE—NEVER MARRIED. Klaus checked DIVORCED. We swore on the Holy Bible. Three minutes later, we stood in front of the justice, and he read the brief words of the ceremony. The secretary stood to his left as witness.

In response to the justice's perfunctory questions, we each echoed, "I do." Then out came the rings we had chosen eight years before—matching gold bands circumnavigated with little square blue sapphires. I had never worn a ring because it got in the way of playing the cello. Now the ring felt foreign but good. Tears seeped from my eyes, representing relief, release, happiness.

Klaus, however, was pale green mottled with gray. His tie had become a noose. His freshly cut hair hung stringily on his temples. The striped shirt clung soddenly. I could only think that our marriage was a profoundly emotional experience. His commitment came from his soul.

Our kiss was chaste. We shook hands with the justice and secretary. That was it, for better or worse, until death do us part. We had no friends nor family as witnesses. I felt it was a private act between the two of us; we did not need to share our intimacy and joy. (And what if he had bailed again?) During the years we lived in Long Island, Klaus had made no friends, and his family was a continent away.

Holding hands, we exited the office to find the car. The parking meter's thirty-minute maximum had not yet expired. The heat and humidity of August had dissipated into a beautiful September day that fueled my growing exuberance.

I'd never seen Klaus so shaky. I was used to his German side—almost cold-blooded, unemotional reactions to any circumstance connected to someone else's feelings. He seemed unable to relate to another's delight or pain. Now seeing him so moved filled me with happy empathy.

We drove back to Georgetown, parked in the hotel garage, and searched for a place to have lunch. A wine bar with a glass facade and charming brick walls was open. Klaus peered in and opened the door for me.

"We deserve a glass of champagne," he said. We sat, ordered, and looked into each other's eyes, tilting the tall, thin-stemmed flutes in a toast. I said, "I want at least fifty more years." The touch was a small, dull thud.

No longer could I doubt that we were one team. From this point forward, I would excise any doubts about his commitment to his love. I would support Klaus's genius and our union.

Back at the hotel, I phoned Anne, who was now living in a beautiful penthouse apartment on DuPont Circle. She was the first to know that Klaus and I were married.

"Oh, honey. I'm so happy for you both. Come for breakfast tomorrow, and we'll celebrate."

That evening, Klaus and I indulged in a five-course tasting menu at the famous Watergate Hotel's five-star restaurant. Klaus was somber. Fires of celebration burned through me, yet my blaze couldn't ignite him. He was burned out even in bed on our wedding night. I decided to enjoy the contentment of the day's outcome, figuring that he was working through his demons.

At ten the following morning, we took the elevator to the eighth floor of Anne's penthouse suite and knocked on her door. She answered, all smiles and warmth. She looked like she hadn't slept, showered, or eaten in at least a week. Hugs went all around.

"I want to make you a beautiful breakfast to celebrate, but please understand I've been practicing ten hours a day." Her fingertips pressed together, her palms springing up and down in tiny, athletic yoga postures. She continued, "In eight weeks, I'm scheduled to perform the first of eight concerts of all thirty-two Beethoven sonatas."

"Anne, are you crazy?" I was incredulous. "Isn't that about sixteen hours of solid playing—all from memory?"

Her palms and finger continued their aerobic springing. I pictured Anne and a nine-foot Steinway piano on an otherwise empty stage. Klaus and I followed her into the apartment, past her concert grand, and to the kitchen. She opened the fridge and peered inside. There was one egg.

"Oh dear. I can make coffee." She seemed distracted, in another dimension. Her feet were floating six inches from the kitchen floor. "Let's see if I have milk."

Klaus, now my husband of less than twenty-four hours, gallantly came to the rescue.

"We'll take you out. Where would you like to go?"

And at that moment, I was so proud. Not only was he supporting me, but he was also taking care of my friend without judgment or complaint.

CHAPTER 13
SECOND THEME

I n the months after our wedding, peace reigned. All our work and sacrifice now had real meaning. I finally felt that we were a team, and my uncertainty dissolved. I redoubled my efforts to support us while Klaus put "every penny toward our future" and saved for his retirement. The only hiccup was his mother's death. But he seemed unconcerned and saw no point in traveling back to South Africa for her funeral.

We had been living in the States for six years and bought the house we were renting. Klaus added a bathroom, acting as plumber, electrician, and tiler, which gave him great pleasure and a release from the pressures at work. I power-washed and spent weeks priming and painting the house's siding. Klaus worked horse manure into the soil, then planted a large fruit garden with gooseberries, raspberries, several varieties of currants, and blueberries. Fruit was his passion and addiction.

We had just come in from working in the yard late one weekend afternoon when the phone rang. Klaus never answered calls. That was my job.

"Is my father there?" The voice was female and had a South African accent. "It's Alexandra."

This was a first. As far as I knew, Klaus had had no contact with her since immigrating to the States. Maybe it was good; they could reestablish a relationship in which I could take part.

I extended the phone to Klaus, who was watching the US Open.

"It's Alexandra."

The TV went silent. Klaus took the receiver from me.

"Lexi." His voice was soft and soothing.

She must be in college by now, I thought as he went to the kitchen for privacy.

A few minutes later, Klaus came back to the living room. I thumbed the mute button on the remote and regarded him questioningly.

"Alexandra and Kurt are together in London," he said matter-of-factly. He didn't seem surprised that they had called or were in the UK.

"How did they find you here?" My mouth went dry. "I thought you were estranged. South Africa to England to Long Island is a huge leap."

"Apparently, Kurt was on a computer search and found me on the Brookhaven Lab directory." Klaus seemed dazed. "Then they plugged in your name. And the telephone number was listed. In a fishing expedition, they put two and two together and tried their luck."

Klaus had always seemed to idolize his children: their athleticism, musical talent, artistic creativity, and, of course, intellectual prowess. It saddened me that he hadn't been allowed to see them for the last seven years, but this development would certainly be good for all concerned. Now that Klaus and I were settled and happy, Kurt and Alexandra might recognize and appreciate the decision their father made when they were still young and unable to understand love.

"That's unbelievable that they would remember my name after so many years," I said. "What's happening? Tell me. Finish the story."

Klaus's look was distant. "I have no idea, since I haven't seen them since they were schoolkids." He collapsed next to me on the sofa. One of the dogs plonked its head on his knee, and Klaus stroked his ears. "They are both at the University of London and want me to come visit. Now that they are away from Ute, it's my chance to finally get to know my children. The connection would be really meaningful to me."

"If you are going, I'm coming too," I said.

I wondered what Ute had told the children about me over the years. That I was a homewrecker? That I had enticed and stolen their father away from a happy marriage, and Klaus was a naive genius seduced by a musical floozy?

Now was my chance to set things right. I wanted Kurt and Alexandra to see the beautiful partnership I had with their father. I knew nothing except the few things Klaus had told me about their childhood. Now they were grown-ups finding their way, probably experiencing their own trials and raptures in relationships. Hopefully they would understand the complexity of what happened between their mother, their father, and myself.

Klaus took his hand off Raoul's ear and cupped the back of my neck. "No. I'll go alone and spend time with them. That will give me a chance to explain the situation."

We talked it through. He wanted to reestablish a relationship and would only be gone for a few days. Memorial Day weekend was approaching. He could take time off from work. I was excluded, but he promised to tell them about our life together and how happy we were.

The holiday weekend arrived, and I drove Klaus to JFK International Airport.

He promised to call me from London, but I heard nothing. Why didn't he call? What was happening? Why had he excluded me yet again?

Four days later, Klaus came home. When I picked him up from the airport, he appeared haggard and even weak. But his arms immediately wrapped around me as if we'd been separated for eternity. We found the car and stowed his bag in the trunk before his story commenced.

"The flight to Heathrow was a total nightmare," he said, sweating despite the mild heat. "The rows in the aircraft were so tight that my knees were rammed into the seat in front of me with my feet cut off at the ankles. I was on an aisle near the toilets, and the entire night there was a constant stream of passengers bumping into my shoulder. By the time we landed at Heathrow, I felt like a living corpse."

I found the parking lot exit and shoved the ticket into the automatic reader, then released the brake.

"Did you recognize them—Kurt and Alexandra?" I asked.

"After the flight from hell and Customs and Immigration, I staggered out of baggage claim, and they were waiting. Alexandra was the first to spot me. She said she recognized me by the way I walk. But honestly, I never would have known her. She'd shaved her head."

I glanced at him as I negotiated the ramp onto the Belt Parkway. He did not look well. His skin had a whitish, jellied mayonnaise–like tinge. Maybe it was the food served on the flight.

I merged onto the highway and listened to his story at a relaxed seventy-five miles per hour. Alexandra was majoring in African and Arabic studies at the University of London, while Kurt was studying for a PhD in astrophysics after graduating from Oxford University. He was living with his fiancée, an actuary, in her flat, where Klaus originally planned to stay. At some stage, there was a rumpus, and the girlfriend threw Klaus out, which I found pretty weird.

He concluded that she was jealous and unstable, so he went to Alexandra's flat in a sketchy part of London. There he slept on a short, lumpy sofa. (For years afterward, Klaus would fondly share the story of Alexandra living in a derelict building, always mentioning that the Indian at the corner store knew her by name and asked to be introduced to her "Dad"—the point being that even the low-rent district was a neighborhood with people who cared, and she was proud to introduce him.)

Throughout the visit, Klaus had been sick. His stomach was delicate even at the best times, and traveling could put him in bed for days. The slightest whiff of yogurt sent his digestion into uncontrollable bleeding diarrhea. Eating cooked onions had a similar dire effect. Perhaps this was compounded by the stress of seeing his kids after so many years.

I couldn't imagine the poignancy of the meeting. He often trooped out well-worn childhood stories: five-year-old Alexandra saving a chicken from execution when their next-door neighbor, a rabbi, chased it around the back garden with a hatchet; Kurt at three calling a horse "a sports cow" and later asking how swaying tree branches created wind. Such vignettes had become his mythology.

When I asked, he assured me that they were supportive of our marriage and wanted to visit us in the States. I had been concerned that they resented me for "stealing" their father and being the "other woman." Now I envisaged an opportunity to connect with these intelligent, sensitive young people and create meaningful relationships with them.

··

I worked systematically on revving up my performance opportunities with piano and chamber-group collaborations. This led to a growing sensitivity to nuanced tone and response. I realized that my bow did not match my glorious Italian cello. Like a car's tire size or the appropriate shoes to accessorize a formal gown, a bow must match both the instrument and the player.

I found no information on how to choose a bow, so as the "research queen" (my brother's nomenclature), I became a detective. I read everything available but was left unsatisfied. It occurred to me that if I needed more guidance, others might as well.

Years ago, my mother had studied graphoanalysis, the psychological analysis of handwriting (I suspect in order to understand my father), and as a "master" was qualified to detect forgeries and had even self-published a book on identifying character traits through handwriting. In her detailed evaluation of my script, which she had analyzed while I was still in Johannesburg, she noted that I had literary ability. I thought she was crazy at the time. I was a cellist, not a writer, but now I thought, *Let me give this a try.*

I interviewed a handful of cutting-edge bow makers in the US, England, and France and compiled the results of my findings in my first article, published in *Strings Magazine* as the cover story of the July/August 1995 issue. My career was expanding and going in a new direction I had not anticipated.

With this accolade under my belt, I approached the president of the world's largest manufacturer of strings, D'Addario String Company, located in Long Island, and proposed that I represent the company at an international cello festival. He agreed. Through this connection, I attended music festivals in Germany, the UK, Russia, and France.

At a cello festival in Manchester, England, I met the editor of the British string magazine *The Strad*. She accepted my pitch, and before long I was a regular contributor. Assignments included festival, concert, and CD reviews, profiles of violin makers, superstar string players, and teachers, product tests, and eventually my own column on cello technique. My journalism assignments led to more travel throughout Europe, the US, Russia, the UK, China, and South Africa. I established a special relationship with the cello festival in Kronberg, Germany, and was commissioned to write a biography of the cellist of the famed Beaux Arts Trio, Bernard Greenhouse.[2*]

Klaus loved the concerts, took pictures of me with the artists, and helped edit articles. Traveling together was exciting and fun. His perspective on music and performances expanded my outlook and experience.

But in my everyday work life, I became a teaching machine. And with so many students and parents traipsing in and out of our little house, we needed more space. To get to my studio in a back bedroom, students went through the kitchen, often knocking over kitty dishes and spilling "crunchies" on the linoleum. And Klaus wanted more land for his garden, especially fruit.

After more than a decade, our days of penny-pinching and saving every cent were finally ending, so we started house shopping. For a year, we spent our weekends inspecting real estate: the North Shore, South Shore, Middle Island. After viewing dozens of houses, we set our hearts on a property directly behind ours, although it was way out of our price range. Every day, we walked the dogs around the block and lusted after this beautiful home on a hill within a huge, fenced-in property. Through the grapevine at our favorite local restaurant, I learned that the property was in foreclosure.

I called the owner, a bank in Texas, and put in a bid at half the list price. The banker scoffed.

---

2   * *Bowed Arts: Reflections of Bernard Greenhouse on his life and music*. Kronberg Academy Verlag 2001.

Finally, after more than two years of playing cat and mouse, we negotiated. I secured a mortgage, our Brookhaven house sold the same day it went on the market, and with a few more financial maneuvers, we bought our dream house. This time I insisted that my name be on the deed. After all, I was paying for a big chunk of it.

The new house was a wreck, but the bones were solid. The former owners, who were evicted by the sheriff, had tried to destroy everything in their vengeful wake. They removed all lighting fixtures, doors, the entire kitchen, and controls for the swimming pool and irrigation system. The place looked like an uninhabited war zone.

When we moved, Klaus assigned me the mammoth task of packing up and transporting the entire contents of the house, except his basement workshop, which by this time was a complete disaster area since he habitually dropped every tool, piece of lumber, or electrical component as soon as he finished with it. He never put or threw anything away. Additionally, he decided to dig up and transplant the entire garden, saying that the new owners would probably pour green cement over it all anyway.

Klaus's energy in attacking the renovation seemed superhuman: replumbing the dysfunctional kitchen, planting dozens of currant, blueberry, and gooseberry bushes from the previous property, establishing a new fence around the four-acre perimeter, and concocting a scheme to turn the kaput swimming pool into a saltwater haven. He inspired me, and I strove to be an equal partner by pulling my weight in our union.

⁂

Shortly after we moved in and were still settling, we heard from Kurt. He had married the British actuary, but they divorced some months later. He was now working in Geneva at CERN, the European Organization for Nuclear Research, where the world's largest particle physics laboratory was situated. He had vacation time. Could he visit? I felt this would be an excellent opportunity for Kurt to join our lives.

He stayed for two weeks, the first of many visits. Since Klaus worked such long hours, he handed me the reins of providing entertainment, though I was also working. Kurt seemed crushed and had little to add to our conversations aside from recounting the torturous hours he spent analyzing data for an experiment with 600 scientists; however, he did not attempt to follow up on my suggestion to take the train into New York City and explore, electing instead to hang around, working from his laptop.

When Klaus came home from work around 7:30, he became the animated host: regaling with stories, entertaining with his wit and knowledge, becoming the master of ceremonies. After dinner, father and son's discussions centered around physics and cosmology—quarks, bosons, string theory.

On subsequent visits, Kurt brought his new girlfriend, and our home turned into a hotel, including the provision of meals, coffee, drinks, laundry, and transportation. I wanted Klaus to set boundaries. I wasn't a maid and worked as hard and as long hours as he did. It wasn't my job to serve his son. This had become a problem.

We invited Klaus's youngest half brother, Petrus (lovingly called Petre), who lived in Pretoria, South Africa. It was his first visit to the United States and an attempt to recover from a recent and traumatic divorce. We connected from the very first hug. I found it difficult to comprehend that he and Klaus were from the same family: one an intellectual scientist, the other an architect by training who chose to grow flowers commercially. Petre was thin and wiry, with a balding pate and sun-scorched skin. His accent seemed more Afrikaans than English South African. He was quick to laugh and be playful.

They enjoyed relating their childhood memories and reviewing their lives. Klaus idolized his stepfather, but Petre was embittered by the rules and restrictions his father imposed, which he considered harsh to the point of brutality. Klaus's perspective was that because he was older and not the biological son, he had been able to do pretty much anything he wanted without reprisal.

The stories were insightful, though a few discrepancies fogged the facts as I understood them. If Klaus's degrees (including a bachelor's, three master's, and two PhDs) were from Oxford University, why did Petre mention that Klaus had graduated from the university in Pretoria? When I asked, Klaus's response was "He's confused. I only took a summer chemistry class there." I let it go.

Not long after Petre's departure, Klaus saw a doctor because of a mole-like growth on the bridge of his nose that kept opening, bleeding, and wouldn't heal. He was sent to a dermatologist, who performed Mohs surgery, slicing away the layers of cancerous skin to analyze under a microscope. Extractions continued until no more cancerous cells appeared. Once completed, the surgeon sprayed epinephrine, an adrenaline, into the wound to stanch bleeding. It turned out that Klaus was the one in a thousand who was allergic to the drug. After the surgery, he complained that his heart was racing and erratic.

A cardiologist sent him to the hospital for a seemingly routine monitoring of his unstable heartbeat. I sat by his side as he lay comfortably in the hospital bed. I was preparing to go home and leaned over to kiss him good night when he turned the color of a stagnant pond. His mouth and cheeks contorted, eyes rolled up, and sweat bubbled from his skin. I started screaming. Nurses careened through the corridor. Within thirty seconds, he was in the intensive care unit. The doctor on duty slapped electric paddles on his chest. With each surge of voltage, Klaus's inert body jumped. The doctor turned to me.

"I have to put in a pacemaker right now, but I need your signature."

"No." I panicked. What did I know? I was terrified. *How can I make such a decision?* "Please call his cardiologist."

The specialist arrived on the scene within half an hour. The staff, in the meantime, had stabilized Klaus with intravenous drugs. The scary part was that his heart was beating between 35 and 205 beats per minute. Klaus was adamant that he didn't want a pacemaker unless it was a question of life or death because of his work in the nuclear accelerator and its powerful magnets.

A week later, the physicians still couldn't diagnose the problem (or find a solution) and decided to pass him on to St. Francis Hospital in Roslyn, which specializes in heart care and has sophisticated machines and specialists. The electrocardiologist tried to correct his unstable heartbeat by sending an electric wire through a vein in his groin to his heart and zapping it into submission—an extremely unpleasant procedure called an ablation. When this failed to remedy the problem, Klaus finally submitted to having the dreaded pacemaker implanted. He now had a battery-operated heart and was dependent upon the matchbox-sized, life-saving device lodged under his collarbone.

The hospital released him with a prescription he dubbed "rat poison," a blood thinner (Coumadin) that he claimed was made from the same ingredient used to kill rodents. This stopped his career in the Relativistic Heavy Ion Collider, with its 2.4 miles of magnets used to accelerate particle beams. My concern was for his physical and emotional well-being. For me, his health was more important than work. Luckily, though he could no longer be exposed to radiation, he changed gears and worked on sustainable energy, specifically the elimination of pollution in burning coal.

Life resumed, and our relationship was peaceful and loving. Financial struggles aside, we got along well and enjoyed many of the same activities: art museums, bookstores and reading, discussing ideas, travel, and, of course, music. We divided the house chores fairly and allowed each other plenty of freedom to spend time alone on our interests. Klaus worked many hours on mathematical equations and read the history of plants and the chemical makeup of their scents as I sat practicing behind my cello or writing articles on the computer. Then we'd walk the dogs.

However, a growing worry was the economic uncertainty of the lab, which relied on government support. Billions had been spent on building the supercollider in Texas, only for it to be shut down, which cost more billions. The Star Wars effort ended with the collapse of communism and the destruction of the Berlin Wall. Interest in nuclear medicine seemed to come and go, and scientists received only a fraction of the funding needed to carry out experiments in fundamental research that required advanced, costly machines and the power to run them.

Pressures mounted as the lab started to drastically reduce staff. Klaus's attitude became increasingly negative. He felt his innovations and solutions to technical problems were not appreciated by his boss and the lab admin. In compensation, the portions on his plate grew, and he gained weight.

Some years before, his left toe had become inflamed, swollen, and turned fire red and so painful that even the bedsheet resting on his foot was excruciating. The diagnosis was gout—the "disease of kings," as in former times only aristocrats had access to the luxury food and drink, like steak, seafood, and red wine, that causes uric acid buildup, which forms needlelike crystals in the joints. Obesity and high blood pressure did Klaus no favors. I began coping with the reality of marrying a man seventeen years my senior. I was forty-seven and in perfect health.

Klaus constantly worried whether he would receive another paycheck. The passion he once had for his work turned to resentment. The hassles at work were almost all he talked about. He thought everyone was against him. He railed against the inane safety requirements. His boss was a "turkey." I wondered if the work environment and his attitude toward it were exacerbating his health issues, but he wouldn't hear it. His disposition became increasingly confrontational and sour; maybe that was why he craved sweets. The added pounds and swollen feet made exercise less enticing. Consequently, Klaus's health deteriorated further.

Frustrated and distressed, I worked out and walked alone, an activity we'd always shared and especially enjoyed with the dogs. I rationalized that maybe having alone time was a good thing as I tried to bolster my spirits.

CHAPTER 14
RECAPITULATION

In 2006, twenty years after I left South Africa, *The Strad* magazine commissioned me to write a piece featuring a grassroots program for young Black string students in a township outside of Cape Town. Klaus and I decided to go together.

I was excited to reconnect with my friend Irit, and our friend Pim planned to be in Johannesburg at the same time, so Klaus and I would stay in his flat. Cape Town, the wine region, and the environs would be lovely in the summer. But how would I feel returning to the place that had brought me so much angst? Well, I'd find out.

It was February. As might have been predicted, we left New York in near blizzard conditions, just managing to escape before JFK closed. The wings of the South African aircraft were de-iced three times while we waited our turn on the runway to take off. Eight hours later, we landed in Dakar, Senegal, on the west African coast. At the same latitude as Guatemala, Southern India, and the Philippines, the previously frozen aircraft's skin seemed to sweat in the humidity and heat.

We observed the refueling and baggage removal from our seats. Then new arrivals boarded. Much to my surprise, these passengers were Muslim and spoke French. And unlike 1980 when I first arrived in Africa with a plane full of only White passengers, now we were the minority.

It was late when we arrived at the O. R. Tambo Airport (formerly Jan Smuts) after a nine-hour flight. We worked our way through Immigration and exited Customs. Klaus's half brother Petre was waiting for us. It felt so good to stretch, feel summer's heat, and see a welcoming smile. We strolled through the hall, and staring down at us from a billboard was a heart-stoppingly gorgeous, sexy, supine young woman.

"Klaus, know who that is?" Petre was jocular. "Your niece, Cynthia, Josi's oldest daughter: Miss South Africa."

This information took Klaus aback. He hadn't been in contact with his middle brother, a pediatric nose, ear, and throat surgeon, and he seemed curious. I was too. What was his family like, and would they welcome me now that we'd been living in the States together for twenty years?

We picked up our rental car. I had heard stories of hijackers, so even in a jet-lagged state, I kept up my guard. Klaus honed his driving skills between the parking lot and the airport exit.

I had lived in Johannesburg for six years and became well acquainted with the city, but I would swear I had never been there. Apartheid ended in 1994, eight years after I left. Now there were eleven official languages, when previously there had been only two, English and Afrikaans. The African National Congress—the democratically elected Black majority party—was in power rather than the White supremacist National Party. With the influx of immigrants from other African countries, especially Nigeria (due to wars, famine, and unemployment), South Africa was overrun with the destitute, many of whom had been brought up amid violence, weapons, poverty, and drug abuse.

For the first time in the twenty-five years we had been together, I met Klaus's other half brother, Josi. The brothers had never been close and hadn't been in touch for years. Josi's

Pretoria property was surrounded by high-security fencing. After vetting, the electric gates swung open to reveal a large, perfectly manicured lawn decorated with grey herons high-stepping near a gently flowing stream. The three brothers and I settled on a wraparound veranda outside the thatched-roof home just as the birds spread their wings in unison like one giant kite. The scene was idyllic, but Josi told us that just the previous week, his five dogs had been shot by men attempting to cut through the fence.

Josi's wife, two younger daughters, and one daughter's boyfriend were friendly and open, but this was a time for the brothers to be together and become reacquainted, so I politely kept my mouth shut, smiled, and observed. I was interested. Who were these people related to Klaus?

The round dining room was lined with a dozen or so glass-fronted terrariums embedded in the walls. They contained all sorts of creepy-crawlies. After dinner, Josi decided to show off his collection. He opened a glass front and stroked a tarantula.

"Oh, she's in a bad mood," he said, putting her back and walking to an adjacent cage. He inserted his arm, and a four-foot black snake languidly coiled toward his throat. He grabbed it behind its head, and the tongue flashed nervously in and out. Then he thrust it toward me.

"Here, take it," Josi insisted. "It's harmless."

"No, thank you," I protested. "Please, I don't want to."

"He won't hurt you." Josi's eyes blazed with the need to control and prove something—what, I don't know.

Klaus wasn't backing me up, and my pleas went ignored, so I took the snake. I was terrified, and yet I did it. Why hadn't Klaus intervened? He was the eldest brother, and I needed protection. Who were these two men—one who wanted a snake to engulf his guest, his sister-in-law, against her will, and the other, my husband, who passively watched and said nothing? Were they as cold blooded as the snake?

Back in Johannesburg, we stayed in Pim's beautiful northern suburb apartment. Just across Oxford Street was the Illovo mall, where my beloved coffee shop, the Brazilian, had moved. Though the venue had changed, the conveyor belt still delivered espressos, cappuccinos, and sandwiches, which created a perfumed nostalgia. Klaus and I scheduled lunch with Kurt and Alexandra there.

Kurt was living with his mother in Johannesburg, and though he had a PhD, he no longer worked in physics. He had visited us in New York several more times while working at Stanford University's SLAC National Accelerator Lab, but his three-year US visa had expired. Now he stayed up all night in front of his computer, day-trading using a complex algorithm he had devised to buy and sell shares minute to minute on the NASDAQ and Dow Jones stock exchanges. He had the dead eyes of someone who peered into the projected light of a computer screen all night.

But it was Alexandra's appearance that shocked me. I had heard of her difficulties, but now I could see her arms were covered in black and blue bruises. Her explanation was sketchy, but we gathered that her husband had one of his bipolar fits and had taken it out on her. Her son, Scott, who was in kindergarten, had thrown up blood and was hospitalized after witnessing the scene.

The reunion was not happy, but the situation was not mine to handle. I merely wanted everyone to feel comfortable, so I chirped away with a synopsis of our flight barely lifting off from JFK in a swirling snowstorm. As usual, Klaus was silent, right forefinger stroking his mustache from nose to lips, a typical gesture that could mean "I'm bored," "I'm deep in thought, solving a nuance of quantum mechanics," or "Lauri will take care of this."

In the following days, I went off with Irit, my Israeli friend from the SABC cello section, to give Klaus time alone with his children. The last thing I wanted was to stand in the way and play the evil, jealous second wife who had stolen their father.

After our Johannesburg stay, Klaus and I flew to Cape Town, where we rented a car and a house. Just as we were settling in and learning our way around the small city, there was an accident at the nuclear power station. All electric services stopped. No lights, no robots (the South African term for traffic lights), no fridges or ovens, no petrol (gas station pumps) or railroads. The beautiful gurgling fountain outside our bedroom window went silent. Most shockingly, the electric gates providing protection from outside enemies became our jailer; we were unable to unlock the doors and gates, so couldn't enter or exit the house. What a reminder that we were back in Africa, a continent of turmoil. This seemed more than an inconvenience. The universe and stars were telling me I shouldn't be there.

A day later, some power restored, we escaped our temporary prison, and I drove Klaus to the University of Cape Town for a meeting with his former colleagues in the physics department.

That evening, we went to dinner with one of the professors, who had been a fellow with Klaus at Oxford University. The restaurant perched on a cliff overlooking the Atlantic Ocean, just outside the city. The dining room was alight with candles, our dinner came straight from the sea, and the wine was South Africa's best.

Then the power went out. No more electricity. No more light. In the pitch dark, we cautiously felt our way down the stairs. Waves pounded on the rocks. There was not a single working electric light in all of Southern Africa, but the sky was ablaze with zillions of glimmering constellations. Gazing above, breathing in the ocean's primordial scents, I was thrown back a thousand lifetimes to a period when our ancestors witnessed these same stars and heard the same eternal surf. I felt us all as one. Tribes, generations, and religions had become a united whole, all sitting together on this cliff. So humbling.

We explored other magical aspects of the Cape: Table Mountain; the Dutch colonial architecture; Kirstenbosch National Botanical Garden with its life-size, serpentine Shona statues, exotic flora, and flocks of wandering guinea fowl; the vineyards of Stellenbosch and Franschhoek; the Cape of Good Hope; and the beach at Hout Bay, with its brightly painted A-frame changing rooms for the surfers.

But despite these scenes of great beauty, I felt edgy and irritable, unable to escape my memories. I ventured into the townships outside of Cape Town to experience and learn about the violin school for impoverished children I had been sent to report on for *The Strad*. The efforts of these dedicated string teachers, who connected with youngsters to help raise them out of their everyday violence into a temporary sanctuary of safety and harmony, both wrenched and lifted my heart.

I was shocked by the structures made from sheets of rusty corrugated metal and lack of running water where the students lived in the township. The SABC National Symphony Orchestra was defunct. The government could no longer justify funding the arts when millions were starving and AIDS was rampant. The country's vibe scared me. I'd heard too many stories of violent crime and warnings about personal security.

But the main culprits for my angst were the ghosts of my past. Kurt and Klaus nagged me to drive the eight hours to Nature's Valley instead of spending the week in Cape Town. That was the scene where, twenty-five years before, I had learned Klaus was married. I couldn't do it. I encouraged Klaus to take the car and go alone. In truth, I couldn't return to the pain, anxiety, and betrayal I'd experienced when his mother threw me out, followed by years of insecurity due to Klaus's broken promises.

We flew back home on February 26. Two weeks later, Klaus was forced to retire. The lab had ruthlessly cut its budget, and his worst fear was realized: no more employment. Despite Klaus's bitterness, I saw the situation as a welcome relief from the stress and black cloud hanging over him. In any case, I'd been the primary income earner for some time. We would be fine. My investments had paid for our house's down payment, and I covered most of the bills. He'd socked away the majority of his income into his retirement.

However, the transition into retirement was rocky. Klaus felt lost and put out to pasture. The beacon of his life had always been his work: recognition, scientific investigation, and creative discovery. Without these outlets, he increasingly needed my attention, reassurance, and support.

Klaus decided to write a "bestseller" ss a diversion.

"I could never get my ideas of a unified theory listened to, let alone accepted," he announced at breakfast one morning in early March.

"That sounds really fun." I could support that. "Do you have a plot?"

"Yes, it will be a mystery with my concepts woven into the story."

He set to work and became obsessed. While I continued my grueling schedule of sixty-five students a week, practice, and writing, he spent hours at the computer in the library upstairs and obsessively reported on his progress. When I asked if I could read his manuscript, he responded, "Let's wait till it's finished." I gathered, though, that it was at least somewhat autobiographical. The hero was a physicist.

He also threw himself into refining several inventions and joined an intellectual property (IP) holding company with a patent attorney, a lobbyist, and a chemist. For decades Klaus had worked on zero-emission coal utilization (ZECU), a process for burning coal with a common earth substance that would convert gaseous CO_2 into a solid. He had tried to sell the idea in its original form to Siemens, the German industrial manufacturing company, during a period when the country was attempting to reduce coal pollution. The other patent was a hydrogen-and-methane nano-bubble storage device that would replace gasoline without toxic emissions. I was excited for the prospects now that he was no longer encumbered by lab restrictions and hierarchy.

Change was afoot for me as well. For some time, I had been searching for a means of edging away from so much teaching and toyed with several options, such as marketing or working in sales for violin shops. One day a startling idea came to me: why work for someone else? I always did my best alone, was disciplined, and had gained considerable knowledge in business, along with supplier contacts through my travels and writing. I registered my business as House of Strings and gradually built the enterprise: the buying, selling, and renting of violins, violas, cellos, bows, and cases. Klaus was enthusiastic and started to rebuild the cabana on our property to be used as my shop. However, progress was slow. He refused any professional assistance and often felt too unwell to work.

That Christmas, just before we left for Dallas to spend the holiday with my family, I listened to a message on the answering machine. In response to recent blood tests, Klaus's doctor was asking Klaus to "please call back immediately." I relayed the message. Klaus remained passive. He'd take care of it after the break, when we returned in the New Year.

Our visit was relaxing and joyous. But Klaus was always thirsty. He drank several gallons of cranberry juice, orange juice, and soda daily. No matter how much he consumed, his tank was always empty. Darrel commented, but we sloughed it off.

Back home, reality struck. Klaus's sugar count was through the roof; he had type 2 diabetes, apparently brought on by years of carb and sugar consumption in the form of potatoes, rice, pasta, bread, cake, cookies, chocolates, sugary drinks, jam, and mountains of fruit. Insulin injections began, along with almost hourly blood tests, added to the blood thinners, high blood pressure, gout, and heart meds.

Breakfast began with finger pricking. I would anxiously await the result, hoping for a low number to indicate the condition was under control. Our conversations focused on how many pills he took, how he felt, and the next medical exam.

I had trouble accepting his pills, pain, doctor visits, and neediness. My ability to empathize was poor. I had never been sick; nor had my family. My father's constant refrain was that illness was all in one's head. For example, when I was five or six, I had an ear infection. The pain was excruciating. My father pulled me onto his lap and said that he'd make it better.

He lit his pipe as I whimpered. A hot funnel of smoke clouded into my ear.

"The hurt is all in your mind," he murmured. "We can simply blow it away. Sickness is in your imagination. It is not real. Don't accept it."

This fifty-year-old mantra circled my head. Anger at Klaus and his illnesses smoldered and ignited.

The strength and vitality I had so admired became a forgotten memory. Every morning, Klaus reported symptoms and said he didn't have long to live. I refused to hear it. I would walk down the driveway to collect the newspaper and think, *I can't take another day.* But there was no way I could leave. He was too sick and needed me. Seventeen years before, I had sworn, "Until death do we part." I took that vow seriously.

CHAPTER 15
FINALE

Tuesday, February 17, 2009

It was early, still dark, and Klaus wasn't well. As usual, I had helped him to the toilet throughout the night and begged him not to fall. There was no way I could pick him up.

"It's a sugar low," he said.

By then Klaus's complaints had become incessant. I quartered an apple and unwrapped a Lindt chocolate bar, then decided to wait until after breakfast to call his doctor. However, his suffering intensified. Finally, anxious and frustrated by the brick-wall answering service, I drove to the office at 9:30, barged in, and was reluctantly given a 3:30 appointment, the only available option.

Klaus was definite. "I won't make it until then."

I dialed 911. The ambulance and police screamed in, disrupting the street's tranquility. Our Bouvier Chianti, who kept vigil in the driveway, disappeared over the fence and into the woods.

All business, the uniformed team pushed up the stairs shouting questions, their walkie-talkies squawking. The lead officer accusingly eyed the chocolate squares and sliced apple on the bedside table. Klaus was lifted into a chair-like stretcher and jostled by two gorilla-muscled techs down the narrow staircase, through the front door, and into the waiting ambulance. Characteristically regal on this final throne, Klaus seemed in command, his faded-blue cotton tracksuit damply sticking to his shivering skeleton, shearling slippers hugging swollen feet.

A burly policeman and blond, pony-tailed emergency crewmember stayed behind, notebooks in hand, squeezing me for details while the ambulance careened back down the driveway through the barren maples. I mechanically explained Klaus's severe diarrhea, diabetes, and general medical condition: congestive heart failure, anemia, and kidney failure.

The three of us stood in the library. I had taken Klaus to so many doctors and tests, sat in so many waiting rooms and on hospital beds, watched erratic heartbeats so often on overhead monitors, listened to and processed so many scary results, and picked up so many prescriptions that there was no reaction left in me. No more nerves. Forget fight or flight. I was in total lockdown.

Questions answered, I grabbed my handbag, phone, and a book. The siren had disappeared in the direction of Brookhaven Hospital. My single thought was to arrive in time to tell "them" that his episode was simply a diabetic low. He was really okay.

Squeezing into a tight parking space, I slammed shut the car door, thumbed the lock, and tried to find my bearings. The entrance was around the perimeter of the hospital. Soundlessly, the glass doors slid open. I took a deep breath and found the window labeled REGISTRATION. With Klaus's insurance card and my identity established, I was allowed to enter.

The ER was total mayhem. My sight fractured; the rows of beds seemed to multiply like acres of tombstones at a military cemetery, each encircled by worried, anxious concerns. Klaus lay on a narrow cot surrounded by myriad plastic sacks hanging from wired sculptures. His uncontrollable diarrhea had become a spray, the smell contaminating the open ward. Though he seemed lucid and upbeat, as if he were performing the role of Odysseus strapped to the mast, I barely recognized my husband. Within the twenty minutes since he had been taken from home, his six-foot-two frame had shriveled. Fear clouded his eyes.

I found a folding chair and positioned my back toward the wheezing agony tethered to a neighboring bed only three feet away. The paperclip-like thimble attached to Klaus's index finger registered oxygen. My eyes followed the two pulsating cords from a tank next to the cot into his pinched nostrils.

His bedpan needed replacing. It sat uncovered in the open corridor. The stench was so overpowering that bedridden neighbors hurled insults. Our friend, Klaus's gastroenterologist, miraculously appeared and even more miraculously stanched the diarrhea with some cocktail of drugs.

As I witnessed the scene, a switch flipped. I instantly returned to another hospital twelve years before, when I sat by Klaus's bed in the intensive care unit. Holding his hand after he had suffered a near-fatal heart attack, I read aloud *The Ides of March* by Thornton Wilder. That book and an African travelogue by the intrepid Irish writer Dervla Murphy had been his distraction and palliative tonic.

I breathed in, shuddered, and took Klaus's hand, this time murmuring lines from *This I Believe*, a series of short essays written by thoughtful "everyday" Americans, based on a 1950s radio show. Each piece focused on an aspect of "core values that guide daily lives." I hoped the simple yet profound insights would inspire, strengthen, and again divert Klaus's attention.

Night approached. The edges of my consciousness sizzled.

The preoccupied staff was unavailable. Klaus's agitation increased. The gauge registered 100 percent oxygen, but he couldn't take it in. By 11 p.m., exhausted, I had to go home. Though his eyes were wild, I said good night.

"Okay." His words were barely coherent. "Here is where we call it quits."

I kissed his clammy forehead, then slid through the doors and out of the hospital with total confidence that he would be fine. After all, we had been through this before. Fifteen minutes later, I stuck the key into our front door, took the dogs out, and peacefully talked myself into going to bed.

Just after 6 a.m., the phone rang. In my sleep I wondered who would be calling this early. Suddenly, I connected and bolted out of bed.

It was Dr. Fahey. Klaus couldn't breathe. She had transferred him to the ICU and put him on life support. The frenzied night nurse had done everything she could. In a state of numbed disbelief, I dressed in the predawn winter light and rushed back to the hospital, where I was admitted to the ICU outside of visiting hours. I ran up the four flights of stairs—faster than the elevator. On autopilot, I didn't even want to think of what I would find.

I pushed through the double doors at the end of the eerily pulsating blue-green corridor and entered the Twilight Zone. Klaus was in a medically induced coma, lying rigid like an Egyptian pharaoh in an open sarcophagus. Tubes and wires crept in every direction, protruding from his limbs and slinking eellike beneath the limp sheet. Transparent sacks of fluid hung from IV poles. His arms and legs were shackled to the bed by straps, his hands encased in white cloth mittens to eliminate the possibility of his ripping out needles and bandages. The low-ceilinged, open room echoed the ghostly reverberation of the artificial lung. Its sucking and blowing accompanied the iridescent green rhythm of the heart monitor scribing the mechanical beats.

I stared past the waxen shape of my husband through the window, which framed the brooding February sky. A lone crow cut across the early-morning clouds.

I began to shake, doubled over, and collapsed. A nurse meted out water in a plastic cup. I was an expert at denial, but my body didn't lie. My first panic attack. I began a mantra to "man up," pulled myself together, and pretended nothing had happened.

It was a blood infection, septicemia. The severe diarrhea had left him completely dehydrated, but he had refused to drink water because his cardiologist had coached him to eliminate liquids to reduce the fluid buildup of congestive heart failure. The self-administered medications for gout had masked the pain of the brewing, force-gathering infection. Now the medical team was trying to determine the source of the poison while pumping gallons of fluids and antibiotics into his prone shell.

"We are optimistically confident. I'd say his chances are fifty-fifty," a doctor told me.

Buoyed by his assurance but still concerned, I called my brother in Dallas from the hospital parking lot. He offered to come on the first available flight. This seemed beyond the call of duty but left me feeling supported.

After a restless night, I returned to the hospital early the next morning, checked through security, clambered up to the fourth floor, walked down the corridor, and hesitated by the too-familiar doors of the ICU. The unknown was the scariest part, but I didn't want to know. I couldn't face the future. *If he was dead, someone would have called*, I thought.

I braced myself and entered.

Klaus's bed was left of the door, just visible beyond shear white curtains that provided a modicum of privacy. Bloated by the gallons of liquid continually pumping into his body, he resembled the Michelin Man.

I approached the bed. His right hand free of the restraining cuff, he was highly agitated and obviously desperate to communicate, but a tubed mouthpiece was jammed down his throat and connected to a machine.

I begged a notepad from a nurse. Klaus made an indiscernible scribble: a heart?

"You love me?" I asked, my voice laced with hope.

His engorged head cruelly twitched a definitive no. Maybe a G. I tried again: "Gout?"

His head bobbed, a tiny flicker. Drenched with sweat, he collapsed further into the pillow. He was in pain. That was our last communication.

I left the hospital and managed to drive the sixty miles to LaGuardia to pick up my brother. Back at the hospital, Darrel and I reentered the nightmare. Klaus was now comatose, and the longer he remained on life support, the less circulation and blood reached his extremities. There were murmurings about amputation.

Every few hours, doctors called asking permission to administer another procedure or drug. After I agreed, the duty nurse came on the line and requested my authorization. I was the first named signatory of the health-care proxy; Klaus's life was in my hands. I knew the time had come to let him go. His body, at this point, was only an artificial scaffolding.

My grim duty was to inform Klaus's children. Kurt and I hadn't spoken since Klaus had thrown him and his new wife out of the house some months before, after they had abused our hospitality one time too many.

I explained the situation to Kurt. "This will be the last chance to see your father."

"I won't come." His voice rang with belligerence. "I hate hospitals."

"That is totally unacceptable." I felt like shaking him. "I'll be waiting for you in the ICU at eight." I hung up. It was imperative for him to make a last connection with his father—if not for his sake, then maybe Klaus would subconsciously know he was there.

Alexandra was in Johannesburg, and as usual her mobile wasn't on or working. I couldn't get through.

At home, I made it through three cello lessons, fed Shiraz and Chianti, and then Darrel and I drove back to the hospital. There was no change in Klaus's condition: comatose.

Ronald, our gardener, was waiting. Tears streamed down his face, and he privately said goodbye while the nurse kindly and patiently explained to me the day's tortures. My only concern was how to relieve the suffering of this living corpse. Would Klaus choose to live like this? He had given me the obligation to decide life or death. The specialists informed me of the options, choices, and chances. The solution seemed clear.

Darrel protested. "I think you should wait until tomorrow. Maybe he can pull through."

With these words, my breath quickened, my heart raced, and I collapsed. Was this my body's way to avoid the reality staring me in the face?

When my strength returned, I found Kurt in the waiting room. He was afraid to enter the ward. His wife was babying him.

"Is your fear stronger than the love for your father?" I cajoled.

Twenty minutes later, he slithered in and stood alongside the bed while I kept a discreet distance. After several minutes, he came to me and admitted, "It wasn't as bad as I thought."

Dr. Fahey called early the following day, requesting my permission to put Klaus on dialysis. I asked for the nephrologist. What were his chances?

"One in a million," he replied.

"No. Do not proceed," I instructed. "We will be there in forty-five minutes."

Darrel drove, parking in the now familiar south lot of the hospital. Though it was outside normal visiting hours, we were allowed entry. The staff and doctors were grim faced. So were we. I turned to Dr. Fahey. A nurse in green scrubs stood beside her.

"We have no choice." I faced her without reservation. "Klaus would not want to live like a vegetable without hands and feet. What is the procedure to take him off the machines?"

I was handed the paperwork and signed what amounted to Klaus's death warrant. It was the weightiest yet easiest decision I had ever made.

The nurse detached the tubes, wires, and respirator within several short minutes. The robotic sucking of the mechanical lung ceased. The hanging bottles with their spidery tentacles were rolled away. Just to the right and above the bed, the monitor displaying his heartbeat was angled toward the senseless audience—Darrel and me. We watched and waited behind the closed curtains.

Dr. Fahey had cautioned that death could take hours. "Talk to him. Tell him that it is okay to go. That you understand. Release him."

I obeyed, cradling Klaus's body as best I could, heart to heart, my arms tucked beneath his squishy and cooling chest. My withered cheek pressed to his hardening, unshaven jowl as his last breath entered my dry nostrils. I whispered the last words he would ever hear.

"Go in peace knowing I love you."

Within three minutes, the dark monitor displayed a straight green line. Life was gone, evaporated. Silently, calmly, the doctor put a stethoscope to Klaus's chest and pronounced death at 10:52 a.m.—our twenty-seven years together dissolved in 2.7 minutes.

Tears seeped from Darrel's eyes. Mine were dry.

CHAPTER 16
DIES KYRIE

In the immediate wake of Klaus's death, I was an automaton. *Right foot, left foot, walk around the bed, part the curtains, sign more papers.* Darrel and I stumbled through the double doors of the ICU, and he gently guided me across the hall to a minuscule, drab-gray waiting room. We were the lone "waiters."

The flat-screen TV was huge and demanding; the rest of the world seemed comprised of talking heads: stock market, weather, and cures for sexual dysfunction. Doctors entered in an unprescribed sequence and pronounced words of explanation and condolence. Ever the performer and pleaser, I tried to put everyone else at ease, teasing history from the Persian cardiologist about his escape from Iran, then from the Korean nephrologist about the successful careers of his musician children.

Finally it was over, and we returned home. The house seemed draped in burden—lonely, sad, and empty. Chianti and Shiraz, jubilant from my early return, competitively raced to the back door. Twenty-two degrees was their favorite temperature. They were not disappointed.

I turned to my brother. "What now?"

Darrel was searching through kitchen drawers. "Where's the corkscrew?"

Somehow, I managed to put together a meal, and from the dining room table I observed the dim February sky—a sky Klaus would never again see. Beyond the windows, behind and between the stick trees, it brooded and churned.

I phoned my South African friend Raymond at his Greenwich Village office. He was expecting my call. His suitcase was packed. Two hours later, Darrel and I drove to Patchogue. The train was crowded, typical of a Friday, and passengers streamed out onto the platform, making it difficult to spot him. We saw only hats, scarves, and black coats. Suddenly our eyes met. Raymond embraced me in comfort and understanding. He was solemn but loving. We drove home the back way, like always.

As a psychologist, Raymond headed up the New York City AIDS Hotline, so he knew about death, whereas I had never lost anyone to eternity.

"We have to let people know." He was all support, action, and distraction. "First, call your parents, then give me names and numbers."

My father answered and shouted to Mumz to pick up the phone.

"I want to come." Her voice cracked.

My father was demandingly practical. "Will you sell the house?"

"You want me to lose my husband and home on the same day?" Anger blossomed in my heart.

Again, I attempted to connect with Klaus's family in South Africa. Alexandra finally took my call. She was trying to get a visa to the US. Johannesburg to New York was a twenty-four-hour trip. There were complications. Petre was also having visa problems but insisted he would make it.

So, in the fading light of early evening, Darrel, Raymond, and I began organizing the events and people that, like dominoes, would inexorably tumble piece by piece into their rows.

Dr. Fahey, who had become a friend through our close social network, arrived with vegetable soup the next morning. She looked like a farmer—down vest, worn jeans, work boots. "Cooking is my form of spiritual cleansing. Klaus was unique. I really tried."

Her distress at losing a patient was heartfelt. It had not occurred to me that doctors and nurses also felt pain; the staff had been so self-assured and confident. Emotion seemed to me to be reserved for the realm of families and relatives, while professional demeanor mandated distance, perspective, and a protective shield. But I belatedly realized that hospitals are not only places to heal; people die there.

Flowers, food, and phone calls followed. In the coming days, the mailbox would fill with cards of condolence and words of sympathy. I had never experienced bereavement, death, or final endings. The outpouring of support triggered a realization: we are here to help one another. Loss is inescapable, inevitable. Here was communal empathy. My friends and acquaintances seemed to feel my loss and connect. I was not alone. Embarrassment and insecurity were set aside and replaced with understanding, compassion, and shoulders to lean on. Two of my friends called me every day for over six months.

That afternoon, the three of us drove to a squat, pillared building—the funeral home—where we were ushered into a hotel-style, floral-wallpapered office with ceiling-to-floor curtains tightly gathered against the direct winter sun. Klaus would have hated it.

We sat with the director, who was somberly dressed in a black suit.

"I want the simplest cremation." This was another easy decision. Klaus believed that dead was dead. He hadn't shown any emotions over his mother's death seventeen years before or attempted to attend her funeral. I knew without a doubt that he wouldn't want to be buried in a casket or have a formal religious service.

"Yes, we can facilitate that." His response was barely a murmur. "After the autopsy and hospital release, we will deliver the body to the county crematorium."

I asked whether I should pick up the cremains there or at the funeral home.

Raymond interrupted and faced me. "You do not want to go the crematorium." He turned back to our host. "Will the ashes be ground?"

I shuddered, wondering if there would be bits of bone and teeth.

"Yes, of course." The director's practiced smile revealed slightly pointy teeth. "Scatter the ashes with the wind blowing away from you." He delicately fingered his tie and briefly outlined the laws of scattering cremains. "Also, be aware that every bank account, credit card, investment, loan, mortgage, Social Security, and car ownership and insurance policy will require proof of death."

He recommended buying extra death certificates. More copies could only be obtained at the county offices upon application, "so buy now through us." I would leave a 50 percent deposit and pay the balance on the delivery of the ashes, which would be in about a week.

My mind started to wander. I was still in a state of disbelief.

Klaus had spoken of death many times during the preceding months, usually at breakfast after reading his blood-sugar levels with a digital device. Next to his bowl of granola lay an index card with columns of handwritten dates and times of glucose readings, along with the vials of nineteen pills he swallowed each morning with Earl Grey tea and a slice of lemon.

"I am going to die." His voice had been flat and his eyes impassive as he said this for the hundredth time one morning.

"You have a bad attitude." I sat across the table, waiting for the reading (hoping for around 100), and tried, unsuccessfully, to ignore his comment. "Think positively. You keep harping on death."

Yes, maybe I should have listened and reacted to Klaus's predictions. I would never know how he felt. I was unable to face the inevitable until it ran me over. I was protecting my heart, which now felt like a desiccated prune.

My mind jerked and pulled me back to the present. I stood, picked up my tired handbag, and handed over the check for the cremation expenses. We all shook hands, the director clasping mine with both of his. The stone on his pinky ring dug into my palm.

✦ ✦ ✦

Alexandra arrived two days later. Her face puffy from crying, she appeared diminished, like an abandoned rag doll.

As I prepared dinner, she asked in a small voice, "Who was my father? I never got a chance to know him. He left when I was twelve, then disappeared for almost ten years. I keep asking myself if he loved me."

"Of course he loved you," I soothed as I chopped the onions. "He loved you very much and often talked about your creativity and intellect. I remember a story he told many times of how, as a little girl, you saved a hen that had flown over the neighbor's fence into your garden. You stood between the chicken and a knife-wielding rabbi."

I carefully considered how to continue. I wanted to support her, let her know that she was loved, yet I felt conflicted. For years Klaus hadn't made the slightest effort to contact her.

I continued, "But he worried about you living in Johannesburg with all the crime and your husband's unpredictable behavior.

You remember our visit three years ago, when you were bruised and little Scott was throwing up blood."

"But who was Klaus?" Her eyes seemed to intensify in color. "When I phoned, he never mentioned anything personal. He always manipulated the conversation back to his work. I need to know who he was."

I wondered how to answer her question but didn't. Twenty-seven years. Where to begin? Darrel lit the dining room candles. Alexandra set the table. The fragrance of hothouse-grown Easter lilies combated the garlicky pasta.

Across from me at the dinner table, Alexandra put her napkin in her lap and raised her head. Unexpectedly she asked, "What did Klaus tell you about his father?"

I was puzzled. "Why do you ask?"

"I've been researching my family history, and the truth is not exactly as my father reported." Alexandra's voice was subdued.

I reached for the grated parmigiana and considered. "Well, he was a German aristocrat, a baron, who died when Klaus was about two. Papa Friedrich was forced to leave Germany after the ancestral properties were confiscated, or should I say reappropriated, with the redivision of lands after the First World War."

I added salt to the pasta and remembered Klaus pointing out the Oder-Neisse region on a map of Europe in what had been northeast Germany, which was subsequently ceded to Poland. We had joked about reclaiming his estate.

"Then Friedrich immigrated to the United States in the 1930s, where he opened a bank in New York City. He was mega-wealthy. He met Marie Gabrielle—your grandmother, who was also German. They married, and Klaus was born. With the outbreak of the war, they fled back to Europe to try to pull together the family fortune."

I glanced up for confirmation. Alexandra's and Darrel's eyes drilled into me.

"There they were in Switzerland," I continued. "That must have been 1941. Friedrich died, and Marie was left scrambling. Klaus said his father was murdered because he was involved with the Allies." He had vaguely implied that the Nazis assassinated his father.

I was reminded of the times Klaus had been asked about his nationality and where he had grown up. Had he ever answer the questions directly? I'd chide him: "Just say your parents were German; it's not like every German was a Nazi." I couldn't understand his reticence. Was he ashamed of his family background?

Alexandra's hand was on her wineglass. "My brother and I grew up with stories of a castle and absconded lands—baronial opulence. But, in fact, I've learned that my grandfather bought the title of baron, 'Freiherr' [in German], through a phony adoption scheme."

This was news. I wondered whether Klaus had been aware of his father's background. *Was his mother privy to this information?*

"Friedrich needed to change his name to enter the United States," Alexandra continued, "because the FBI was suspicious of his political activities and the crimes he was accused of committing during World War I. Therefore the double-barreled name: von Österberg-Bauer. Von Österberg was the adopted name. A shady agency connected down-and-out broke aristocrats with those willing to pay for a title. With his connections, he founded a lucrative business laundering money and selling German securities for the Nazis and the Third Reich."

Through the candlelight, Darrel and I stared at her, our fettuccini growing cold as Alexandra held court. She had been researching reports from newly declassified FBI documents, blogs on Axis.com and Ancestory.com, and historical accounts of how Hitler financed the war. Her grandparents had fled New York and escaped to Switzerland because Friedrich's New York City bank was blown up by a bomb. Consequently, the FBI suspected him of heading up the Gestapo in the United States and of involvement in murders back in Germany.

"He was a wanted man, a criminal." She caught her breath. "But maybe this is boring."

"Are you kidding?" Darrel was riveted. "Keep talking."

I didn't know how to react. Even if this were true, it didn't change who Klaus was. He wasn't his father. I'd never heard him say a derogatory word or act with hostility toward Jews.

Alexandra picked up her fork and explained that Hitler had needed to fund Germany's expanding empire. "After the First World War, expatriated Germans were dead scared of possible internment. Look what happened to the Japanese here in America.

"Apparently, my grandfather's role was to find those ex-German citizens, whether in the US, Scandinavia, Portugal, Japan, South America, or Manchuria, and offer them outrageous exchange rates for their dollars, yen, kroner, pesos, whatever, if they would return to Germany. The Nazis confiscated money from German Jews and offered it to Aryan Germans returning to the Fatherland in exchange for their hard foreign currency. It was business, and he made a fortune."

I couldn't believe what I was hearing. *Was Klaus's father a murderer, a money launderer, a Nazi higher-up?* Klaus had always presented a fairy-tale version of his childhood. *Was none of it true?*

Out loud I said, "Do you think Klaus knew this?"

Alexandra finally glanced down and twirled pasta around her fork. "I spent hours with my grandmother," she sighed, "especially when she was sick. She only reported stories of private dressmakers in Paris, first-class passage across the Atlantic, the tragedy of trying to put her life together after her first husband's death, and finally the immigration to South Africa."

My voice was flat as I recounted a memory. "Whenever we were in a new social situation, the question of Klaus's name, accent, and nationality arose. Invariably he'd reply, 'My ancestors were German, but my name is Russian.' In fact, now that we're mentioning it, I remember back in South Africa, a Russian violinist pointed out that Klaus is not a Russian name. I never really questioned his background, and, as you know, he could be an impenetrable safe, refusing to talk or reveal anything about his heritage."

Darrel turned to Alexandra. "So, what do you think?"

"I want to know who my father was." Alexandra's tone was expressionless. "He abandoned us while I was still in grade school, so my memories are vague and colored by my mother's hurt. Over the last few years, whenever I phoned Klaus on his birthday or a holiday, his voice was soft and loving. He called me Lexi, my pet name. But there was nothing personal in our conversation. He referred only to work and his accomplishments. I find myself overwhelmed by the need to know where I come from. I think about my son's biological inheritance and background."

She seemed so sincere and in obvious pain. Though I didn't know this young woman, I wanted to help her. But Raymond had cautioned me to be circumspect with what I shared with her. He did not trust her motives.

After dinner, Darrel drove Alexandra back to Kurt's basement apartment. I had just finished washing the dishes when I heard the key in the lock. Darrel pushed open the door and blurted, "You've got to talk to Alexandra about Klaus. She is desperate to know if he loved her. She is in a foreign country, separated from her family, and didn't get a chance to say goodbye to her father. Make it your priority."

Of course I would do whatever I could. Perhaps we could reassure one another. Daughter and wife had both lost someone we cherished.

Darrel and I said good night and climbed the stairs to our separate rooms. After turning down the bedsheets, I went to my bathroom sink, squeezed paste onto my toothbrush, and considered my relationship and history with my stepdaughter. I had seen her only three times in twenty-five years. I could vaguely picture her in the back seat of Klaus's car. She was timid and shy at eight years old. That would have been in the early 1980s, when the three of us picnicked together at Zoo Lake in Johannesburg.

The next meeting was in London more than twenty years later, around Easter. I had been commissioned to write a piece focusing on the education of elite young string players in Prague. Headed for the Czech Republic, Klaus and I had planned to visit Alexandra and meet her husband.

Our flight from NYC arrived at Heathrow early in the morning, and Klaus was struggling with a diabetes-induced sugar low. We managed to lug our suitcases up to a coffee place on the mezzanine. Our croissants were barely buttered when we heard an announcement: "Klaus, your party is waiting for you outside gate twelve."

He quickly found Alexandra and her two-year-old son, Scott. They had just arrived from Johannesburg, a twelve-hour flight. Alexandra's face was blanched and her eyes ringed, though I calculated she must be just over thirty.

"Giles was so mad that he buggered off, leaving us stranded." Alexandra's nose reddened, and her lips tightened. "Yesterday, going through passport control at Jan Smuts, I was told that Scott needed his own identity papers to leave the country. His name on my passport wasn't good enough, so I ran from one closed bureau to another, trying to get photos taken. When I asked for help, Giles got so pissed off that he disappeared into a bar. I was sure we'd miss the flight."

Alexandra drew out a tissue.

"I carried Scott through business class, dragging the stroller and diapers on our way back to steerage, and we passed Giles. He had upgraded and left us to fend for ourselves in the rear of the plane. When we finally disembarked, I realized I had no money or credit cards."

This was only the second time she had seen her father in more than twenty years. She was dead tired, upset, and not connecting. Klaus remained in a speechless fog. *Why isn't he handling this?* I wondered, then softened. He was jet lagged, needed food, and, I assumed, was suffering along with his daughter. I shifted into gear. "We'll take you to your hotel."

"I don't have the slightest idea which hotel or its address."

Scott clung to her neck, diapers smelly and sodden. The four of us checked into our Knightsbridge hotel. When we finally found Giles's hotel, he had locked his family out.

Our subsequent encounter was five years later, in Johannesburg, and she was covered in bruises.

Now I stood in front of the bookshelves, looking for a palliative bedtime story. On a lower shelf, next to *Quantum Field Theory and Methods of Mathematical Physics*, stood a row of composition notebooks—the kind schoolkids use. I estimated about twenty, all filled with his script in pen and more difficult to read than the typed pages in the half dozen or so folders. I chose a red one. I had never pried or snooped, but these pages might divulge something of who my husband had been.

Inside was a thick stack of printouts. A quick examination revealed numerous drafts of the same few chapters. Each chapter appeared to have only a few words changed between iterations. I selected one at random and read:

IBROS

The fact that Ibros was a major personality was obvious at first sight to all but the dullest. That this was so, despite his reserved and quiet nature, stemmed from a mercurial intellect that instantly set alight his enthusiasm for the most diverse range of subjects. This genuine display of interest charmed and flattered and gave him a sparkle that compensated for the absence of the ebullience he admired in Emilio. That he was handsome and athletic did not escape notice with women and alerted in males the instinctive hostility toward rivals. In turn he strongly favored the company of women and was bored by exploits that gave expression to male camaraderie. It was not only a blatant sexual response; he genuinely liked women.

But there was a dark side that puzzled even those who were close to him. It arose from the melancholy born of habitual immersion in deep thought. To combat this state of mind, Ibros immersed himself in whatever task was at hand with relentless vigor. In the same spirit he imposed draconian demands of excellence on himself, such as he would not have dreamt of expecting from anyone else. This merciless self-discipline was widely misinterpreted as extreme competitiveness, which it was not in the least.

Ibros was undoubtedly Klaus. I immediately recognized this as the "bestseller" Klaus had been writing over the course of several years, which I had encouraged so he'd have a focus. I read on.

Through her open shirt, where buttons had come undone during the rugby game, Ibros was confronted with a close-up view of her breasts. Fully pendulous as she arched over him, and pleasingly ample, they presented an outline of compelling beauty. Shiny beads of sweat were running along the summit line, coalescing before dropping heavily. On a sudden impulse, he plunged his hands under the sodden fabric of her shirt, working it loose where it was plastered against her back. He gripped her firmly about the waist with the fingers of both hands stiffly outstretched, and trembling a little, began slithering his palms slowly up the sides of her torso, indenting her breasts deeply as his thumbs passed. Her gaze remained absent and far away, neither rejecting nor acknowledging his attentions. But when his hands reached the limit of vertical travel, his fingers lightly touching her in both armpits, she gave a strangled yelp and leapt upwards and back as if electrocuted, heedlessly diving for safety in the sand. Ibros executed a hasty twist onto his stomach, and he was uncomfortably aware of the laughter in her eyes as she taunted: "I'm hot. Last one in is a sissy!" and ran off into the surf.

The Klaus I knew was thoughtful, creative, sensitive, and erudite. I had slaved relentlessly day after day, week after week, beaten into pulp from teaching, while he was spending time writing pulp. I would stagger out of my studio at 8:30 to find him waiting for dinner.

His words rang in my ears, both admonishment and sympathy. "How can you do it? It must be torture."

Now I knew the fruits of his efforts. It was more than I could process and way past my bedtime. *Time to close down and end the day.* I didn't have the energy or emotional strength to read on. It was too much, too soon, though my thoughts lingered on the pages I'd found on the shelf. Alexandra and Kurt had begged for copies of Klaus's book. Kurt claimed that the contents held Klaus's best physics ideas, the ones too advanced for the physics community at large to understand and accept. Alexandra wanted to understand her father. I needed to comb the pages for clues and possible insights before sharing.

With my compulsory sit-ups, stretching, and push-ups finished, I showered, turned off the light, and tucked myself into bed. Upset and alone, my thoughts ricocheted between the image of Klaus's bloated body in the hospital bed, the candid sexuality of his writing, and his Nazi father. Forget sleep.

The night was long, my bed sweaty yet cold, my breath shallow and stifled. Finally, the spongy gray light of dawn seeped past the curtains. I threw off the blankets and dressed.

While the coffee brewed, I felt an overwhelming urge to start clearing and cleaning. I climbed the stairs and reentered the library, Klaus's space. His habit had been to dump every bit of mail and papers on the library table (the mountain was over a foot high) and jam his closets with socks, underwear, shirts, sweaters, old computers, bills, correspondence, and books. His "compost" piles drove me crazy, but I had judiciously picked my battles and never complained. Now I looked at the desk and remembered his words: "I take papers from the top; the problems on the bottom seem to disappear." My first thought was that he never even bothered taking from the top. What would I find at the bottom?

I approached the library closet and slid the louvered door to the right. Underneath rumpled shirts, suit jackets, and a few old shoes were four plastic storage boxes. I pulled out the furthest one, which was jammed into the corner under a shelf to the far left.

The bin appeared to be full of internet printouts. I assumed it contained information on solar panels, wind turbines, or clean fuel production. I picked up the top sheet and read, catching my breath. The article, in a low-quality printout, screamed of the libidinous effect of urinating on the opposite sex. My heart pounded. I raised the next page and then the next. The pile of pornographic articles was at least eighteen inches deep. I stopped, knees turning to gelatin. My husband was a scientist: cultured, sophisticated, intellectual. Yet here was a mountain of smut.

I dragged the box into the middle of the room as Darrel walked in.

"What's wrong? Are you okay?" He looked worried.

"Please, take this garbage out of here." I pointed accusingly at the offensive heap. I trusted Darrel to keep me in check if I was overreacting and going crazy.

He casually glanced through the stack. "Okay, but this doesn't look like any big deal to me. Relax. Bear in mind, guys are different. Pictures don't mean anything." He lifted the box and carried it down the stairs and out to the curb.

A poisonous worm entered my mind. *What else don't I know?* I scanned the piles of papers, notebooks, and boxes. First Alexandra's news concerning Klaus's Gestapo father, then the "novel," and now these disturbing printouts.

A couple of days passed. The phone rang and rang. Darrel answered and recorded names, numbers, and condolences. Food and flowers streamed in. My mind couldn't keep up. My heart was shuttered.

Darrel and I made a to-do list. Number one was finding and pulling together the assets, which might allow me to stay in my house. I searched through files to find records of bank accounts,

Social Security, and investments and realized that this was going to be a full-time job.

We then outlined a plan to reconfigure the cottage Klaus had begun to build with Ronald, our gardener and helper. The intention had been to move my business out of the house, but the project had languished over the past months. Klaus hadn't had the strength and refused to hire a builder to complete the work. Now we considered the viability of the space as an income producer, which would mean installing a kitchen, taking out the wood-burning stove, and adding central heat via an oil burner—an expensive proposition, but it made long-term sense.

We'd barely begun when Darrel flew back to Dallas, his life, his home, his reality. He left just before the next winter storm. I no longer had my closest relative there to look out for me. I would need to be circumspect in what I shared with Alexandra. Just because I was facing the shadow side of Klaus didn't mean I had to puncture her heart as well. I wanted to protect her.

CHAPTER 17
MISTERIOSO

Midmorning, the snow began a stately waltz. The dogs needed exercise, so we ventured out into the thickening weather. Shiraz and Chianti vibrated with anticipation as I aimed the toy, but uncharacteristically, their energy soon flagged. With a yearning only dog eyes can express, their need resonated straight to my core: *"Please, let's go inside."*

We marched as if connected by rubber bands. Three of us, ten legs, shuffled back toward the gate. My spirit began to crash. I was numbed by the cold and my husband's illness, lies, and loss. We entered the back door as a frigid gale blew from the north over the house's eves. A cave of stalactites extended from the roof, a visual expression of the ice building in my heart. Why hadn't Klaus told me about his father? Why had he pretended to be writing a physics mystery? What was that pile of porno all about? Why the secrecy?

Didn't he trust me?

Shiraz and Chianti settled. The wind sang at a high pitch, careening around the dried lavender stalks, throwing howling sheets of aggression across my fragile environment. Sorrow and an urgency to bury the present overwhelmed me. Doing was escape. I continued excavating.

Later that night, as Alexandra watched TV, I rummaged through the fridge and arranged a dinner of camembert, pâté, bread, and salad. Poised on the coffee table, I angled the corkscrew into a bottle of Cote du Rhône.

Alexandra took the plates and glasses from the tray. "What movies did Klaus like to watch?" Her eyes met mine.

In response, I chose one of his favorites, *Caio, Professore!*—a charming Italian film starring a cadre of delinquent six-year-olds. We zipped through the bottle of red wine. I ejected the VHS tape.

"Tell me about the last twenty-plus years." Alexandra's curiosity was unquenched.

I pulled out the bottom drawer on my partner's desk, carried it to the sofa, and sat beside her. The drawer held hundreds of pictures documenting everything Klaus and I had done together over twenty-seven years.

Recollections of good times flooded back. Before Klaus's health declined, he had joined me on many fabulous trips: Germany, China, Russia, Italy, France, Spain, Holland, England, Switzerland, and South Africa, as well as in the US. Alexandra found the pictures of her brother and Klaus the most interesting. Kurt and his father stood at the Eiffel Tower, in front of the pyramid at the Louvre, leaning on a red phone booth in London, on the lawns in Greenwich, and miming sculptures at the Pompidou.

Also from the drawer came photos of her with Klaus and two-year-old Scott in front of the National Gallery in London. It had been a hot, sunny day. Klaus wore a navy polo shirt with the logo of the Oxford Cello School, where I had taught. The grass was green. Grandfather and baby were mutually engaged in loving but sweaty smiles.

I had duplicates, so Alexandra took them all, even the shots of Klaus with our last two decades' worth of dogs and cats—our delight, companions, and solace.

The evening ended late. I needed to talk, to share, to be comforted. Alexandra was searching and questioning. Comforting her comforted me.

CHAPTER 18
SF—SUBITO FORTE

After the night's blizzard, the Bouviers led us through two-foot snowdrifts the next morning. My shovel cleared the buried gate behind the swimming pool. Their exuberance and nature's pristine freshness momentarily lifted my mood.

The night before, I had again spent too long combing through more pages of Klaus's "novel," leaving me feeling raw and duped. Now the sun bounced off the Disneyland of ice and asked me to surrender to its beauty. I threw the ring to Shiraz. It arced through the air and sank into a drift. Her head pivoted, tail erect, erratically searching. Chianti's nose followed an unseen leader.

"I remember when we met in London a few years ago and sat outside a restaurant, having lunch." On my left, Alexandra's voice was as soft as the snow she was seeing for the first time. "You referred to Klaus as your husband. I thought you must have had a private ceremony in your home or something. And I saw you wore matching rings."

"What do you mean?" My eyes stayed on my black dog pouncing on the white landscape. "We've been married for years—seventeen in fact." I turned and stared at her.

"Lauri." Alexandra's voice remained soft. "My mother and father were never divorced."

The ring was now at my feet, Shiraz's expectant eyes drilling through ice-covered eyebrows. I reached for the green orb, dusted off the snow, and threw the toy. I had two simultaneous thoughts: *I knew it* and *She is lying.*

"Impossible. We were legally married." My gaze fell across the frozen desert.

Her expression clouded. "When you and Klaus were in South Africa three years ago, he promised my mother that she would inherit half of his estate."

I wore dark glasses against the sun's shimmering glare, but I needed more than shades for protection. My husband had died four days ago, and his daughter was claiming that he was still married to her mother and had promised to that wife, upon his death, half our combined assets. This was crazy talk. Klaus and I had executed our wills and given everything to each other.

"Did Klaus make a will in South Africa?" I asked, squinting at the fence's boundary.

She shook her head.

I scanned my memory of the last testaments we had written in 2003, six years earlier. If Klaus predeceased me, which was now the case, I was executor with Darrel as second. We had considered and discussed at length how to distribute our assets. He gave everything to me except "all property in South Africa," which he divided between Kurt and Alexandra. At the time, I thought this meant only a sixth share of the Nature's Valley house since he had given the Johannesburg house to Ute in their divorce settlement.

That portion of the vacation property, which he had inherited when his mother died and was the scene of the fateful first contact with Ute, had always been a mystery to me. Klaus's mother had left one-third to each of her three sons. Why would she give a third to each of the two brothers but split the other third between her eldest son and his divorced wife? Klaus's explanation had been "She was just trying to cause trouble, as usual."

I threw the ring toward the gate. I had decades of experience in emotional shutdown. The habit kicked in. "Let's go in. I'm cold."

We high-stepped between drifts to the back entrance. The dogs gleefully led the way. I cracked open the back door, and Shiraz pushed through, hurling snow from her coat onto the furniture and carpets. Chianti charged in after her. As I unwound my scarf, Alexandra and I stamped off the snow. It felt no warmer indoors. My bones were chattering. The piles of snow outside seemed inconsequential compared to the avalanche that had been dumped on me.

I was removing my arm from the parka when my legs started to quiver. I only just made it to the sofa. My knees gave away, sweat pouring cold from my scalp and armpits. My breath heaved, my heart hammered, and my limbs went limp with uncontrollable shaking—like in the hospital when I first gazed upon Klaus's prone body.

Alexandra put her arm gently on my back. "Are you okay?" She remained silent as my lungs heaved.

I managed to gasp and reached for the phone. My friend Deborah Birnbaum was on speed dial. She coaches singers at New York City's Metropolitan Opera, specializing in breath control.

I could barely gasp, "Help me."

"Listen very carefully." Deb's voice was gentle. "Do you hear me?" She spoke as if to a child. "Am I registering?"

"Yes. I'm listening," I choked out.

"Good. Now find a paper bag and hold it to your mouth. Breathe in through your nose to the count of six, then exhale through your mouth smoothly and steadily, counting to eight.

Fill the bag with air. Slow-paced, deep breathing will begin to calm your nervous system and relieve the anxiety."

I straightened my back and breathed through the diaphragm, imagining the air filling my lungs down to my hips while internally chanting, *I am calm and in control.*

Alexandra's voice shattered my concentration. "I know you feel bad, but in ten minutes, we have an appointment with Dr. Fahey."

Klaus's doctor lived only a mile away, but I could barely stand, let alone maneuver a car. I took another deep breath.

"You'll have to drive." I pointed to the staircase. "The key is in my bag."

She was defiant. "No way. In snow and ice, and on the wrong side of the road, going to a new place?"

I chanted to myself, *Alexandra needs you. Alexandra needs you. Alexandra needs you.*

Half an hour later, we pulled into the driveway in time for tea. The three of us sat at the doctor's kitchen table, a plate of homemade oatmeal cookies between us. Alexandra's demeanor was respectful, almost coy. She had become the same eight-year-old girl who sat in the back of Klaus's BMW, wrapped in a crocheted shawl. With a penetrating solemnity in her ice-blue eyes, she asked, "What happened to my father? Why did he die?"

"His condition was all related to diabetes." Dr. Fahey poured the boiling water from the kettle. There was a hint of damp mud on her khakis.

I sank into myself. *Is that true? Could the damage to his esophagus, liver, kidneys, and heart be due to diabetes?* For years, he'd swallowed nineteen pills a day. He had several heart attacks, a pacemaker, and congestive heart failure. He tried to manage gout, but the chemical brew festering in his blood created all sorts of conflicts. What about the mega-doses of blood thinner that he called rat poison? My cotton-wool-clouded senses couldn't absorb her medical speak as she sat and explained.

My thoughts continued to zig and zag. *Why did he let himself go?* Back in "the good ol' days," he would nudge me awake to walk before breakfast. We jogged, rode our bikes, and swam every day during the summer. He had been a bull, devouring chores—plumbing, construction, pruning, gardening.

At what point had his attitude changed and his standards relaxed? Perhaps once he became confident in the knowledge of my devotion and admiration. Our home life was secure, without emotional challenges. He had insisted his health depended on potatoes, pasta, rice, and bread, and he often indulged in sweets.

I pictured him standing and contemplating the shallow end of the swimming pool but never dipping in for a single stroke—he who bragged of his Olympic prowess. Once, I had complained to a friend about Klaus's lack of exercise, framing every transgression in minute detail.

"Does accusing and cajoling help?" His response had the ring of truth. "Is he convinced? Does he change?"

I confessed. No.

"Then stop."

I took his sage advice and shut up, but my frustration increased. In so many aspects of my life, Klaus had been my motivation, encouraging me by example to work hard, think big, take risks, dive into new subjects, and stay fit. But his energy had abated, especially sexually. I wondered if it was not only him changing but perhaps me too. Disappointment and disillusion had grown as it dawned on me that Klaus was no longer the man I fell in love with; I slowly extricated my emotions and built protective barricades.

The doctor suddenly stood and adjusted her glasses, our interview concluded. I had barely registered a word. With appreciation, we said our goodbyes, and I cautiously backed out of the driveway, maneuvering the car between the fenceposts buried in snow.

Back home, I edged the car into the garage. We entered the house, stamped our boots, and hung our coats. From the shelf in my office, I chose Bach's *Goldberg Variations* and switched on the amplifier and CD player. The room, and my nerves, needed the music's somnolent soothing. Alexandra sat. The sofa held three decades of memories: exuberant parties, intense intellectual discussions, myriad overnight guests, unmeant poisonous words, arguments, and lovemaking. Also, cat claws.

My first words accompanied the exquisite Baroque counterpoint as I sat beside her. "When I quit the SABC orchestra in 1986 and left South Africa, I said to Klaus: 'Find me when you are divorced.' Each time we spoke, he reassured me at least a thousand times that he would come 'next week.'"

I saw I had her attention.

"He was desperate to leave Johannesburg, his dead-end job, and your mother."

I told her about the job offer at Argonne National Lab outside of Chicago, though the promised contract never arrived. And when I phoned the lab's director to find out what was happening, he said that Klaus had not been given a position.

I concluded, "Klaus had said, 'Go to Chicago, find a home, move everything, and we will be free to make a life together.' But . . . there was no job." I took a breath. "What do you make of that?"

Alexandra's face turned ashen. "He said the same thing to us. 'Buy winter coats. It's cold in Chicago.' I even said goodbye to my friends at school. We were planning to come, to move to America. He left first to get settled, but weeks would pass, and we heard nothing. Then he'd finally call and say he was so broke that he was living in a bookstore or sleeping in his office.

It wasn't long before we could no longer reach him. He had disappeared. I was thirteen, and my father was gone."

My head exploded at the duplicity—like Nature's Valley when he set me up to meet his wife. Had Klaus really planned for his children to live with us?

Alexandra was still talking. "The next time we saw him was two years later, when he came back to South Africa and took us to the Kruger Park on safari."

My mind raced, though firing on only half its cylinders. Would I ever reach the bottom of this unending pile of deceptions? To gain time and avoid her blue-eyed stare, I stood.

"Let's make lunch."

I opened the fridge, then turned abruptly.

"Wait a minute. That must have been when Klaus drove me to catch a flight to Chile for a South American concert tour and announced that he was flying to South Africa the next day. He claimed his mother had had a heart attack and he had to help sort out her financial situation, which was dire. There was something about selling a portrait by his stepfather to the national art museum in Jo'burg."

"That's true." Alexandra's gaze was innocent. "I accompanied him downtown to the museum, and the museum bought the painting. Then we went as a family, the four of us, to the Kruger game reserve."

"You mean the story about his mother being sick was just that—a story?" I put Manchego and olives on the table.

Alexandra reached into the cabinet for the glasses. "It was the last time we were all together, but there were promises, encouragement, carrots dangled."

"What was that like for you?" I felt empathy for that young child. How sad to be abandoned.

She couldn't look at me. "I wanted the family to be together."

"And Kurt?"

She filled the glasses with water. "Kurt was getting ready to go off to Oxford to pursue physics. Klaus helped organize it."

"And your mother?" I needed to know. "She was okay with the arrangement of Klaus living in the US and the two of you staying in Africa? Twenty-plus years away from her husband worked for her?"

"She knew how important Klaus's work was to him."

I remembered the trip in question. Klaus had been concerned and worried about his mother. When I asked whether he would see his children, he reinforced the mantra that Ute would take her vengeance out on the kids if he did. He claimed that his estrangement protected them from her wrath and abuse. I had experienced her outrage and believed his every word. Alexandra presented an entirely different perspective. *Is it true?* I loved Klaus. He was gone, and though I respected this young woman, I didn't know her.

"What was it like when your dad left South Africa the first time?" I finished chopping tomatoes.

Alexandra pulled out a chair from the dining table. "We said goodbye at Jan Smuts airport. He took only a battered red suitcase and his bike. All his books and papers were left behind. That gave me hope that he would return, but we hardly heard from him for years on end."

I brought the salad to the table and sat, placing the napkin in my lap. "Klaus told me that if he ever contacted you or Kurt, your mother would make life impossible for you. He left to protect you. As weird as it sounds, he convinced me that it was better for you and your brother. You know how magnetic and compelling he was. His attitude toward your mother was like St. Anthony slaying the dragon. Klaus was the savior."

"My mother was barely able to scratch together enough money to feed us."

"At least she had the house and his pension." I stood and touched a flaming match to the candle wick. The conversation needed light and warmth.

Alexandra's hands rested in her lap, a frown creasing her face. She drew the glass of water to her lips. "No, the house is still registered in Klaus's name. My mother needs a copy of the will to change the title over to her."

"When I asked Klaus about alimony, he told me he gave his pension and the house to your mother in the divorce settlement."

Her face was empty. "Then there would have been checks coming in, but there were none."

I picked up the fork and knife. *How can this possibly be true?* For years I had heard a different story. *Is she lying, ill informed, or messing with me? Is there a pension?* Maybe she had come to spy, as Raymond had warned. I abruptly pushed away the plate, my appetite gone.

CHAPTER 19
RETROGRADE

I gratefully excused myself from the table when the phone rang. Maybe it was a student or condolence call.

"This is Robertson's Funeral Home." The voice was low pitched and grave. "We have your husband's ashes. Please feel free to come anytime."

Lunch no longer held our interest. Alexandra and I gave up and drove to Patchogue. I parked behind the squat, pretentious building. Inside, a black-suited undertaker took my hand in both of his.

"Please accept our deepest sympathy for your loss." There were almost tears in his eyes. The plastic flowers in the corner of the room reflected his sincerity. Then his earnestness increased. "Your husband was a big man. The ashes weighed over eight pounds. May I help carry him to your car?"

His manicured fingers edged the invoice across the polished desk, cutting off a partial reflection of the fluorescent bulbs. I took out my checkbook.

Alexandra gathered our coats, and I gathered my burden.

"Shall I take him?" she asked.

"No, I'm good."

I lifted the cremains of my dearest intimate, someone whom for twenty-seven years I thought I knew and loved so deeply. Only a week ago, I had cradled his body in my arms as he died. Alexandra and I turned to go. The doors of the funeral home whispered open automatically. We crossed the icy tarmac. I pressed the remote lock and squeezed the square, plastic "urn" onto the floor between the front and back seats, taking care not to jostle the synthetic flower attached by a rubber band. We drove home.

The heavy ashes needed to rest in a place of respect where I wouldn't have a constant visual reminder, so together we lifted them on top of a bookcase near the kitchen. That resting place would do until I could plan an occasion to give his brothers, son, my parents, and our close friends the opportunity to respect his life with an appropriate ceremony.

The next day, I took Alexandra to New York City. She knew Pim from South Africa and wanted to meet his husband. Though Raymond was a psychologist, I primarily thought of him as an amazing cook, divulger of recipes, and fun shopping and gallery-hopping buddy.

From Penn Station, Alexandra and I trained downtown and met Raymond for lunch at Markt, a small Belgian-style restaurant near his office, just north of Ground Zero. He had managed to escape from work and was costumed in an elegant dark-green suit and red silk tie. His low-hung halo of curly black hair was neatly tethered with a red band. We glanced at the menu and collectively ordered soup to start. My companions' South African accents seemed extra pronounced.

"After Lauri called, Pim and I met and bawled like babies."

Alexandra's calm demeanor softened her penetrating blue eyes. "You knew my father for decades, and I assume, because of your profession, you are a keen observer of character. I really need to know who my father was."

Raymond took up his spoon and looked straight at Alexandra. "Klaus was a sociopath—a brilliant man who manipulated people into showing sympathy toward him. He was a narcissist with no empathy for others or their feelings."

There was an uneasy silence as his words hovered between us. *What is Raymond talking about? Aren't sociopaths axe murderers?*

Alexandra was the first to speak. "I don't understand. What do you mean, sociopath?"

Raymond's voice was steady and firm. "If you want to know your father, look at yourself."

Wow! I knew Raymond was adamant that Alexandra had ulterior motives and didn't trust her, but to call her a sociopath?

Generic sandwiches arrived, and the conversation followed suit as we traversed previously trodden ground. Through my mind ran Raymond's initial advice: "When you are tempted to reveal the details of your life, step out the front door, show Alexandra the workshop, then walk around the back to the gooseberry bushes. She can get to know her father through his activities." In other words, reveal nothing.

I had not followed this advice. Alexandra was staying with me, and she was needy in the wake of her father's death. I wanted her to trust me and felt it was my duty to help and trust her. Had I rearranged reality by projecting my feelings onto her?

⁂

My brother-in-law Petre finally managed to get a flight from Cape Town after waiting over a week for a visa. The problem seemed to come down to surnames. Dr. Fahey had written a letter explaining the circumstances of Klaus's death to help expedite Petre's travel, but Klaus's surname was von Österberg-Bauer, while Petre's was Richter. Same mother, different fathers. The

United States government couldn't understand this and had belligerently denied his entry into the country.

I parked in the lot outside JFK's terminal 4, rushed in, and waited, my eyes glued to the arrivals board. An interminable stream of overloaded carts oozed out of Immigration. Weary faces brightened in recognition, followed by excited reunions. Arms wrapped joyously around shoulders. Families enthusiastically welcomed loved ones. I impatiently yearned for the same embrace.

Then he was there. For an unbearable moment, we were separated by the Plexiglas barrier. We spoke no words as we crashed into each other. I hugged a pillar—solid muscle. Eleven years Klaus's junior, Petre remained wiry, slim, and sun leathered.

The experience of touching another's body delivers many messages. This one communicated profound sympathy and need. He barely choked out, "I can't accept death. My father, my mother, now my brother."

This was Petre's second time to the United States. Our first encounter occurred five years before, when he visited us after the disaster of his divorce. Then, he was swimming in a sea of misery. Now we drove back to Bellport in a swirl of disbelief, denial, and nostalgia.

I have pictures of the three of us, Alexandra, Petre, and me, on the beach in Southampton that day. The winter sun was low but bright, and we wore sunglasses. The dunes glowed whitish yellow, the waves scant with a meager sponge of foam.

The day was warm enough that we ate lunch out on the deck of the American Hotel in Sag Harbor. The sun's rays shot colored spectrums off the crystal wineglasses. Over salad, we reviewed the horrendous crime situation and upcoming election in SA. Alexandra's politics leaned further to the left than her uncle's. During the seafood course we lamented the inescapability of experiencing the deaths of friends and family and how we missed Klaus. While sipping espresso, we discussed Kurt's defection from nuclear physics after working at CERN in Switzerland and SLAC at Stanford University and choosing day-trading from his home computer.

Finally, Alexandra brought up the subject of Klaus's father and his Nazi connections.

"What!" Petre exclaimed. "I never heard a peep about this."

"Are you surprised?" she countered. "Your mum kept this hush-hush and took it to her grave."

On our way back home, we dropped Alexandra at Kurt's basement apartment. Her flight was the next day. Two weeks was the longest she had been away from her son, and she was anxious to return. As a parting gift, I gave her my Nikon camera and a significant cash advance for a picture I commissioned her to paint for my studio.

Saying goodbye was hard. I felt a connection of mutual closeness, shared grief, and intensity of need with this young woman, who I thought of as my stepdaughter. She had such a sympathetic and gentle nature. The car door closed, and she was gone. As we drove away, I felt sure that the revelation about Klaus still being married to her mother would sort itself out and go away.

CHAPTER 20
REQUIEM

Two days later, I drove to the airport, this time to meet my parents, who flew in from Texas. My every nerve registered dread. I decided to call my bro.

He picked up. "Sis, how ya doin'?"

"Mumz and Dad arrive in twenty minutes, and I'm freaking."

"Yeah? Tell me." He seemed interested yet calm.

"You know the situation." My heart was racing. "Their son-in-law might be a bigamist, their daughter, *me*, was involved with a married man. Klaus lied to us all. There's way too much I can't share." I was pretty good at concealing my thoughts and feelings, but my situation ratcheted up the difficulty.

"I get it. Stay cool. Don't say anything. That info would cause way too much anxiety and all-around misery. Plus, there's nothing they can do about it except worry and ask questions that you don't want to answer."

"That's what I thought." Just hearing his voice was a tonic. "Can you imagine me going through all that ancient history and the latest revelations? I'd end up having to support them. I don't have the strength."

"Better that you play the distressed widow."

"That won't be difficult. I'm living that truth."

I brought my parents home and installed them in the upstairs guest room. Petre helped provide a diversion. He was gregarious, lively, and engaging. Immediately, he and my father connected through their love of art. He flattered and joked with my mother. My parents both remarked on how different the two brothers were. Klaus's philosophy was "I come down from a dizzy height," which I'd seen for decades and accepted as the way he operated, just as he had put up with my desire to nurture and accept others. His brother's attitude was "I love people and learn from everyone."

***

The time came to bury Klaus's ashes. The temperature had climbed a few degrees, and the March wind vibrated through the crystalline air. Steely daggers of cloud pierced the skeletal trees as I angled the chair uncomfortably on the uneven ground. I was numb, but not only from the cold. Too many raging conflicts were rocketing through my nervous system to feel invested in this ceremony. *Let this be for everyone else who cherishes Klaus's memory and wants to honor him*, I thought.

Our little family group scattered on the incline around the hole that Ronald, our handyman and gardener, had dug. The dormant Japanese maple with its cherry-red bark would overlook the garden that within a few months would yield red currants, gooseberries, blueberries, and raspberries—Klaus's pride and joy.

Petre wanted to bury the urn. No. We would release the ashes. He tipped Klaus's cremains into the cavity while I played Bach. My husband's Bach.

D minor is the key of sorrow, grief, and mourning. My spirit was in my fingers, my soul in the bow. We had shared a love of music, but this performance was for my family and me. Klaus was gone. The final chord of the Sarabande evaporated into a tragic, etheric release. I lay my cello on the near frozen earth and, dropping white lilies over Klaus's ashen remains, recited Lord Byron's poem "When We Two Parted."

> In silence I grieve,
> That thy heart could forget,
> Thy spirit deceive.
> If I should meet thee
> After long years,
> How should I greet thee?—
> With silence and tears.

This last stanza seemed to be extracted from my heart and express our parting—the silent kissing of Klaus's cold cheek as he died. I felt obliged to keep the secret of his deceptions as we positioned the naked tree over his ashes and tossed flowers and earth into the roots, saying our goodbyes in memory of the man we had loved. My heart, once filled with the petals of roses, now felt wrapped in thorns.

Petre's architectural and design skills proved valuable. I asked his advice, and like a terrier after a rat, he took to transforming the cottage initially meant to house my growing business into a rent-producing entity. He evaluated the situation, took measurements, researched supplies, and submitted a plan.

As he predicted and is often the case, the work ended up being much more extensive than the initial analysis. However, over the past few days, I had dipped my toe into the uncertain waters (that would prove to be an ocean) of making decisions on my own. This was one more rehearsal for a performance of living life solo—a considerable hurdle for anyone who has had the luxury, or frustration, of working with a partner. I was learning "man stuff," which I'd previously left up to Klaus.

We began the renovation by removing the wood-burning stove and installing an entire heating system separate from the main house. The apartment required a kitchen: cabinets, appliances, sink, faucet, granite. Then my builder discovered that the water supply Klaus had connected to the house was only twelve inches underground. Code is thirty-six inches to prevent frozen pipes, so the driveway had to be excavated and the foundation of the basement drilled through. Construction started immediately, and soon there were as many as eight trucks in the driveway and twenty-two men per day anting their way into the apartment.

The price tag skyrocketed. "How could Klaus screw up like that?" I asked Petre. "He seemed so capable."

Petre's eyes blazed. "You could never tell that bastard anything. He always had to have the last word."

* * *

The need for a memorial service remained on my mind. I didn't need to expose the corruption of our relationship or reveal any fractures. There were so many who respected Klaus; why desecrate those memories? And I still loved him. I couldn't bury the image of the man who had been part of my identity for over half my life. What would Klaus have wanted? Definitely not a funeral. Since music was an important part of his life, I decided to give a concert and reception in his memory.

After booking the musicians, I practiced, oblivious to the nuances of the musical colors, phrasing, and articulation. I dialed it in. The tangle in my head felt like a steel wool pad scratching, irritating, and flaking off bits of hardened, burned debris.

We scheduled the first rehearsal of Schumann's Piano Quintet, probably one of the top three crowd-pleasers in the chamber music canon, in New York City. Together with my parents and Petre, I drove west on the Long Island Expressway (locally known as the world's longest parking lot) and dropped them off at the Metropolitan Museum of Art on Fifth Avenue, then continued through Central Park to the West Side, where we were rehearsing at Columbia University's Teachers College.

The first violinist and violist were young men with competitive personalities. The testosterone-fueled banter ricocheted across the quintet, interspersed with the occasional subtler discussion of interpretive details. I listened to these harmless insults in abject silence while desperately trying to focus on the romanticism that so poignantly expressed Schumann's joy, pain, and humanity. The work was dedicated to his wife, Clara, a concert pianist who relentlessly promoted her husband's compositions.

But focusing wasn't easy. Klaus had died two weeks ago and might prove to be a bigamist, and I had houseguests, a large building project, and was presenting and performing a full-length concert in his memory in eight days. Over the past week, I had contacted hundreds of people and arranged the players, the rehearsals, the program, the venue, and the food and drink. Invitations had been sent and acceptances acknowledged.

The day of the concert, a Sunday, with the help of a couple of the South Country Concerts board members, I set up the chairs, food, and drinks, positioned the piano, and adjusted the lighting at the local Episcopal church. More and more guests pushed through the door. I accidentally overheard my parents' discussion.

"I think she is going to crack up," my mother murmured.

"No, she won't." My father's jaw was set.

The comment gave me the backbone I needed to pound down all emotion. Hadn't Dad always said when I was a child, "Stop crying, or I'll give you something to cry about"?

My friends prepared food for over a hundred people. The scent of lilies misted over the shrimp and spanakopita. Our music was exactly right: a string trio by Beethoven, a duo for viola and cello by the British Victorian composer Rebecca Clarke, then the Quintet. But I was on another planet, probably Pluto—frozen, numb, and playing and acting on remote control.

+++

That evening, after I'd repeated the circumstances of Klaus's death over and over to well-wishers full of concern and support, cleaned the hall, driven home, then fixed dinner for Petre and my parents, I was completely empty, an arid desert vulnerable to every passing storm. All my reserves had been flushed out. Mumz and Dad went to bed early while Petre and I were left with the unfinished bottle of red wine.

As we sat across from each other at the kitchen table, Petre picked up his glass. "Did Klaus tell you about his bank account in Germany?"

My stare was blank. *Please, no more surprises.*

"When my mother died in 1992, she divided her money and gave one-third to each of us: Klaus, Josi, and me. My uncle, who now has Alzheimer's, seems to have invested the money wisely. It's still sitting in a little bank in Northern Germany."

I held my breath for a beat. "You're kidding." Would the revelations of Klaus's subterfuges never end? "That means it was set up just after we got married, and this is the first I've heard of it. I never even saw a bank statement."

By the look on Petre's face, I knew he was not kidding.

"Klaus had the statements sent to me in South Africa. He said that he didn't want the US government to find out about the account and tax him. Let me call the bank first thing tomorrow morning and see what I can find out."

"How much do you think it's worth?" *Is this possibly good news?*

"I'm not exactly sure, but he never withdrew a pfennig. Let me think. How long has it been? Fifteen, eighteen years?" He took a sip of Merlot and calculated. "Perhaps €100,000."

"You mean to say that during all these years, while I've been slaving my guts out to support us, and he kept saying, 'I wish you didn't have to work so hard,' I didn't need to?"

His shoulders peaked toward his ears as his eyebrows lifted. The meaning was clear: *"Don't ask me."*

Early the following day, Petre called his uncle in Germany. No luck. But he got through to the bank manager. Petre's German crescendoed as his frustration increased. Finally, he ended the call by slamming down the receiver. He hadn't received a straight answer on the account balance or how to get moneys transferred.

"Those bloody Germans and their rules. I'm going to fax over Klaus's will. Let me have a look-see."

I fumbled through the growing pile of legal papers stashed between towels in the laundry closet upstairs, found what we needed, and handed him the long document printed on thick-bonded, cream-colored paper.

"Okay, that's great. Now, how do I work this blasted machine? I'll just tear out this staple so I can run it through the feeder."

The deed was done. Some days later, the German bank informed me that to release the funds, I would have to apply for a certificate of inheritance through the German consulate in New York City. When I explained the situation to one of my students, an attorney, he was flabbergasted.

"By ripping out the staple, you've invalidated the will. It's now compromised," he said. "Not good."

My heart sank to my stomach.

CHAPTER 21
INTERPRETATION

Shortly after Alexandra returned to Jo'burg, I received an email obviously written by her husband. The legal wording would have come easily to him as a journalist. This was not her style.

> Dear Lauri,
>
> I wish the circumstances in which this note is written were different. However, there are practical matters that require very urgent attention. My mother finds herself in an unnecessary precarious state of affairs. As Klaus was still legally married to her at the time of his death, the ownership status of the Johannesburg property must, in fairness, be resolved to guarantee my mother absolute security of tenure. As things stand, she possesses 50% of the equity vested in the property after having established from the title deed that her marital regime was in community of property. [This, I later learned, was not true. They were married in England, where there is no such "regime."]

The letter went on to request the contact details of my attorney, an "original copy" of Klaus's will, and the date it was scheduled for probate so her mother could claim her rightful share as surviving spouse.

My insides dissolved, and the belt around my chest tightened as I tried to contact the lawyer who had drafted our wills six years before. Tracking her down took several calls and as many days. I finally learned that she had retired. However, a secretary promised to forward my request for her to contact me.

The next day I answered the telephone and recognized the pronounced Boston accent. It was Ruth Clark, the attorney. She remembered us.

"I was impressed by your devotion to one another and the care you took in crafting the wishes for your legacy."

When I told her that Klaus passed away and I needed her help in verifying the integrity of the original will, she was confused.

I explained. "Klaus's brother ripped out the staple while attempting to fax the will to Germany, where Klaus had a bank account. Now I need your confirmation that the document has not been changed or tampered with."

"That was a very bad idea." Ms. Clark was all business. "I will have to provide you with certification testifying that no changes have been made. Your brother-in-law must swear that he did not alter the document in any way and, without forethought or evil intention, unwittingly took out the staples. I will corroborate his affidavit after a careful comparison of the two documents. When I am convinced, I will forward my sworn statement to the attorney representing you in settling the estate."

I took a deep breath. "That may take some time since he is in Cape Town, South Africa."

There was a brief silence. "Yes, I see the problem."

"Thank you, but there is an even bigger problem." This was becoming complicated. "After Klaus died, his daughter came from South Africa and claimed that he never divorced her mother. She asserts that he is a bigamist and they are going to come after me to claim his assets as their inherent right."

"Stop right there." She was abrupt. "Don't say another word. If I'm called to court, I must be able to testify that I know nothing. Who is representing you?"

"I hoped you would." My voice weakened.

"That is out of the question. Give me twenty-four hours, and I'll phone you back with a list of at least three attorneys who I feel can expertly represent you. Call each one, paint the general picture, and request a consultation. My advice is to go with whomever you feel most comfortable. This is not going to be easy. I predict that you are in for a brutal, nasty, and expensive battle."

The following afternoon, as promised, she phoned with her recommendations. My habitual course of action would have been to seek referrals and references from everyone I knew, but I wanted to avoid gossip. Despite feeling pressure to move quickly, I sensed a seed in my heart, a loyal commitment that wished to protect Klaus's image as a brilliant quantum physicist, inventor, music and art connoisseur, naturalist, and charming conversationalist.

Maybe I also needed to protect my image as the grieving widow. How could I admit my role? Who was I that I could let this happen? So, I kept my mouth shut and took Ms. Clark's advice.

Stomach roiling, breath shallow, I called the office of the first attorney on Ruth Clark's list. Three days later, carrying copies of the wills, asset lists, bank statements, a death certificate, and myriad other documents, I was escorted into a stark conference room by a clerk wearing a shiny tan business suit and similarly hued, coiffed hair. I guessed that she was approximately my age.

The atmosphere was formal yet edgy. We sat across from one another at a small table.

My speech was prepared and brief. She shuffled through my papers, maintaining an imperious air. I glanced out a picture window overlooking the choked Long Island Expressway as she notated my details in a tightly precise hand on a yellow legal pad.

"From now on, stop calling Klaus your husband." Her first bullet hit the bull's-eye of my heart. "You do not have a copy of his divorce papers, so we haven't yet ascertained if your marriage was legal."

In a single sentence, she had deleted almost two decades of our attachment as husband and wife.

Forty-five minutes later, I was shown into the partner's office and shook hands with a small, balding, immaculately dressed gentleman with round, wire-framed glasses and a trim mustache. His bow tie was dotted and hand tied. He quickly glanced through the clerk's notes.

"We need to first determine whether or not the family has the right to seize your home." He turned toward the clerk. "Ms. Brown, would you please find volume fourteen so we can reference the law?"

She approached the floor-to-ceiling bookcase and stepped onto a short ladder. My eyes followed her index finger as it skimmed the rows of hardbound volumes above her head. The tome's cover was a pristine burgundy with gold lettering, just like all the rest.

"Thank you, Ms. Brown." He adjusted his spectacles. "Now, let us see. I believe the ruling is on page 462."

His focus drilled across the fine print, and he almost immediately found the citation. He raised his head. The narrow-set eyes found mine. I held my breath while the ever-increasing adrenaline surge sparked my nerves. His gaze returned to the page.

"This appears inconclusive." His voice was icy and without expression. "However, I'm not at all convinced I can help you retain your property and assets if you have no proof that there was a legal divorce. Without the dissolution of his first marriage, your marriage will be considered null and void, and, therefore, you are not his wife. This will is as valid as a used piece of toilet paper. We might as well flush it away for all the good it will do you."

Dread trickled down my spine. It seemed he was telling me that my home and life savings could be stripped away from me.

He named a figure he would need as a retainer to represent me. I took out my checkbook to pay for the consultation. The pen twitched so wildly I could barely sign my name.

We stood and again shook hands. I placed the documents securely in my satchel and retraced my steps back to the elevator, then decided on the stairs. Suddenly feeling lightheaded and dizzy, I couldn't breathe. I tried to pull in air but choked. I struggled to exhale, but my lungs had seized. Was the air going in or out? For a terrifying moment, I thought I was losing consciousness and would topple down the concrete steps. I grabbed the banister, dropping my purse and papers. The cement was cold as I sat to collect my belongings and my composure.

"I'm okay. I'm okay. I'm okay!" I took myself firmly in hand. "Pull yourself together. Crumple or prevail. Which will it be?"

Shakily, I stood, picked up the scattered documents, and pushed through the exit. As I sat in the car, I knew with certainty that although this attorney was highly esteemed by his peers, he was not the right attorney for me.

The next day I found the courage to call the second name on the list. I left a message, which was never returned.

With number three, a shrill, caustic voice with a strong Long Island accent answered: "Randazzo and Randazzo, please hold."

I waited while listening to the prerecorded hold music: Beethoven's Trio for Clarinet, Cello and Piano. A good sign.

"May I help you?" The receptionist was back.

"Yes, I'd like to speak with Ms. Randazzo."

"Who's calling?"

"Laurinel Owen. I would like to consult Ms. Randazzo concerning the estate of my deceased husband."

"Please hold while I see if she is available."

Mozart briefly replaced Beethoven.

"This is Sheryl Randazzo." Her voice was neutral.

I began my prepared speech, which was almost immediately interrupted.

"Hold on." Now she was firm. "This is way too much information. Put together a timeline from the very beginning, bring all documentation: wills, asset lists, bank and retirement statements, correspondence. When can you come in?"

It was the last week in March when I parked my car next to a frozen snowdrift and found the law firm's imposing double glass doors. Readjusting my laden satchel and feeling the dampness on my neck, I pushed the door's handle and stepped into a bright, airy entrance. After registering, I immediately sought the ladies' room. My mind ricocheted between the facts I needed to present and the interview I'd had only a few days before.

Ten minutes later, a young woman, very pretty with thick, long, dark hair and brilliant blue eyes, exploded into the waiting room, hand extended. Since she wore heels, we were the same height—five foot two. I followed her past an open office scattered with secretaries, staff, and piles of files.

She indicated a room on the right. "Please, sit down. May I get you a coffee or water?"

She slipped across the hall, giving me a chance to glance around—thankfully, no lawbooks. Rows of citations covered one wall. One proclaimed Ms. Randazzo was the president-elect of the county's bar association. She was also accredited in feng shui, having introduced its principles of design and layout to improve the ambiance of law offices. On the opposite wall, above a waist-high bookcase, were framed family photos. The overwhelming theme was a tiny, blond girl sitting in the laps of several different Santa Clauses, each with decorated spruce trees in the background. Compared to my last experience, the atmosphere was warm and welcoming.

By the time Ms. Randazzo reemerged with the proffered glass of water, my heart was pounding so hard that I thought a percussion ensemble was rehearsing in my chest. Nonetheless, I outlined my situation and showed her the will, the email from Alexandra, and details of Klaus's retirement accounts and the assets I had accumulated and funded. I had registered those investments as joint tenure, whereas Klaus excluded me from his.

"This seems clear." Ms. Randazzo went straight to the point. "From what you have shown me, there is no estate. The bank and retirement accounts will all have beneficiaries assigned and are outside the purview of the will. Give Kurt the books and papers, as stipulated, assuming you don't want them. There is no need to register the will or go to probate. We don't need to involve the court. All other assets are held jointly, so everything automatically goes to you as the surviving spouse. If it is challenged, then it will be up to the family to prove there was no divorce."

Her confidence soothed like a balm. She took out a legal pad and, in crabbed script, devised a to-do list:

1. Get an original of your marriage certificate from the State

of Virginia.
2. Claim the retirement accounts. We don't know who the beneficiaries are, but as the wife, you are entitled.
3. Close your joint checking account.
4. Claim the $220.00 Social Security death benefit.
5. Close the safety deposit box. Everything in it is yours, even though it is registered in both your names.
6. Take Klaus's name off all your investments that you registered jointly.
7. Put the title of the house and all insurances in your name.
8. Draw up a new last will and testament as well as a healthcare proxy—assuming that you no longer wish to give Kurt and Alexandra half of your assets.

Her eyes softened as she pushed the pad over to me.

"You know, I'm probably the only lawyer in Long Island who truly understands your situation. Someday, when this is all said and done, I'll tell you about my ex-husband. But in the meantime, my advice is to do nothing. We will not register the will because, as I said, there is no estate; everything goes to you. Let the family sort out the property in South Africa. Go ahead and apply for the money in Germany. If you decide you need representation, I'll ask for a retainer and draft an agreement."

Her tiny frame belied a formidable intellect and commanding demeanor. I almost felt relieved as she wrapped up the interview and I took out my checkbook. Now I had a plan that seemed to offer me a bit of security. Control was out of my reach, but she acted without hesitation, and I preferred this response to not knowing whether I could keep my house.

CHAPTER 22
A GERMAN REQUIEM

With attorney Sheryl Randazzo's advice to claim the German bank account, I called Pim and asked for help, as German was one of his eight languages. Would he mind looking into what it would take to obtain the obligatory certificate of inheritance from the German consulate?

He had just returned to New York City from Johannesburg after the shock and violation of having his apartment vandalized and robbed. The brick-faced, iron-barred front entrance on the second floor of a security-protected building had apparently been smashed through with a sledgehammer. The door and padlocked iron gate were in place, but the supporting wall was no longer supporting. The thieves walked right through the broken wall. Dutch and Indonesian antiques, silver, and precious artifacts were stolen.

This defilement was the final straw. After years of fighting corruption, crime, and unpaid invoices for his artist management services, he threw in the towel and permanently moved back to New York City, where Raymond had been holding down the fort for the last twenty-plus years.

Pim was eager to help. "The consulate is across from the United Nations on First Avenue. I'll look it up, but I think it's around Forty-Ninth Street. That will be a nice little outing, and it should be easy for me to find out what you need."

The next day, he walked from his West Side apartment to the German Consulate General at the United Nations Plaza and spoke with the vice-consul, who gave him the application and said I should phone her with any questions. (This proved impossible since the telephones at the consulate are never answered.)

Pim sent me the paperwork, and I immediately realized there would be difficulties. The form required names for all the deceased's relatives, including previous spouses. It also required an official certified translation of the will into German.

I searched online for a "certified" translator and reasoned that someone nearby would be an advantage. An appealing moniker with a "von" and hyphenated surname immediately popped up, and she was based close at hand in Long Island. She responded to my email straightaway, quoting reasonable rates. We agreed on terms. With German efficiency, the translation was completed within a couple of days and sent to an agency that certified and formatted the document with the proper stamps and seals. I received the document upon paying the fee.

After a dozen attempts, I finally got through to the German vice-consul and booked an appointment. The day arrived, but I needed someone to hold my hand.

Naho Tsutsui and I had taught as a team at Ross School, a newly minted, chichi private school in East Hampton. She taught the violin and viola students in small-group lessons; I looked after the young cellists. Together we conducted a beginners' string orchestra. Her language is Japanese, mine English, but we shared a respect for discipline, a systematic approach to teaching, and a profound desire to communicate and express music with a sense of humor. Our twenty-year age difference and East-versus-West ancestry seemed more of a connection than a barrier.

We met in front of Bloomingdale's on the Upper East Side of Manhattan, one of her regular haunts. Our hug was peremptory. She was dressed "to kill."

"Let's go in and take a quick look at shoes," she suggested. "I think boots are on sale."

"Are you kidding me? I'm shaking in my boots. My entire future is riding on this meeting, and you want to shop?"

She looked shocked—but not about my future. "I just thought we could take advantage of a sale."

"You're so practical," I countered. "Take me downtown before I change my mind and bail on this meeting."

Exiting onto Lexington Avenue, we walked east toward First Avenue. Along with all the other New York City pedestrians, we crossed against red lights, dodging SUVs, limos, and the ubiquitous yellow cabs as we headed for the United Nations and the international consulates. As soon as her right foot connected with the curb, Naho's attention veered toward the showcase windows. I poked her in the ribs with my elbow.

"Naho, focus," I begged. "That must be it on the right."

"How do you know? I don't see anything."

"Are you blind? Can't you see that enormous black, red, and yellow flag? Maybe you need glasses. It has a huge, threatening, scary-looking eagle that overpowers the entire block."

"I'm not impressed." She was blasé. "Remember, my mother comes from a line of samurai."

The tinted glass doors led into a security-enforced checkpoint. Theoretically, we were in the Bundesrepublik Deutschland. A small group of tall, blond men in brown suits gathered with us at the glass-fronted elevator as a cordial, even jovial guard pressed the up button. While he joked, I held my breath, choking back the fear lodged in my throat as we ever so gradually rode up to the third floor. We exited the lift and briefly waited until the vice-consul herself ushered us into her small, tidy office. After introductions and formal handshakes, I presented the completed application and supporting documentation.

Surprisingly, she typed the application and translated it into German while we waited. As the document zipped out of the printer, Frau Bautz alerted me to the small print: imprisonment if I lied on any of the questions. I swore on a Bible "nothing but the truth," then signed on the dotted line. My fate was sealed.

My throat and voice were tight as I handed back her pen. "What can I expect now?" I asked. "What is the procedure? How long do you think it will take for the German government to process my request?"

"There are two possible scenarios." Frau Bautz aligned and stapled the pages. "One: the German court will rule that you are the sole inheritor and will release the money. Or two: the court will send a copy of the will to all the involved parties to ascertain if there are any conflicts. If there are, it is likely that the funds will not be released until the US court decides how to disperse the moneys."

I took out my checkbook and paid the hefty fee. (I was getting good at this.) Naho and I left the consulate, then headed back uptown to an Italian restaurant the vice-consul had recommended.

Comfortably surrounded by water gurgling over golden bricks, starched white tablecloths, and antipasti, we ordered lunch. I unfolded my napkin.

"What did you think?" I asked.

"Well, I thought the interview went smoothly." Naho was tentative, which was unlike her.

The wine arrived, and I swirled it around the glass, stuck my nose deep into the bowl, and signaled my approval to the waiter, who expertly poured the six-year-old amarone with a delicate splash. Together we breathed in the vibrant perfume, touched the rims, and locked our eyes in a toast.

"To your success," Naho murmured.

"Will you visit me in a German prison?" I wasn't joking.

She almost choked on the Tuscan nectar. "Why do you say that?"

"I signed the affidavit swearing that I know of no conflicting circumstances. Don't you remember? There is the small detail that Klaus may have two wives."

Maybe the German court would reward me the moneys. Maybe the will would be sent to Kurt in Long Island and Alexandra in South Africa. If so, I would be forced to register it with the probate court. Either way, the waiting game had begun.

CHAPTER 23
PIANOFORTE

The next Friday, at 12:02, I pulled into the Patchogue train station to meet Pim. Standing outside my car, I heard the earsplitting shriek of the double-decker's approach.

Ding, ding, ding. "The 12:05 from Babylon is operating on time."

The doors slid open, and I immediately laid eyes on the familiar figure: slim and stylish, silvery-blond hair, an onyx-studded signet ring on his right pinky.

When I saw his swagger, my heart lurched. Our greeting was quick, overwhelmed by the thunder of the departing Hampton-bound train. Conversation on the ride home was scattered and superficial: the train ride, the weather, and the just-budding foliage.

Twelve minutes later, we pulled into my garage. Hearing the key in the front door, Chianti and Shiraz proclaimed their jubilance at this reunion, their little tail nubs jerking and jaws slinging toys from side to side.

Over a simple lunch of brie, *sopressata*, bread, greens with sliced tomatoes, then fruit with espresso, we revisited the past: the hospital, details of Klaus's death, forcing Kurt to the hospital to say goodbye to his father, Raymond's help, Darrel's visit, Alexandra, revelations about Klaus's father, the memorial concert, and resting Klaus's cremains under the coral maple near his fruit garden.

At the same time, we hashed out our questions: Why hadn't Klaus divorced Ute? How could he have left me with this mess? What was the story with the German bank account? Had he known about his father laundering money for Hitler? Was the house in Johannesburg still in his name? How could he have been such a dear friend and yet perpetrated such deception? What was Alexandra trying to achieve by coming? Was she a spy?

We each needed support, reassurance, and confirmation. Our lives had been intimately intertwined for nearly three decades and extended back to our time in Johannesburg.

"What do you make of all this?" I voiced aloud what I had thought a hundred times. "How could Klaus do this to me?"

"He seduced us all, not only you." Pim lifted his knife to scrape more butter onto his bread. "I remember like it was yesterday, though we're talking at least twenty-five years ago. I was standing backstage at city hall in Johannesburg after a symphony concert. You were holding your cello. A gorgeous, tall, deeply tanned man wearing a white linen shirt and khaki slacks walked past me toward you, and I thought, *WOW*."

He paused to enjoy a bite and reminisced how he had met Klaus at Penn Station only a few months ago and accompanied him to a meeting with lawyers from an Australian mining company. Klaus had recently acquired a patent for extracting carbon toxins from coal.

"I met his train," he continued. "Klaus was unable to walk even a few feet, so I grabbed a cab. Wasn't it anemia?"

"Yes." I thought back to all his medical complaints. "He was so sick his doctor forbade him to go, but he insisted. You were his guardian angel."

"Right," Pim agreed. "Anyway, we were led to a conference room and sat at a table with half a dozen or more 'higher-ups.' Klaus made his presentation, handing out only one sheet of paper, yet he had the audience gripped by his story and execution. We were riveted, but where was the backup data? These guys needed pie charts, a business plan, and especially a financial breakdown of expenses. He was asking for a million dollars of 'seed' money."

"That sounds like him. He could lead an army with his intensity."

"For sure." Pim became thoughtful. "Klaus was supersmart, charismatic, and thought he should rule the universe. Now we can see him as weak and narcissistic. He wanted it all and was used to getting it. He manipulated you. You were a young ingenue when you met and didn't know better."

This was confirmation of thoughts I'd never dreamed of expressing out loud. I liked to think of myself as an equal partner, not a Barbie doll who allowed a man to make all the decisions.

When the doorbell rang, I excused myself to teach my first lesson of the afternoon.

"It's now three." I checked my watch. "I'll be finished at seven. What do you want to do? Read or watch TV?"

"How would you feel if I pruned the privet hedge in front of the driveway? I'd like to tidy it up a bit."

I wasn't so sure but conceded. "Okay, why not? Ask Ronald for the clippers. There should be electric shears out there somewhere. He'll know."

During the next four hours, I chugged through five students, correcting intonation, fingering, and posture and advising on tone production and repertoire selection. Finally closing the door behind the last pupil, I left my studio and glanced out the kitchen window. My gaze swept down the driveway. I felt momentarily electrocuted. The hedge had shrunk from eight feet down to four—or was it three? The feathered barricade between the house and street was now naked sticks. No, it was more like spindly twigs. Shocked, I considered the possible advantages. I couldn't think of any.

Pim blasted through the front door, sweaty and exuberant, with grass clippings sprouting over his grimy, bunched-up socks.

"What do you think?" He was radiant.

"I think you need a shower before dinner." I paused. "The hedge sure looks different."

"You're going to love it. The branches will grow back thick, and now you have some visibility. Just wait and see. For years I suggested that Klaus should open up the driveway."

I let it go. How reassuring it was to let someone else make decisions. *If Pim wants to play in my garden,* I thought, *it's okay.*

The routine continued every weekend as my friend attacked saplings, chopped down mature Norway maples (our native weed tree), then cut the trunks into two-foot chunks, which he stacked to form barricaded pathways through the emerging openness. We ended the evenings with dinner and conversation. His visits became my anchor, soothing and calming my growing anxiety. Instinctively, I knew I had to change my environment.

Between Pim's weekend visits, the weekdays proved more difficult. Twice I packed my little station wagon to the ceiling with Klaus's clothing and drove to the Salvation Army: 123 pairs of socks, 94 underpants, 46 slacks, 32 silk ties. I was scandalized when I found unopened packages containing dress shirts buried beneath sweaters my mother had knitted. All were jammed waist-high in two closets.

Stuffed behind the mountain of clothes, I discovered a locked Samsonite briefcase. I had spotted a tiny key in a small silver dish on the fireplace mantel in his office/library (where he had spent so many happy hours writing his "novel"). It fit. The lock popped open. Staring back at me with arched back, huge, naked breasts and bleached, wig-like hair was one of dozens of Playboy foldouts. I swallowed my anger.

Beside the offensive contraband was a cardboard box. With trepidation, I pulled open the folded flaps. There was our unofficial marriage certificate. SEPTEMBER 11, 1992, was handwritten along with the court and location.

On the left were several ring binders. I took out the top one and placed it on the desk. Opening it, I found hundreds of pages of mounted postal stamps. This was the childhood collection Klaus had described many times as his schoolboy window into geography. Most were from European countries. Hundreds from Africa. A large portion were stamps from the Third Reich, immortalizing Hitler. I had no idea why he would want to keep the latter. I closed the box and immediately knew what to do. I picked up the phone.

"Dad?" I explained the situation. "Can you help?"

My father was an enthusiastic philatelist and had collected stamps for decades. As a child, I remember a jeweler's magnifying orb lodged beneath his prescriptive lenses like a glass eye in a skull. He spent countless hours comparing color, perforations, and condition. Tweezers in hand, he sorted through thousands of precariously balanced stacks heaped in tidy rows on the dining room table. A few choice examples he purchased and meticulously cataloged in binders behind light-inhibiting film. Most were retied with sewing thread into equal-sized cubes and sent back to auction houses. As a teenager, on numerous occasions, I had threatened his precious piles with the vacuum cleaner.

I knew that sorting through this collection would bring him pure joy. He could feel that he was helping me—and he was.

CHAPTER 24
STRINGENDO

The first blowback from my attempt to secure the German inheritance certificate came five weeks after the application process. I walked to the mailbox and, skimming through the junk mail and bills, I picked out a thin brown envelope addressed to Frau Laurinel Owen. I took a breath, sliced through the flimsy seal, and murmured with courage I didn't feel, "Lauri, man up."

My eyes registered the stylized profile of an eagle on the letterhead. The stationary was taller and thinner than the American standard, and the words were really long. I turned to retrace my steps to the house. The paper started to tremble, or was it my vision? My hands followed, and then my knees. Everything became blank as I tensed, anticipating the inevitable impact.

I caught my breath and tried to read, applying my thirty-years-ago high school German. Useless. What could the worst case be?

Thoughts looped around my head while I waited two excruciating hours for Pim, who was again arriving via the Long Island Railroad. We drove back to my house, and finally, as Pim leisurely approached the fruit trees to breathe the vaguely salty air from the Great South Bay, I pushed open the front door and grabbed the letter. In the garden, standing next to the micro apples delicately hanging within their protective leaves, he read and translated the court order from the German court.

My nightmare had come true. The court had sent copies of the translated will and accompanying request for the certificate of inheritance not only to Klaus's son and daughter but also to his first wife, Ute. The court had canvased their permission to allow me to receive Klaus's German bank account, which, until a couple of months ago, I knew nothing about. For five months, his family had waited to learn how much Klaus left them. Now they knew the truth: he left everything to me except the South African properties and his scientific papers.

The document from the German court included the family's notarized tirades. Each had enumerated why I should not inherit the account.

Letter from the German court:

> In the matter of the estate of Klaus Maximilan von *Öster*berg-Bauer, Ms. Ute von *Österberg*-Bauer and the children of the deceased have voiced concerns about the validity of the last will and testament, as can be seen in further detail from the attached letters. It is in particular claimed that the deceased was never divorced from Ms. von *Österberg*-Bauer.
>
> You have the opportunity to respond within 4 weeks.

Letter from Karl to the German court:

> I, Karl von *Österberg*-Bauer have several concerns about the issuance of an inheritance certificate

for Laurinel Owen.

Firstly, the last will and testament is invalid, because my father is still married with my mother Ute von *Österberg*-Bauer and did not get a divorce from her.

Secondly, she kept the last will and testament a secret from me. I went there several times and always found out that it still had not been published, probably because she had found out after the death of my father that her marriage with my father had been illegal.

We are going to contest the last will and testament, because it excludes us.

From Frau Ute von Österberg-Bauer to the German court:

Dear Dr. von Behren,

Klaus and I were married in Oxford on Oct. 19, 1968. I am attaching a copy of our marriage license and document.

At the time of my husband's death on Feb. 20, 2009 we were still legally married and not divorced. My daughter, my son and I learned with horror and dismay of the second wife/marriage when my daughter traveled to New York. Laurinel also kept secret from us the will. If you had not advised us of the existence of such a will, we would even today be unaware of its existence.

In New York Laurinel advised my daughter that she had attempted 6 times to marry her father. On that same day of marriage they both registered their last will and testament together.

I would further like to add that my husband and

I were in no way estranged. He had promised to give me 50% of his pension. He also paid for the education of both children and always supported me financially. The fact that he was a bigamist came as a great shock to all of us.

To: County Court of Bücheberg

From: Alexandra Gupta

Dear Dr. von Behren,
I, Alexandra Gupta, hereby declare that all that my mother has communicated to you in writing is true.
I would also like to declare that I oppose the distribution of the inheritance as prescribed by Laurinel Owen and that I am opposed to the validity of the last will and testament.

Pim rifled through the pages again. We stood in bewildered silence. Eventually, I spoke. "These are half-truths mixed with distorted facts. What do you make out of it?"

Uncharacteristically, Pim was slow to respond, but his answer was unequivocal. "Looks to me like you need legal representation from the German side. Without help, you'll never survive."

"I don't understand why Alex says I am the one prescribing the distribution of inheritance. Klaus wrote that will, not me. And where do they get off on us getting married and rushing out to write wills together? There was a twelve-year gap."

"This is only about money. Klaus was their ATM. I bet they were blackmailing him and now they want their final payout. I'm telling you, you need backup."

"Let's say you're right." I considered his assessment. "How am I supposed to find a lawyer in Germany when I can barely order a coffee in the language? Maybe you hadn't noticed, but I live six thousand miles from there."

"Let's call my son in Kronberg. I bet he can advise you."

We immediately dialed Mark, a banker living near Frankfurt, who came up with three recommendations. Right there and then, that Friday morning, I tried phoning each one. With a time difference of six hours, it was late afternoon in Germany.

The first contact was on vacation until August.

The second contact was out of the office. Third was a charm. A voice in Hamburg answered speaking perfect English (like all the rest). I asked to speak to Frau Müller. I was told that she no longer worked there and had transferred to München.

"Who then, in your opinion, is the best attorney in the firm?" I asked.

The answer was immediate. "That would be Dr. Meyer. Please hold. I'll connect you."

Dr. Meyer spoke heavily accented English. I briefly told him the story:

Klaus was born in New York City, died in Long Island, and was an American citizen. He never lived in Germany. He married his first wife in England and inherited the German bank account from his mother, who died in 1992 There was another account here in the US that his family contested my right to inherit. I was the beneficiary, yet they claimed his first wife, Ute, was legally entitled to half. My attorney in New York said that my marriage of seventeen years was good enough for the US government and it was not my responsibility to prove whether he was divorced or not. The outcome was pending.

His tone was serious yet buoyant. He instructed me to email him an outline of the relevant events up through the request of the certificate. At that point he would contact the judge, explain the situation, and ask what documentation would be needed.

Based on the information I gave him, Dr. Meyer's opinion was that whether or not we were married, Klaus clearly indicated that he wished most assets would come to me. After speaking with the judge, Dr. Meyer would send me a power of attorney agreement, which I should return along with a retainer of €5,000 (about $7,500 at the time) so he "could get started."

My mind raced. This sounded like a lot of money, but what was I going to do? Shop around for an attorney in Germany? The apparently sizable German bank account that Klaus had inherited after our marriage was at stake. That evening, I sat at the computer and put together a framework of the basics, with facts and dates.

One week later, the shadow of my postal delivery person flitted across my front door. Patty smiled and handed me an envelope with a green strip across the top. "It's a certified letter that requires your signature."

The return address read: JOSEPH HANLEY, ESQUIRE. I scrawled my name and staggered back into the kitchen. I knew but didn't want to know what was in the letter. Like a child scratching a scab, I knew it would hurt but couldn't help it. I ripped through the seal.

The attorney had learned through Ute that I had in my possession a legal document, and if I didn't register the will within twenty-one days . . .

My hand was forced. The next day, I phoned my lawyer.

"Randazzo and Randazzo. How may I direct your call?"

The static in my head was so strong that the voice barely penetrated. It sounded far away and vaguely underwater, or like when my brother and I attached a string between two tin cans and talked through our "telephones" as kids.

Sheryl came on the line, and I dove right in.

"Hi, Sheryl. I just received notification from a law firm in Nassau County that Klaus's family has a copy of his will. Obviously, they found out about it through the German court and are now requiring me to file a probate petition with the Suffolk County Surrogate's Court within twenty-one days."

"Okay. Fax over a copy of the letter. I'll mail out a retainer agreement. Sign and send it back to me with a binder of a thousand dollars if you want me to represent you. I'll prepare the required paperwork. We have to register the will to make sure that you will be appointed executor by the court, and not Klaus's son. It's imperative you retain control. Let's plan to meet as soon as possible. You are aware, I hope, that this could get very nasty and expensive."

My intuition told me to trust her. I believed she could represent me in an intelligent and supportive way, and losing everything Klaus and I had worked for was not an option. The gauntlet had been thrown, and I had to defend myself. I couldn't lie down and play dead.

Three days after Sheryl registered the will with the Suffolk County Surrogate's Court, I received an official certified South African document from Ute contesting my claim to the estate, citing the fact that as the surviving spouse, she could not be disinherited and was exercising her "right of election." In other words, she was suing me.

Was this really happening? Was Ute still married to my husband? How could she have put up with her husband living on a different continent for over two decades? Why hadn't Karl told me or confronted Klaus? Would US law and a marriage sanctified by the government protect me?

In the meantime, I awaited a decision from the German court. I contacted the woman who had translated Klaus's will into German for some insider knowledge. She suggested that I ask her father, a retired German judge. In an email, I described the circumstances and asked his opinion on how the court might view the situation of my legitimacy to inherit Klaus's bank account. After several back-and-forth scenarios, he concluded, "Probably the court would wait for the ruling in the US." This was not what I wanted to hear and exactly what German vice-consul Bautz had predicted.

CHAPTER 25
DAL SIGNO

My life was shattering. A constant whirlpool of thoughts spiraled, keeping me awake at night. Seeking relief and exhaustion, I would fall on the floor for several rounds of push-ups only to climb restlessly back between the sheets. Disinterested in food, I drank more and more coffee, trying to stay awake.

I needed solace, so in the fall I attended the weeklong cello festival in Kronberg, Germany, my seventh visit. My world was broken, but I felt confident and welcome in this cultural oasis. Music was my language and salvation, and in Kronberg, music's expression was of the highest caliber.

The Lufthansa flight left JFK in the early evening and arrived the next morning. The Frankfurt airport was huge and Germanic—hospital clean, with designer shops representing Italy, France, and Scandinavia and selling leather, liqueurs, electronics, beer steins, and the ubiquitous T-shirts. Anything for a price. After visiting the *Damen* (ladies), I followed the yellow arrows to *Gepäckausgabe* (baggage claim).

On carousel 3, I retrieved the new suitcase that had replaced the one I'd used on my trips with Klaus. I quickly cleared Customs and Immigration. The uniformed official barely glanced at my face to compare it with my passport photo. (Just as well, since even my mother wouldn't have recognized me.) I ventured my lesson-one German phrase: *"Guten morgen."*

I was rewarded with a thwack of the entry stamp.

Susanne—who had translated into German a biography I had written of Bernard Greenhouse, the cellist of the Beaux Arts Trio—found me fumbling with the strange euro coins as I attempted to pay for a cappuccino at one of the generic kiosks serving *Kaffee* and fresh *Brot*.

She was Valkyrian, her confident stride clearing a well-defined path. The delicate gold chain slung over her left shoulder supported a tiny, feminine leather handbag.

I swigged the dregs and turned joyously, grateful to be swallowed in a maternal and much-needed embrace. What comfort it was to reengage and leave my problems at home. The new environment spit me out of my downward vortex (at least temporarily) and into a welcoming cocoon of sympathy and understanding. Distracted by talk of the flight and New York weather, we walked to the parking garage.

Together we hoisted my suitcase into the trunk of her aging Volkswagen. I recognized the long white cat hair clinging to the upholstery, then buckled in and was thrown back into my seat as we shot north onto the Autobahn.

Fifteen minutes later, Susanne's right blinker indicated we were taking the next *Ausfahrt* off the highway, and we slowed in front of a Braun factory, a Mercedes dealership, and waving gold, black, and red national flags. The road narrowed. Posted on the streetlamps and bus stops were banners picturing cellists. The gray, overcast day was bright with celebration. We glided past shops, restaurants, and, finally, the town's center, which by now was reassuringly welcoming. The gold and orange of the autumnal trees diffused their natural calm into my transatlantic psyche. I felt some of my tension transmute from dark despair into the light of excitement.

My hotel, Schützenhof, a third-generation family-owned inn, was on the town square. Susanne confidently bumped onto the cobbled sidewalk, the car askew, and cranked the parking brake. We decided to meet in a half hour for lunch. I scrambled out and wrestled with my bag as she deftly made an illegal U-turn into the underground parking across the street.

The hotel's gated entrance led into an Italian pizza place. The waiter, wearing a floor-length white apron and skin-tight black shirt, opened a drawer under the espresso machine and extracted a key. He handed it to me and pointed up the stairs. Owen was penciled on a sticky note. That was check-in.

I manhandled my luggage up the two flights to *Zimmer* 5, turned the key in the oak door, and took a deep, grateful breath: *I am here.* The massive, double-paned windows filled my eyes with a vista of tiled roofs overlooking half-timbered facades: a bookshop, market of fruits and vegetables, bakery, and butcher. Tiny figures peddled bicycles carrying loaves of crisp, golden bread pillared in panniers. Pudgy dachshunds, panting German shepherds, and silvery, yellow-eyed Weimaraners led their owners, most of whom wore green felt hats adorned with feathery plumes. The narrow, curved, red-carpeted street proclaimed, Cello Festival!

I was too excited to settle in. A cursory swish with my toothbrush and gurgle of water sufficed. I pulled the door shut behind me, ran back down the stairs, crossed the street, and skirted past the bronze Rostropovich Memorial honoring the recently deceased, celebrated Russian cellist who had inaugurated Kronberg as the "World's Cello Capitol."

Reaching the glass doors to the *Rathaus* (town hall), I pushed through. "*Guten tag. Wie geht's?*" (How goes it?)

I happily accepted the packet of tickets. The program was thick: a week of master classes scheduled simultaneously in three nearby Catholic churches, with concerts held in each location every two hours starting at five and ending after midnight.

At the top of my agenda was interviewing five of the guest soloists for a documentary film that Deutsche Gramophone was producing in coordination with the Kronberg Academy. My notes and questions were prepared. Cello was a language I was fluent in. The five interviews were filmed over two days. How inspiring to hear such diverse answers and approaches to interpretation and technique!

The week was both insightful and a distraction. One night, after attending two master classes, two concerts, and a ten o'clock dinner, I finally slipped exhausted under the goose-down duvet on my bed. I reached for the switch on the bedside lamp and deliciously closed my eyes. Just as my body surrendered to sleep, my senses jolted me awake. It was an A string, then the fifths down to the D, G, and C.

My neighbor was tuning, clearly getting ready to practice. The clock confirmed it was past midnight. My ear was attuned to cellists, especially after the previous twelve hours. This was no beautiful melody but endless scales up and down the fingerboard, in every key and in rhythm with the insistent beat of a metronome. Shifting exercises, then double-stops, thirds, sixths, octaves. I stuck my finger in my ear—useless. I wanted to break down the door in a screaming foreign tirade: "HALT! STOP! The scales are perfect. I need to sleep."

I regrouped, let it go. I was a guest.

The next evening was the festival's finale: a three-part, six-hour concert. I sat in the eighth row and heard one of the most riveting performances of a weeklong extravaganza where the extraordinary was the standard. It was Penderecki's Viola

Concerto performed on cello, from memory, with the composer conducting. The half-hour tour de force was an indescribable display of pyrotechnics, virtuosity, powerful passion, and the avant-garde. After seven days of extreme stimulation and sensory overload, I sat dumbfounded and thrilled. The audience clapped together in rhythm, demanding an encore. Finally, as the applause subsided, the lady sitting beside me turned. She was gray, thin haired, and crooked but rosy cheeked as she said something to me in German.

"I don't speak German," I apologized.

"What did you think of the cellist?" she asked, this time in English.

I gushed my heartfelt enthusiasm.

Her face was alive with radiant pride. "That is my son."

Together we climbed the four stairs and pushed through the curtains backstage to congratulate the handsome soloist. In that moment I realized he was my scale-practicing neighbor, whom I had seen at breakfast in the inn's dining room, eating the same rock-hard boiled eggs I'd been served.

The following morning, I met Maria Kliegel, superstar cellist. She had written a book on cello technique that we hammered into "good" English. We had spent grueling hours on the phone—she in Essen, while I sat in front of my home computer—discussing, deciding, cajoling, explaining, and compromising. Through the meticulous process, we became friends, and she had invited me to visit her home.

Three days later at the Düsseldorf airport, I breezed through security and selected a *Bar* to enjoy a last German coffee before boarding my plane back to New York. The bag slid off my shoulder, and I was suddenly jolted by the thought of what I would find at home. Robbery? A burned-down house? Had I left the dryer tumbling for ten days? Insidious images of disaster niggled at the corners of my brain.

Driving home from JFK on the Long Island Expressway, I tried to focus on the moment rather than my anxiety. At exit 63, I turned north under the highway to collect Shiraz and Chianti at their spa. My two hairy, black Bouviers bounded into my little station wagon.

"Let's go home, Mom," they panted excitedly in syncopation. The right blinker anticipated our turn into the driveway. We slowly approached, passing the old rhododendrons and ancient maples that protected the long entrance leading to the house. I looked to my left. The house appeared abandoned, lonely, decaying.

A mirage flashed across my sight. It was as Charlotte Brontë's Jane Eyre must have viewed the burning Thornfield Hall. My eyes imagined fiery clouds of smoke that spewed memories instead of ash. I was back to face Klaus's financial infidelities, a court battle to establish if my marriage was real or fraudulent, and the urgent need to protect my investments, which could possibly be up for grabs.

From the safety of the garage, I popped the trunk's latch. Finally released, the dogs charged from the car, asserting their freedom and reconnecting with their territory. There was a rush of scratching nails, flapping tongues, and eager enthusiasm as they bolted, panting, pawing, and pushing, through the gate into the backyard. I dragged the luggage and myself up the cracked step and fought the front door with key in hand. Finally unlocking it, I entered the house. I was alone.

All was cold and silent. Mail stacked high, mostly bills. The voicemail blinked with dozens of messages. With the heating oil low, email overwhelming, laundry heaped, fridge empty, and no one with whom to share the excitement of the trip, the trauma I had tried to escape came rushing back. I called the dogs, gave them their bedtime treats, dialed up the thermostat, and crawled alone into my icy bed.

The next morning before coffee, I threw the ring for Shiraz in the backyard. Chianti was not himself. He stumbled toward me and collapsed. No amount of encouragement or treats could entice him to his feet. His giant head lolled as I supported it in my lap. His legs remained stiff and unresponsive. *How can this be?* He was only a young adult at five years old. *Is he dying?*

I felt my life slipping away alongside his. Together our hearts constricted, and as one, our breaths became shallow. Somehow, I managed to get inside and call the vet. "Could be neurological" was the noncommittal response.

It was Columbus Day weekend. All clinics were closed. The only option was emergency service. I went back outside to my beloved pet, where he still lay prone on the grass beyond the gate. From above, the sky's energy-laden clouds pressed down with their dark weight. I cradled my sick dog and remained next to him on the cold, wet ground, wishing the earth would devour us both, as Hades had consumed Persephone. In that moment, I was struck by a thunderbolt as if from Zeus: *I can't make it; I need support.*

"I love you," I whispered into Chianti's floppy ear. "I need you. Please don't die."

As I would handle a baby, I hand-fed him tidbits of food, one morsel at a time. I sensed a small shudder of effort. Gently easing my arm under his ribcage, I encircled my fingers around his waist in a supreme effort to help him find purchase with his semiparalyzed back legs. He rallied, and we staggered up the brick path to the warmth of the house. And he did seem to improve. So, as usual, I ignored his condition and did nothing.

CHAPTER 26
STURM UND DRANG

Engulfed in darkness, I stopped eating. There was nothing left to feed. No feeling remained except a cyclone of thoughts and a withering constriction in my heart. I suspected I was to blame for all that had befallen me. When I took inventory of myself, I couldn't find anything I liked.

My poor sick dog seemed to embody my mental state, and when I had to face getting him to a vet and what that would entail, I couldn't cope. I needed help. I picked up the phone and called my neighbor Joyce, a psychoanalyst. We were both trustees of our local public library and drove to meetings together. At eighty-six years old, she was one of my icons: smart, artistic, politically active, intellectual, kind, and beautiful. I had complete trust in her opinion; plus, I knew nothing about therapy. Joyce gave me two names. Naomi's office was closer.

"I'll call her first and ask if she can fit you in." Joyce sounded concerned. "Her schedule may be full, but I'll let you know as soon as I hear back from her."

Later that day, I received the okay and dialed Naomi's number.

"If I don't respond within twenty-four hours, kindly call again," said the recorded voice.

Speaking to the answering machine, I referenced Joyce and choked out, "My husband recently died, and I'm being sued by his first family. I can't do this alone and need the support of a professional."

The following day, when I answered the phone, the voice in my ear was calm.

"Grief is my specialty." Her tone was *mezzo piano* (medium soft) and expressionless.

I jotted down the directions and a week later drove to Naomi's home office, located in a gated community just north of the Long Island Expressway. The entrance was meticulously groomed, with vibrant autumn-orange, white, and purple chrysanthemums, red-berried holly, and Montauk daisies. The barrier's arm was down. As instructed, I stated my name to the attendant (whose knitting I interrupted) and announced, "Naomi." The pudgy uniformed guard placed the call, nodded, lifted the barrier, and I proceeded at a cautionary crawl of fifteen miles per hour.

The serpentine road swung through an immaculate private golf course. I eased over speed bumps, stopping several times for electrically powered golf carts manned by sedentary retirees. Naomi's condo was on the right. I parked beneath a young, golden-leafed maple, walked up a short driveway, turned right and then left around the south side of the building past the main entrance, and went down three wide steps. I now stood beneath a balcony overlooking the still-green, undulating lawns.

On the right sat a small cement figure, eyelids half-closed and its elongated, upturned, overlapping palms resting atop crossed legs—the Buddha in his eternal pose. I turned and jabbed the bell with a jittery forefinger. The lock buzzed, and I leaned on the door and walked into a low-ceilinged entrance with an off-white tiled floor. Lined with framed World War II posters, the long, fluorescently lit hall seemed to tunnel into the unknown.

Naomi stepped forward with her right arm extended. Short, seventy-ish, blond, and artsy, she offered a nonthreatening smile. We shook hands, and she led me to the second door on the left—the waiting room. I sat on a small rattan sofa surrounded by framed certificates, merits, degrees, and citations. A high-voltage light glared over my slumped shoulder. She handed me a mountain of insurance forms. I felt no nervousness or unease; I was putting one foot in front of another, just like I did every morning when simply attempting to get out of bed and get dressed. I expected relief and was following through.

Naomi handed me an intake form entitled "Grief Scale." I was to rate on a scale of one to ten (one low, ten high). There were eighteen categories.

Both my pen and mouth were dry as I struggled to rate my feelings. I debated whether to admit to being human and answer honestly or portray myself as stoic and superhuman. I opted for not seeming too bad and circled fours and fives for almost every question except loss of appetite, sleep problems, and disbelief. Those I would have marked twenty.

But as I fiddled with the ballpoint pen and juggled the clipboard on my lap, I wondered: *Do "normal" people need therapy?* I wanted this lady to gather the fragments of my shattered self, glue the pieces back together, and explain what happened. Why had I failed? For years, a day hadn't passed when I wasn't grateful to be with Klaus. Why had my eyes been closed? For years, I had paid most of our bills so he could "put every penny toward retirement." All the while, he might have been married to another woman he was supporting with my income. Why had I believed him? I had allowed him to control me through his nonparticipation. I wanted to understand. I wanted a remedy and explanation that would take the pain away.

Naomi returned. I handed over the questionnaire and followed her into the next room. "Where would you care to sit?" She pointed to a small, black leather chair against one wall, where a tangled vine hung over a bookcase like Rapunzel's golden locks. "Or there?"

Across the width of the room was a white leather sofa with two tiny pillows leaning against the low arms like lazy sentries. That seemed the better bet. I wedged myself midway between the two guardians, hands shoved between my legs.

Inhaling a shaky breath, I studied my surroundings. The blinds were discreetly drawn halfway. The distant golf carts scrambled back and forth like targets in a video game. To my right the wall was paved with books. The complete works by S. Freud with their lime-green jackets caught my eye. (Wasn't he the guy who said I was there because I wanted a penis?) I became subliminally distracted by a staticky, low-pitched hum that threw me back to childhood when I would awake after 11 p.m. in a La-Z-Boy recliner and the TV station was finished for the night. This was the same electric snowstorm.

"It's so no one will overhear us." Naomi's explanation was bolstering. "Originally, I thought ocean waves would work, but it proved to be too metronomic."

I pretended it didn't gnaw at my senses. *What's wrong with a metronome?* For years I used one for hours every day. (And still do.)

Her right ankle was cocked over her left knee, notebook in lap. I wondered how she could write holding the pen between her first and second finger. Silence fell, except for the carpet of white noise.

"Would you rather lie down?"

Is she kidding? Adrenaline was my language. Give me a choice between the couch or sixty push-ups, and I'd choose the floor. But the clock was ticking, and I needed to tell the story. I started with a basic outline and introduced the cast of characters. By the time I was done, I felt no better. I clamped my hands together, tightly lacing my fingers.

"That's about it," I concluded.

"We can continue next week then."

My narration seemed to neither shock nor bore her. Perhaps she had heard this same story hundreds of times. Naomi shifted in her chair and appeared to look at me, though her glance might have been aimed at the clock beside me.

The truncated (forty-five-minute) hour ended. She watched me write the check. We negotiated the next appointment as she pulled out her spiral-bound desk calendar. I edged closer to see what day she was referring to. It slammed shut. The message was loud and clear: *"This is private and secret. Your eyes are prying where they shouldn't be."* The atmosphere was about control—hers. The first session had been purely informational, with me informing her. The relief I anticipated would have to wait a week.

A few minutes before noon the following Tuesday, the buzzer allowed entry. Remembering the white carpet, I removed my wet shoes and, rather than forging through to the waiting room, chose to stand at the entrance. I didn't want to sit like a caged bird in a windowless room.

The same smile greeted me, and I timidly found my seat on the sofa. I was empty handed except for the cash to pay Naomi's fee and my car key. I had felt compelled to leave my purse in the car like so much extra baggage.

"Before we begin, I'd like to teach you how to meditate."

Naomi walked to the picture window and pulled down the blinds.

"This technique will help relieve stress and calm your nervous system. I've taught it to thousands of patients."

Anything to calm my ratcheting anxiety, I thought as she dimmed the lights.

"Place your hands on your lap. Sit with a straight spine," she advised. "Yes, that's good. Feet flat on the floor. Close your eyes. Breathe regularly. Follow your breath in and out through your nostrils. Now say to yourself: *I am calm, I am calm, I am calm.* If a thought arises and interferes, dismiss it as if you were sitting on the train traveling to Penn Station. At each stop, passengers enter. You are reading. You look up and then return to your book. Dismiss that thought and continue the chant: *I am calm.*"

I had tried Transcendental Meditation in the mid-'70s when a boyfriend had enrolled me for instruction and paid (what seemed to me) an outrageous fee. I wanted to please him, so I willingly jumped in. The process seemed secretive. I was strictly forbidden to reveal or share the mantra that, I was told, had been selected specifically for me. I understood that if I divulged this unique syllable, the transformation I sought would be in dire jeopardy. That minimal effort ended when I no longer sought my boyfriend's approval.

After a few minutes of breathing and a tortuous and failed attempt to focus, she restored the lights.

"Start with ten minutes twice a day," Naomi said, handing me a blurry photocopy of a decade-old article describing the process and its merits. When she had settled into her chair, which I now noticed was surrounded by clocks, all facing in her direction, I self-consciously resumed the narrative of my travails.

"I feel so betrayed. After I gave my lifeblood, I know now that I was only a convenience. Please tell me where I went wrong."

There was a faint nod. "What do you mean?" Her tone was neutral.

"My training as a musician was a master–student relationship. My cello teachers were masters whose instruction I tried to follow, striving for 'perfection.' Then I worked with conductors, who acted like gods. Their every demand was my command. When I'm a member of a quartet or trio, we aim to be a single entity. Listen, adjust, cooperate, share. Ideally there is no boss. We operate like an octopus. Each tentacle has a task that works for the benefit of the whole. None can decide on its own, but each can inspire the whole, which then reacts to the communicated nuance: imitating, expanding, developing the idea."

I'd wondered how these experiences and my training had shaped my relationship with Klaus. Certainly, in the early days I saw him almost as a deity—sensitive, intelligent, well educated, knowledgeable, experienced, and stunningly handsome—and did everything I could to please him. There was the model of my parents' marriage, with my father reigning over his kingdom and directing my musical education when I had no choice but to cooperate or risk losing his appreciation and love. I had behaved and acted in the role of "good girl" for fifty years.

I averted my eyes. "Any confidence I may have had has been eroded. I've been stripped and need someone to tell me what to do to make me feel better."

Naomi was unmoved. "That's not my job. I'm not here to build confidence, though I hope you will find me supportive. I will listen and feed your words back to you. Together we may be able to discover habits of faulty thinking."

Faulty thinking indeed.

CHAPTER 27
SOTTO VOCE

As my life steadily crumbled, my friend Cara Mia visited from Minnesota. We first met as teenagers at music camp in Los Angeles. She was a fabulous instrumentalist who had been principal second violin in the Saint Louis Symphony but left the orchestra on disability due to severe arthritis in her back, which made playing excruciating.

Cara Mia was raring to go. "Now that I'm here, I want to help."

"Great. What's not to like about that offer?" I pointed to an outbuilding on the other side of the driveway. "While I'm teaching, how about going out to Klaus's workshop and throwing away junk? Aside from all the tools and building rubbish everywhere, he brought about a hundred boxes back from his office at the lab when he retired. They're piled along the walls. Start anywhere."

"Sounds good. I can work with that plan. Any instructions about what to keep and what to chuck?"

"Chuck it all. I don't care."

A pile of debris grew outside the workshop doors until halfway through the second day of clearing, when Cara Mia came into the house to find me.

"You'd better come have a look." She did not look happy. "You're going to have to go through these boxes yourself."

"Uh-oh." I was immediately on guard. "What'd you find?"

"You said that all that stuff was from Klaus's office?" She was matter of fact. "In addition to ninety-one library books that I've piled on the table saw, there are tons of personal papers. I'm guessing you're in for another shock."

I took a measured breath as I followed her unsteadily down the brick path and entered the workshop through the french doors. Boxes had been stacked four high and littered the floor. We opened and dug through the first few. Mixed in with electronic components, small motors, and dozens of pens and pencils were years of bank statements, fading faxes, check stubs, photos, letters, postcards, and printouts of emails.

I rifled through the contents of several boxes and brought an enormous heap into the house. A cursory glance revealed evidence documenting tens of thousands of dollars Klaus had sent to South Africa.

Twenty years of records detailed the moneys Klaus had paid toward college tuition for both Karl and Alexandra, which I could understand. That was right. But he had told me he was estranged from his children and was not allowed by law to contact them. I'd ask: "Why are we so strapped when we both work so hard?" He always answered: "I'm saving for retirement so we'll be okay. You know I gave Ute my pension and we have to catch up." Why had he lied and hidden the truth?

There were letters from Ute, many in German. The ones in English were hostile in the extreme, always demanding more money. An article from *The Argus*, a South African daily newspaper, proclaimed the bloody murder of a young woman in their Johannesburg neighborhood. Her handwriting screamed, *"Why have you abandoned us? Your daughter could be next!"*

I discovered their method of communication: a post office box with the laboratory zip code. Obviously, Klaus had sent and received correspondence for years without my knowledge. That would explain one of the keys on his key ring that didn't match any locks at home.

Mixed in with graph paper and pencil stubs was an interview of a prize-winning scientist who claimed he became a physicist because of a class he took at the University of Cape Town, taught by a young, enthusiastic, Oxford-trained physicist: Klaus. After this scientist's first semester, apparently Klaus left his teaching position and absconded to England. He never submitted his resignation or informed the administration of his whereabouts or intentions. He left the UCT physics department and all the students in a lurch. He chose to bail rather than explain.

This sounded alarmingly familiar. He abandoned his family by taking me back to Johannesburg from Nature's Valley and again to come to me in the States. What was that psychology about?

While we were still scrambling through the debris, the phone rang.

It was Ruth Clark, the attorney who drafted our wills in 2003.

"Do you have a moment to talk?" she asked. "I need to find out what's going on. I've been subpoenaed to release my notes and the documents relating to those wills. The court and a law firm representing the von Österberg family wants all the records relating to Klaus's and your assets."

I started to update her regarding the litigation, but she immediately interrupted with a warning not to reveal any details.

"Remember, if I'm called to testify in court, I need to be able to honestly report that I know nothing. I can tell you, however, that I have very little material: a few letters from you, which you might have retained copies of, and an asset list, which is now six years old."

Her statement did nothing to assuage my fear. The family was playing hardball. Did this mean they meant to interrogate her regarding all our financial records?

CHAPTER 28
PESANTE

A small reprieve and distraction came when I was invited to an Upstate New York university as artist in residence. The assignment was to teach and perform chamber music with undergraduates.

I reconnected with a longtime friend of forty years from my student days. Patti Schlechter and I had shared apartments in La Zona Rosa over several summers while playing in Filarmónica de las Américas in Mexico City.

In addition to being professor of violin and chamber music, Patti was a certified instructor of yoga and the Feldenkrais Method, a body movement system that aims to remediate ingrained, habitual bad posture and muscle misuse contributing to repetitive stress injuries and chronic pain.

After a grueling day of teaching, rehearsing, and coaching, we finally relaxed over a glass of wine and one of Patti's amazing Mexican chicken concoctions. We settled into a postmortem of the day's classes.

Then she said, "Do you realize you aren't breathing?"

"No." I was taken off guard. "What do you mean?"

"Start to notice your breathing patterns. You almost never breathe. I'd guess you feel dizzy most of the time."

At first, I was silent. "How did you know?"

"I'm trained to notice." She lifted her fork. "This is not simply a bad habit but a sign that you are holding in a great deal of pain. Somehow, you've got to find a way to express the hurt and let it go."

My arms crossed over my chest. She had struck a nerve.

"The only time I see you breathe is when you play the cello," Patti continued. "You breathe with the musical line and phrasing."

We went to her studio. I lay on a yoga mat as Patti methodically encouraged my breath to enter my nostrils, continue through the throat, and expand into the base of the lungs. Instead of my upper chest rising and falling, the goal was to push the air down so the abdomen would lift and fall. "Expand the diaphragm," she instructed. I managed three inhalations but soon felt ants crawling through my skin and muscles.

The lesson continued in small increments: feeling air expand the outside of the ribcage and the back, holding the breath to counts of eight and exhaling to ten, then extending the beats. I was going out of my mind: the ants became spiders weaving webs through my systems.

The next day, my throat felt raw, even sore, just from breathing. At the breakfast table, Patti poured strong, aromatic coffee into handcrafted mugs.

"I think you should start meditating to calm your mind and nerves. Has that been at all on your radar?"

"Yes, my therapist said the same thing, but every time I try, my heart starts racing, and I feel nauseous and sick."

"Okay. Don't pressure yourself. Begin slowly and take micro steps. All the agitation and anxiety will mess with your nervous and immune system. Like I said yesterday, you've got to find a release."

Patti pushed away from the stool and reached for the sliding glass door to let her huge dogs out and the frigid air in. She sat again as I aimlessly poured cream and swirled it through my coffee.

"The release I'm getting is through all the changes I'm making to the house. Every time we discussed making improvements to the house, like finishing the cottage for my business, Klaus would reply: 'It's on the list but hasn't made it to the top one hundred chores yet.' Yet he'd do nothing. I became increasingly frustrated and stewed in a thickening soup of anger. The poison was boiling in me, waiting to explode. Then I'd remember how sick he was and suppress my irritation. Now my inner tiger has been freed, and I am on a mission."

The colossal dogs pounded back into the tiny kitchen, eager for their treats.

"I'd say that your instincts to clear the negative energy from your space have been activated."

"I guess that is one interpretation," I agreed. "This summer I had as many as twenty-two workmen and carpenters coming in and out of the house while Pim chopped down over two hundred trees. My biggest thorn, though, is the mountain of building rubble Klaus piled in front of the property. I've become lifelong friends with the attendants at the dump. I've been there every weekend for months now."

"Sounds passive-aggressive to me." Patti spooned another dollop of yogurt into her bowl. "He got his way by continually assuring you he was working while in fact there was no action. He tied your hands."

I suddenly remembered to breathe. "When I suggested calling in a contractor to finish the cottage so I could expand my business, he replied: 'You'll kill me if you do that.' For the last three of four years, I was a time bomb ready to detonate but felt that this was a battle not worth the fight."

"See what I mean? It was all about control. He controlled you so he could feel potent. Maybe there was also self-denial.

He couldn't face the illness that was bringing him closer to the end of his life. Did the two of you ever talk about his death and how it would affect you?"

My private torment was not a subject to discuss before coaching Beethoven. "On a few occasions, when he was checking his blood-sugar levels and counting out the morning's two dozen pills, he'd say, 'I'm going to die. I won't live much longer.' I thought he was just trying to get my sympathy. Contemplating his death was way too painful. I'd tell him he had a negative attitude, to please think of something positive to say.

"Of course, I was also in denial. I assumed that my future was taken care of, since he gave me everything in his will and had been 'saving for us' for so many years."

I picked up my bowl and spoon, stood, and placed them in the sink. Behind me I heard Patti's lowered voice. "Did you love him?"

I turned on the hot water in the sink. "Yes, passionately."

But the last three years had become almost intolerable as I realized his promises had no backbone. The phone would ring, and he'd answer and have a brief conversation.

"Any news?" I'd ask.

"That was John [or Steve or Bill] in Colorado [or Australia or Canada]. He runs a multibillion-dollar company interested in supporting research on my clean coal patent [or extracting oil from shale or wind turbines]. They're allocating a quarter million dollars in two weeks with options worth hundreds of thousands."

How many times did I hear that before it became white noise?

Then I remembered all the mornings I'd walked down the driveway to get the newspaper while the coffee was brewing, my mind a static buzz, thinking, *I can't stay one more minute.* But I did. Klaus was too sick. I couldn't abandon him. There was so much history, and our finances and emotions were so intertwined. Though I was starting to feel liberated, I couldn't dismiss all those years. Our relationship and my love deserved the vow I gave him, through sickness and health. I felt I had no choice.

CHAPTER 29
DA CAPO AL FINE

When I wasn't practicing, teaching, managing house restoration, or sorting through files for my attorney, I continued to bury myself in books, which I hoped could fix me. Not only was my nervous system in shreds, but my heart and head were sick. I plowed through advice on positive thinking and optimism, books dealing with grief and forgiveness, spiritual canons by Gary Zukov, Deepak Chopra, Thomas Moore, and Eckhart Tolle. The voice swirling around my head echoed, *How could this happen to me?* My world had imploded, and I suspected it was my fault.

I should have taken more interest in Klaus's health and medical procedures. Perhaps I could have prevented his death. My unspoken attitude had been "Come on, pull it together; illness is all in your head." If I had been more attentive and faced the truth, I might have acknowledged the red flags. I hadn't run away when I found out he was married, we married without his divorce papers, and I never checked his investments to see where his money was really going. How many things had I allowed to slide? Why had I trusted him?

Before breakfast, while throwing a toy for the dogs, I listened to recorded books. I was seeking answers, if not salvation. *The*

Power of Now by Eckhart Tolle inspired me for the third time. The dog's green ring arced yet again, and Shiraz skittered to the right as Tolle's slightly accented voice intoned, "The greater part of human pain is unnecessary. It is self-created as long as the unobserved mind runs your life.

"The pain that you created now is always some form of nonacceptance, some form of unconscious resistance to what *is*. On the level of thought, the resistance is some form of judgment. On the emotional level, it is some form of negativity. The intensity of the pain depends on the degree of resistance to the present moment, and this in turn depends on how strongly you are identified with your mind."

As I fed the dogs, I reflected on Tolle's words. I was very strongly associating with my mind and resisting the present moment. I could not accept the profound betrayal, the possibility of having my home taken away, and that the foundation of more than half my life was being swept away by a tsunami of unforeseen events. *Is my resistance some form of judgment? Yes, definitely.* I was judging myself and coming up short. I was not the person I wanted to be.

Every day, all day, cortisol and adrenaline gushed through me; I constantly felt as though I were about to walk out alone on the stage of Carnegie Hall to perform the six unaccompanied suites by Bach from memory. To combat the nervous energy, I became addicted to push-ups, day and night. I jumped out of bed every couple of hours, fell on the floor, knees stiff, arms pumping, cortisol racing, and counted to sixty, followed by a short break for sit-ups, then repeated. I listened to music and pumped. I left dinner parties to get down on the floor and push. I became a walking machine, covering miles daily even as the temperature dropped into the teens—or lower.

I stopped eating. My weight plummeted. At a yoga class, I writhed on the floor because my bones pierced the little flesh that was left. I was starting to look like a starvation victim and became so sleep deprived that simply driving the five minutes to the grocery store threatened danger, as I almost immediately fell asleep behind the wheel.

I was barely holding on when Pim and Raymond decided to leave after living in New York City for nearly three decades. Raymond resigned from his position with the health department. The travel addict Pim left for Portugal, assuming Raymond would quickly follow. With their announcement to emigrate, my world finally collapsed.

There was a snag, however, with Raymond's departure. Ashley the cockatiel couldn't cross international frontiers without an avian certificate guaranteeing the parrot was disease-free. (Birds can fly across countries, but don't try to take one through Immigration.) Raymond felt forced to stay behind.

There had been weeks, if not months, of nightly phone calls when Raymond had tenderly listened, metaphorically holding my hand and extending loving guidance. The time had come to repay the friendship. I dolled up the cottage, installing shades, a shower curtain, a bed, several chairs, and a carpet so Raymond and his bird could live in comfortable privacy (and apart from my dogs and cat).

That Christmas Eve, several days after Raymond moved in, I made a special dinner. Though separated from our partners, we were together, bound by thirty-plus years of memories. He passed the salt and pepper and looked up from his plate.

"You've got to stop telling Klaus stories."

"What do you mean?" My guard went up. "You've lost me."

"You continually talk about all the bad stuff Klaus left you with." Raymond's eyes were getting shiny. "He made humidifiers that don't work. There's no heating system in the cottage. The water pipes were installed only a foot underground. There's the Nobel Prize he bragged he would win, the porno 'novel,' the twenty tons of garbage dumped in the front. What am I leaving out?"

I felt more than competent to answer that question. "Well, we could include the patents that were going to make us rich, the leaks from the upstairs shower that he blamed on Pim. How about a Nazi father who was Hitler's banker and a secret German bank account? May I include possible bigamy?"

Raymond was unperturbed by my aggression and finally sampled the roasted veggies. "All this negative repetition is linking you with the past and deepening the already damaged ruts in your memory. You need to shed those thoughts rather than reinforce them."

I stared across the table at my friend and wondered if he was right—if the "stories" were keeping me from facing the indescribable pain of my nightmares. Who was Klaus, and who was I? I had no understanding of that level of duplicity and deceit, let alone a way to process it. Dealing with the trivia seemed easier than facing the core issue: the fact that I'd turned a blind eye for years.

"Okay. There is an entire laundry list of deceptions and betrayals that would take me this entire bottle of wine to detail."

I sipped the champagne to emphasize my point.

"Clearly, I was inaccurate in my perception of reality and who he really was. But all that is superficial compared with his clandestine communications with another family and the hundreds of thousands of dollars of our combined assets he diverted to a woman he may still be married to, who, as you know, is suing me."

"The Lauri I know is the research queen," Raymond countered, "and she had all the information on Klaus for the ten years before she married him. You ignored the facts."

I put down my fork, smearing cranberries on the white tablecloth, and averted my gaze. Squeezing my eyes shut, I took a slow breath. *Whose side is he on?* For a long moment, I communed with the candle.

"Every second of your day is crammed full of doing." Raymond wasn't finished. "You never stop. The bottom line is that you work as a distraction from feeling."

I started to disassociate and shut down. "Explain, please."

"Isn't it obvious?" Raymond's voice rose along with my blood pressure. "If you are constantly putting out fires, answering calls, seeing clients, teaching, running the house, instructing builders, putting together marketing material, updating your website, writing articles, exercising, when do you take time to process? Do you have emotions? Can you feel?"

"You sound like my therapist." This was supposed to be a special dinner, but I felt trapped. "Besides, I've been working like that for years. Probably I was making up for the fact that for the last several years, Klaus could do nothing except lie on the sofa, watching TV. Our conversations revolved around how he felt and how many pills he took. I wanted an equal partner. Maybe I find it easier to focus on the minutia rather than these larger issues, like the fact that I gave and he took."

"Well, stop it." He was adamant. "How can you become calm and ease your anxiety with all that activity?"

Is he right? For years, I'd filled every second of my day. The more demanding Klaus became, the more promises he made of riches from his patents, the more I buried myself in work and achievement (a compulsion sanctioned and even encouraged by society). To the outside world, I looked successful. Yet my spirit had erected an impenetrable shield. I'd become bulletproof.

Emails, students, customers, orders, exercise, building, and the garden were diversions from overwhelming pain. Sometimes, I even thought I missed Klaus because there was no one to whom I could prove how hard I worked.

At the end of the meal, worn out from exposing my bruised heart, I hugged Raymond good night. He grabbed the flashlight to illuminate his passage back to the cottage, and I clung to the banister to support my ascent up the stairs.

The curtains were closed, so I undressed with the lights on and stood naked outside the shower, adjusting the water temperature. The steam rose and my thoughts drifted. I was not living my life; I was hardly even a participant. The weight of worries and demands suffocated my ability to connect with reality.

How could I find peace when Klaus had left me in a situation where I couldn't even grieve his loss?

CHAPTER 30
AGITATO

In therapy, Naomi pressured me to talk about myself, which intensified my unease. I couldn't stop shaking. She asked if I felt she was judging me. *Yes.* She complained that I censored my responses. *True.* When she analyzed me, I shut down and couldn't hear what she was saying. My mind went blank, and I only registered moving lips on a soundless face.

"I'm sorry. Could you please repeat that?" I tried to jerk my attention back to the present and focus.

I finally focused and heard Naomi ask, "Is there anyone who really knows you?"

Crossing my arms tightly over my chest to keep my hands from twitching, I replied, "I don't need anyone to know me. It's an illusion that one person can really know or understand another. We may each be unique, but don't we all have the same desires and motivations, though in different proportions? Don't you hear the same old problems over and over: relationships, jobs, money, health?"

She propped her ankle over a knee and pushed a loose hair off her forehead, a habitual gesture. "Do you think your experience, successes, and challenges are just like everyone else's? I'm hearing you say that you feel insignificant."

I was feeling completely useless. *Why would I admit that?* I needed immediate help, relief, and advice on how to cope. I answered, "No, but don't our experiences result in similar joys and trials? Aren't there only a few stories, though the details vary?"

Naomi's eyes surreptitiously slid to the left, where one of a dozen clocks faced her but away from me. "We can continue this discussion next week."

As I drove home, the unanswered question of why Klaus lied about small as well as monumental things looped through my addled brain. I desperately wanted the puzzle pieces to fit into a digestible package. Naomi suggested that liars are layered in insecurity. They need to control every situation and will say whatever they feel is necessary to please their audience or dodge an uncomfortable situation. Maybe in Klaus's case he lied to impress. Perhaps he was subconsciously competing with and comparing himself to his father, whom his mother might have portrayed as a larger-than-life hero. She had been an absent parent and hired multiple surrogates to raise her young son. This didn't seem like a recipe for emotional peace.

Klaus certainly knew how to control me and how to garner sympathy or adulation. His reaction to tense circumstances was to erupt in anger, pound his fist, and insist everything he said was authoritative and accurate.

✢ ✢ ✢

For months, Naomi had been pushing me to go on medication. My reluctance stemmed from a belief that I should be able to cope independently. But as I kept spiraling, the time came to reach out my hand from the pit and ask for help.

The psychopharmacologist's office was near the Queens–Nassau border. There was no receptionist, only a waiting area surrounding his glass-enclosed office. I had ten minutes to pull myself together before an elderly couple emerged, shaking the hand of a thin, balding Indian gentleman who wore a dark suit and somber tie. The pair shuffled out, and the physician approached me with a warm greeting. He ushered me into his office. I sweated across from him, distanced by a moat of Formica and pressed board shaped into a huge desk. Both of us were swallowed by its enormity.

"Why are you here?" His intonation was singsong and soothing. His fingers, like dark pencils, subtly and rhythmically thrummed his open notebook.

A lightning bolt shot through my heart. I felt myself detach so I could have the strength to relate the basics. My goal was to get medication and relief. I looked into the sympathetic brown eyes and forged ahead, trying to ignore the linen blouse sticking to my back. I capsulized my situation: twenty-seven years, visits with kids, hundreds of thousands of dollars sent to South Africa, years of illness, bigamy, and a lawsuit on three continents. Then I tried to breathe.

His hands fell still. Unlike me, he seemed relaxed.

"I've been listening to stories for a long time, but I've never heard anything like this. May I ask you a few questions?"

Perspiration coursed around my left ear and down my neck. I wiped wet palms across my thighs and nodded.

"Do you have pets?" His manner was gentle. "Do you play with them? What do you enjoy doing? How do you sleep? Tell me about your diet."

I answered simply and as honestly as I could. Question one was easy: yes. Number two: still okay—yes. Three: push-ups didn't seem likely to win a gold star. Sleep was a solid "badly," and diet was simple: almost nothing.

He lifted his head from his notes. "You are not depressed, or you would get no pleasure out of life. I'm going to give you a prescription for tranquilizers. I recommend starting with a very small dose, no more than one to three times a day. See how you respond. My guess is that when your lawsuit is finished, you will be okay."

I took the slip of paper to my local pharmacy and received ninety tablets of clonazepam. I googled the drug; it was addictive. After months of avoiding medication, I decided to start with a quarter, which was a challenge to dissect because the pills were tiny. My response was almost immediate. I hadn't felt that calm in months. No cloudy or fuzzy thinking. The problems had not gone away, but there was respite from the symptoms. For the first night in weeks, I slept, breaking the pattern of habitual insomnia.

CHAPTER 31
DIMINUTION

In January 2010, I signed the papers opposing Ute's claim against the estate to present to the probate court. Two weeks later, I received the amended documents.

Not surprisingly, I had to prepare my defense, which included compiling two decades of our financial history: all bank accounts, investments, assets, documents pertaining to the mortgage, proof of earnings, tax returns, investments, and spending history. I read the emails Klaus had printed and saved, collected bank statements from accounts I never knew existed, and calculated the thousands of dollars he had sent Ute and the kids over the twenty-two years we had lived and worked together in America.

I relived the betrayal with each new realization. Nights became a nightmare as I tossed and turned alone in bed. My thoughts churned through a food processor, going in whole to be spat out in shreds. My life, confidence, past, and future were hacked into fragments that I couldn't imagine piecing back together.

In early March, I received an email from my attorney in Hamburg. He had called the judge in Bücheberg, who said he was inclined to give me everything. *Good news? Is it possible?* Just as I started to celebrate this potential victory, the phone rang.

"Good morning, Lauri. It's Sheryl. I just heard from Ute's legal team."

My knees almost buckled as I held the receiver in a death grip.

"She is demanding half of Klaus's pension, savings, and all Social Security benefits. We are playing with fire here. Can you find out who owns her house in South Africa and its value?"

A sledgehammer struck me with full force. *Don't tell me I have to engage an attorney in Johannesburg.* I went to the computer and typed out a quick plea to the attorney husband of my friend Irit. David replied that he had someone who could check the records for real estate. However, for an assessment, the appraiser would have to go into the house, which Ute would surely never allow.

The next day, the postal carrier handed me an envelope containing a new retainer agreement from Sheryl and the discovery requirements from Ute's legal team. The demands were so extensive—such as copies of all photographs from the last twenty-seven years—that initially it seemed bogus. If this was about pressure and intimidation, it was working.

Sheryl scheduled a meeting. I asked Raymond to accompany me because when I became anxious, my mind filled with static, and nothing registered. On Monday, we were led into her office and sat around a table, surrounded by pictures of her toddler.

I dove right in. "I don't understand why Ute should get anything when Klaus already sent her thousands of dollars. She put nothing into his life here. I can't follow the legality of this."

"Listen to me, Lauri." Sheryl was deliberate. "The law and fairness are not always the same thing. The law says that a spouse cannot be disinherited. Klaus's will does not provide for her, nor is she a beneficiary of any of his financial assets, which fall outside the parameters of the will. If Klaus in fact never divorced her, she is the legal spouse, and your marriage will be considered fraudulent—null and void. Unless she signs off and says she doesn't want any of the money, by law she is entitled to fifty percent of all bank and retirement accounts, plus one-third of all other assets, which means Klaus's percentage of your house and the investments that you funded and put in joint tenure with him. All that is rightfully hers."

Raymond was taking notes. "Lauri needs protection. What can we do?"

"We must do everything possible to establish that she was financially involved in building up these assets."

"How can I do that?" My voice was barely a squeak.

Sheryl's gaze sought mine, trying to penetrate the obvious glaze. "You are going to have to go through every piece of paper, statement, canceled check, tax return, fax, email, letter, whatever else, so we can assemble a watertight case that your income helped purchase the house and that you funded the joint investments."

I left the office so stricken that I could barely unlock the car doors. As I backed out of the parking space and pulled hesitantly onto New York Avenue, Raymond and I began to debrief.

"How am I going to get through this?" I moaned.

"You are going to put one foot in front of the other." His voice was gentle but firm. "You have no choice."

"But how? You haven't seen the extent of the mess Klaus left me with."

"Now you're sounding childish. Can I tell you your two biggest problems?" Raymond was in therapist mode.

My car started to feel like an air-deprived space capsule, a cage hurtling through Long Island's bumper-to-bumper traffic. Raymond continued, "You are immature because you've been criticized, instructed, and told what to do for twenty-seven years by Klaus, and before that your father. You chose Klaus because you were comfortable with a father figure. You married your 'father,' and now you're holding the baggage of anger and resentment."

Silence fell, but Raymond wasn't finished.

"The fact that you rush to please and take on the concerns of others is due to how much and how often you've been criticized. You take responsibility for everything. Now you wonder why you can't cope. Taking so much responsibility is like the egoistic child who thinks the breakup of her parents' marriage is her fault. Every situation rotates around you. You're stuck in childhood."

I cursed at an idiot driver trying to cut me off.

"I can't wait to hear my second biggest problem."

"You are too impatient." Raymond's foot shadowed the brake pedal from the passenger seat. We didn't speak as a car passing on our right shot into my lane. At this point, annihilation would have been a welcome relief.

✣✣✣

Sheryl had asked me to pull together the numbers related to Klaus's Social Security contributions. The nearest office was a fifteen-minute drive. I sat on a folding chair, expecting a long wait; almost before I unfurled Tuesday's *New York Times*, my number flashed on the screen. I handed over my ID, marriage license, and Klaus's Social Security card and death certificate. From a printer on the other side of the room popped out the application Klaus had filed upon his retirement (three years before his death). As his wife, I was entitled to a "death benefit" of just over $200.

Anxiously, I drove home, pulled into the garage, unlocked the front door, tossed the papers on the dining room table, and threw my coat and myself onto a chair. I opened the document.

At the bottom of the page was Klaus's signature. He had verified his first marriage, Ute's birthday, and the date and place of their divorce. I immediately went to my files to check these details with the marriage certificate I'd received from Germany, which included Ute's paperwork. Nothing coincided. He had invented every detail on the government form: the date of his first marriage in England, Ute's birthday, and their divorce date (which I calculated would have been impossible). It was all a fabrication.

There was no time to bury myself in muck. I put those thoughts on the back burner since I had to catch a flight that afternoon to Switzerland, then to Spain. My suitcase was almost packed. I threw in an extra sweater and T-shirt before jumping into the shower, then recorded an outgoing message on the answering machine, locked the windows and doors, and drove to Queens to board the Swiss Air flight to Zürich. The transfer to Barcelona would be easy.

My cellist friend Olga had grown up in Mexico and was fluent in Spanish, though not Catalan. She had rented a Barcelona apartment with a second bedroom, and I jumped at the chance to join her and enjoy a bit of relaxation, foreign culture, and adventure. The central location meant we didn't need a car since we were near Las Ramblas, a boulevard that seemed to be a combination of New York City's Fifth and Madison Avenues, spiced with Paris's Champs-Élysées.

After three days of surreal bliss, it was almost dusk when I arrived back at the flat. I began to enter the security code to the outside door, then suddenly decided to backtrack to an internet café to check my email. My two words of Spanish, a smile, and a couple of euros did the trick, and I logged on while the patron deftly sold coffee, cigarettes, and lottery tickets. I entered my password, and an avalanche of unread messages blasted like

July 4 fireworks. Ninety percent I quickly deleted. Then my eyes fixated on a familiar name: Raymond.

I'M LEAVING TOMORROW FOR PORTUGAL. ASHLEY'S CERTIFICATION CAME THROUGH. I'LL TAKE CHIANTI AND SHIRAZ TO THE KENNEL AND SET OUT FOOD FOR THAÏS. SEE YOU SOON. LOVE, RAYMOND.

I thought, *I'll be home in a few days. You can't wait?* I couldn't blame him, but after four months as my guest, another four days of keeping an eye on my pets would have given me a modicum of peace.

That news was unanticipated but registered low on the emotional scale. As I scrolled down, my nervous system exploded with an adrenaline rush. I double-clicked on my brother-in-law's name. The greeting was short, followed by a jab to the jugular. Ute had asked him for a copy of his (and Klaus's) mother's will. She wanted to know what was happening with me. My impending nightmare lived thousands of miles away, but one sentence threw me back into a miasma of fear and anxiety. Continents and months stretched between me and what might or might not happen. Running away had always worked for me. Now my life was chasing me.

After the beauty of art, architecture, food, flamenco, and companionship in Barcelona, I flew back to Zürich and staggered onto the high-speed airport train. As the doors airily joined, forest sounds accompanied a soothing Germanic voice. The birds twittered, and the language changed to French. The tree leaves rustled as the wind caressed the branches. Then it was Italian. An alpenhorn's steady tone cleanly penetrated a frog-and-cricket chorus. Just as the English message asked us to prepare for our exit, a distinct and low-pitched *moooo* and expressive cowbells cleared the slightly nervous air. We all visibly relaxed.

All too soon, I was home. The dogs and Raymond were gone—complete desertion. Clues indicated an early evacuation: the heat in the cottage turned up to eighty degrees, the food in the fridge rotten, piles of mail, and the answering machine overdosed with messages. I drove to pick up Chianti and Shiraz at the kennel.

Upon my return, I was struck by a thunderbolt. My wound was so fresh and open that I was utterly incapable of going through and organizing the evidence of Klaus's deceit. I needed help.

The next morning, I walked to my local library and knocked on the director's door. I'd been on the board of trustees for several years and was now the president, so I had a good connection. Could she recommend a trustworthy staff member to assist me in sorting through extremely personal and sensitive financial data? She suggested and I immediately contacted the library's bookkeeper. What a relief to hand her twenty years of bank statements, files pertaining to the house purchase, tax returns, years of emails, and Sheryl's to-do list.

She systematically worked through the twenty-two years of our financial life together and made a spreadsheet detailing Klaus's income, the money he sent to South Africa, and our expenses. The numbers showed that he couldn't have paid our mortgage alone, thus giving me leverage to establish ownership of my home. This evidence also proved that I had solely funded the investments held in joint tenure. The family seemed to think that Klaus was the big money earner, the rich, powerful one, while I was an artistic dependent—an impression he encouraged.

When the demands from Ute and Co. for the dispersal of assets arrived, I arranged to open the packet with a friend. Sheryl believed the contents would be so upsetting that I needed someone to keep me stable.

Ada was on the South Country Concerts board and had studied with me as an adult beginner for a couple of years until life took over. She removed the contents of the FedEx envelope while we sat in her garden room, surrounded by the first feathery maple leaves and golden forsythia. She rifled through the pages and quickly sorted the documents into two big piles. There were twenty to thirty letters from Klaus telling Ute of hard financial times, embellished with descriptions of the beauty of wild turkeys outside his office window and groundhogs confronting him upon his early entrance to work. These were accompanied by pages of wire-transfer records detailing the funds he sent to South Africa. Even at a glance, we figured he sent her hundreds of thousands of dollars. No wonder I had to work so hard.

The following day, I went to Sheryl's office. We spent three hours hammering out the questions she planned to ask Ute and Karl during deposition—our chance to question their involvement in this gross deception. She already had fifty pages of notes.

As we sat again at the round table in her office, she carefully placed her pen beside the yellow legal pad and met my eyes. "I have to warn you that the chances of you being 'the wife' are becoming slimmer and slimmer, so if Ute and Karl won't agree to a settlement, we'll be forced to sue Klaus's estate for fraud, on the grounds that he married you under false pretenses. It looks like Ute is going to show up at court, and Karl is trying to weasel out of it. I'd advise you to prepare an offer for a settlement."

I suspected this was coming and replied, "Do you really think that strategy will work? I need this to be over."

Was it possible that Ute would come over after so many years? It would be her first time in the US, though her "husband" had lived here for twenty-two years with me. I couldn't imagine how she had allowed all that time to slip by, unless she was just using Klaus as an ATM and was blackmailing him. Certainly Karl knew the situation, since he had visited so many times and lived only a few minutes from us. This whole exercise seemed to be about cashing in. And there was probably a lot of stored-up anger and resentment. Klaus was dead, so I had become the target.

My eyes traveled across the wall of degrees, accreditations, citations, and images of the golden-haired toddler. Then I responded to Sheryl's suggestion.

"How does fifty-fifty sound?"

Sheryl was incredulous. "Hold on. Reel it in. Way too generous. We need a much stronger position. While I put together a compromise, read through these questions that I'll ask Kurt and Ute at the deposition. My job is to represent you in obtaining the best outcome. I don't want to see you stripped naked and homeless."

I fell silent. While I couldn't disagree, I was ready to move on with my life.

CHAPTER 32
DECISO

The hearing was scheduled for 10 a.m. in Riverhead at the Suffolk County Surrogate's Court. My French friend Chantal had loaned me a navy-blue linen suit from Chanel with big, heavy gold buttons on the cuffs and down the front of the jacket. Delicate, pointy black shoes completed my disguise as a sophisticated, in-control adversary. I brewed extra-strong coffee and left the house early. Completely unaware of the cars hurtling past me, the traffic lights, the natural beauty of the Pine Barrens, I drove east at the regulation fifty-five miles per hour.

The morning light shone at a sharp angle, and as I struggled to see, I felt myself disassociate. The car's steering and power seemed out of my control. I had only been in court once before, in Johannesburg, for speeding, and the judge had worn a white wig and sat high above me while I stood in the "dock." That was fifteen years earlier as I awaited prosecution in a court on the other side of the world. As intimidating as that was, this would be far worse. I could lose almost everything—my home, investments and faith in the man I'd loved. The uncertainty and disbelief in the situation I now faced meant that the stakes were far higher. A simple slip of "Your Highness" wasn't going to work this time around.

I parked in the court parking lot, entered the building, and was immediately funneled through a metal detector. To the right stood a flight of stairs, which I climbed and found the ladies' room. I came out of the stall and looked in the mirror. Staring back at me with raccoon eyes was an emaciated, pale face bordered by lank, straight hair. In horror I saw, smeared down my crisp, gorgeous suit, bright-orange pollen. It appeared as though Shakespeare's Puck had sprinkled his love powder and missed his intended victim, the jackass.

I twirled the handle of the towel dispenser and soaked the paper with water. The dust spread further down my lapel, and shards of tearing paper lodged into the linen. I tried soap. I was getting wetter. I started to hyperventilate. My lipstick was smearing. I gave up and pushed open the door. Standing directly in front of me in a huddle were Karl, his wife, Ute, and three men in dark suits with good haircuts and designer ties.

Sheryl was pacing. "Where were you?" she admonished. "We were supposed to start deposition ten minutes ago."

She opened heavy-looking, seven-foot-tall doors, and we entered the high-ceilinged courtroom with its cold fluorescent lights. Sheryl turned to a smiling woman with striped blond hair and orangish lipstick.

"This is Lisa. She's the court stenographer and will record the depositions." Sheryl turned to the darkest suit. "We're ready. Let's go."

There was momentary indecision from the opposition team while Sheryl and I stood at the back of the empty courtroom, waiting for the three attorneys to decide who would question me.

"What's happening?" I whispered. "What are they going to ask me?"

"I didn't want to coach you since you have to speak for yourself, but they will try to get you to admit that you knew Klaus was married and that you forced him into a bigamist relationship so you could inherit his money. After they finish with you, I get to grill Ute and Karl." She indicated her legal pad. "The judge will read the depositions and decide how the assets are to be split. If we don't like it, we sue the estate for fraud."

One of Ute's attorneys interrupted us. "May we have a word in private, Ms. Randazzo?"

Sheryl and the three suits crossed the hall and entered a cavernous room on the right, leaving me standing just outside the door, still trying to dry. The stenographer and I matched in an absurd way—her orange lips and my smeared jacket.

"Come sit down next to me." Lisa indicated a seat in the hallway.

I sat. I was there and yet not there. As the stenographer chatted about the bizarre cases she'd recorded for the court, I felt myself float out of the chair. A whisper of me was down the hall, protecting myself against Ute and Karl; my ghost was in the next room, wondering what Sheryl was working out with the lead attorney and his team; and another fragment was still attached to Klaus. I somehow thought his spirit would save me from this inferno.

Thirty minutes later, Sheryl emerged. I stood.

"We have a possible settlement." Her eyes were burning darts. "I've decided that I can't let you go into deposition. You'll never survive in the state you're in."

Sheryl spelled out the proposed division of assets while a fifth of me listened. The other four-fifths had evaporated into the ether.

"They want all South Africa properties, the German bank account, two-thirds of Klaus's retirement investments, and his

Social Security. You can keep your personal investments and the house."

Suddenly, out of nowhere, I stood up for myself. "No. We will split the German funds evenly, and in exchange, they can have the three paintings I have by Klaus's stepfather." The idea came unpremeditated from a voice deep inside me.

"Okay. I can't guarantee they will accept, but I'll try." Sheryl stormed back into the conference room, a determined pit bull ready for a fight. The mahogany door creaked closed behind her, then slammed.

A long minute later, the three intimidating Al Capone clones strode past me toward Ute, Karl, and Karl's wife. Some interminable minutes passed before the lead attorney returned.

"Yes, we accept your offer."

I waited while Sheryl hammered out a few final details with the opposition. She finally reappeared, and we walked together along the corridor to the staircase. Ute stopped me as we passed. The last time I had seen her was twenty-five years before, in the foyer of the Roodeport Theater, when she screamed to the world that I was a whore who had stolen her husband.

"I want to thank you for taking care of Klaus," she now said.

What was I to make of this? One side of me wanted to reach out to comfort her for all the years of hardship she seemed to have endured since Klaus abandoned her and her children. The other side saw her as a money-grabbing opportunist who couldn't pay her own way.

I turned to Karl. "You knew about this for years."

His demeanor was defiant, proud, and smug. "Yes, and I never said a word to you."

Two days after the court appearance and working out a settlement with Ute, Karl, and Alexandra, I invited Sheryl and two friends for a celebratory dinner. We toasted with Veuve Clicquot, the widow's champagne. Sheryl brought the final agreement to the restaurant. Time was of the essence because Ute had to sign before leaving four days later for Johannesburg. That Monday was Memorial Day, and all delivery services would be suspended. Saturday, I signed, had notarized, and sent all the papers via FedEx to Ute's law firm. We had agreed, and there was simply the formality of signatures.

But Ute flew back to Johannesburg without signing.

Several days later, I received an email from Karl requesting all the German bank records. Klaus had opened the account in the early 1990s and had the statements sent to his brother in South Africa. I had never seen any correspondence from the bank, and Petre told me it had been years since he had been in the loop. Unfortunately, Karl didn't believe my assertion that I knew nothing. His lawyer contacted my German attorney, which put me in a catch-22 situation: The German bank wouldn't release any information until the US court ruled, establishing an heir, and Ute wouldn't sign the agreement until she saw the bank statements. Obviously, she thought I'd siphoned off money.

Six weeks after I thought the settlement was settled, Sheryl sent me documents to sign, asking the German bank to send all statements to Ute's attorney. As much as I wanted to blame this ruthless triumvirate, I knew that they were only interested in money. Klaus had been the catalyst of this international fiasco.

The longer I pondered his actions, the more I concluded that Raymond was correct in his assessment that Klaus was a sociopath who hated women. I remembered how Klaus talked about his mother, how he'd treated Ute and me, how he left his retirement to Karl and not Alexandra. He was unable to empathize, understand another's pain, or care. He was a narcissist, extremely clever at manipulating the feelings of others and portraying himself as someone powerful and insightful yet sympathetic. He had betrayed me, Ute, and his children. This entanglement was of his making.

Five months after I signed the settlement agreement, I received notice from Dr. Meyer, my Hamburg attorney. He reported that Klaus had set up the German bank account in December 1992, three months after we were married, and had never touched it. Almost every day, Klaus had said, as I finished work at 8 p.m., "I wish you didn't have to work so hard." Here was hard proof that I never had to. Why had he kept those funds a secret? Why had he never taken any money out of the account when there were times we needed it so desperately? He had told me he received nothing from his mother's estate. Another tick on the lies and deceptions scale. Would it ever end?

With all the loose ends of the lawsuit finalizing, the last of the attorneys' bills rolled in. I'd already sold a cello I'd had commissioned to my specifications and a vintage Porsche. Now most of the German money would evaporate. I kept telling myself that the lawyers hadn't gotten me into this mess; Klaus had.

In November 2011, six months after we had appeared in court, Sheryl called to explain the final details of the settlement. Just before Ute's attorney was scheduled to come to her office and exchange signed documents, she asked that I deliver the three paintings. At the same time, I arranged with Germany to send half of the moneys to Ute's attorneys.

※ ※ ※

In May 2012, a year after meeting for depositions in the courthouse, Alexandra emailed requesting contact.

"We were all put in a situation," she wrote. She had encouraged my confidences, distorted my words, taken my money with promises of reimbursement, and been part of the legal action against me. I couldn't trust her and had no desire to play a game of accusations. I couldn't even consider sharing my life with her so felt no need to condemn, confide, or communicate and did not respond.

Sheryl was sworn in as president of the Suffolk County Bar in June. It was a glorious, formal affair held in a swishy ballroom. There were at least 200 guests, and one could only see the far tables on the other side of the room with binoculars. I sat next to Sheryl's brother Ralph, her law partner. This was our first opportunity to meet and discuss the case, which we dissected between courses of salads, seafood, grilled meats, and roasted vegetables.

Ralph reported that legally I didn't have a leg to stand on and was lucky to have gotten what I did. My seventeen-year marriage was a complete sham, and Ute could have wiped me out financially. I should have felt relieved that I didn't have to sell my home, but a profound sadness engulfed my heart.

CHAPTER 33
FUGUE

The mechanical arm was down as I approached the guard's hut at the gated community. I murmured the sacred password: Naomi.

Barely crawling so as to avoid potential rogue golf carts, I edged toward her unit and parked. I locked the car, walked past the fading daffodils and tulips, and turned left under the deck. The cement Buddha remained in the lotus position, one hand over the other in the dhyana mudra. Little pebbles rested in his upturned palms. I turned my back on him and rang the doorbell. With the electronic buzz, I entered. Again I stood in a corridor festooned with World War II posters. Was Uncle Sam demanding that I join?

Naomi emerged from her office with a smile.

I sat on the edge of the white leather sofa and described walking into the court building covered in orange pollen, feeling assaulted by the three lawyers who represented Klaus's family, our negotiations, and the final agreement.

"You were in a 'fugue' state, a condition where you were able to function but couldn't take in what was going on," Naomi concluded.

I considered how a musical fugue introduces a theme or subject, and as it develops, another "voice" joins in imitation, then another and another in order to create an intricate, multilayered texture of complex imitation and counterpoint, the combination of several melodies on top of each other all played at the same time.

"Now that it is over, I want to move on." I had been anticipating the moment when the lawsuit was behind me; now I needed to understand what had happened. *Why?* kept hammering through my head.

"What will that look like?" she asked, sounding interested.

"Well, I have to continue fixing up my house and clearing out all Klaus's junk: the huge pile of building rubble in the front of the property, the workshop, the library."

Naomi repositioned her hands on the chair's armrest. "And do you think your memories will dissolve and you will find peace?"

"Maybe now I'll be able to sleep." I was seeking the upside.

"How many tranquilizers are you taking a day?"

I didn't have to think. "I've stopped. The pressure is off; the stress is over. I'm done."

"Careful," she warned. "Stopping cold turkey is dangerous. Those pills are very addictive. It's crucial that you ease off gradually."

"I can do it. Mind over matter and all that."

"After everything that has happened, are you at all curious about how your mind works?" She had become a terrier after a rat.

"No, I'm interested in 'fixing' it."

"Maybe you're used to being good at everything and don't feel like you are 'good' at this. Therapy, I mean. Perhaps if you understand your problems, you may be able to fix them."

My mind countered, *Isn't it arrogant to spend so much time thinking about myself?* She wanted me to be open with her, but she was not open with me. All this blah-blah about the past wasn't teaching me anything. We seemed to be going in circles, covering the same ground over and over. I was tired of doing all the talking. It was time she put in two cents.

Naomi leaned back in her chair in an all-too-obvious posture of relaxation. Her hands dangled over the armrests, her rump slid forward, and the cocked calf slipped over her thigh. I imagined her seated in the bar at an expensive hotel, soliciting a pickup. Body Language 101 told me she was trying to get me to relax by imitating her posture. No way. I sat curdled and intimidated.

I grasped onto a safe topic. "My mother visited, and as you advised, I asked about her childhood."

I told her of my mother's poverty-stricken Texas youth with an uncommunicative, flighty father and a bossy, controlling mother.

"It seems to be the pattern you described," I concluded. "We marry one of our parents. In her case, she married her mother."

Naomi was playing the "silent" card, so after a short pause, I continued.

"She said I 'was born an adult.' Even as a toddler, I took responsibility and was totally reliable. She would tell me to take care of Darrel, my baby brother. He was one, and I was three. Then, while we were talking, she started crying because she had been such a 'bad' mother."

Now Naomi's posture was less relaxed. "And what was your reaction?"

"I freaked out seeing my mother cry and left the room. I simply got up and walked out."

Her expression registered *"You are an unfeeling heathen, letting your mother cry alone while you turn your back on her."*

"I completely shut down. It was the same when Klaus said to me, 'I'm going to die soon.' I just couldn't bear to hear it."

"And then?"

I thought for a minute. "I stood in the kitchen, pretending to get more salt or something equally important, and suddenly said to myself, *Lauri, your mother is in the other room crying, and you abandoned her. Try to show at least a little compassion.*

"I brought the salt to the table and said, 'Relax. I don't feel bad about my upbringing. I think I've turned out okay. I'm a responsible adult and don't pass on blame.'"

"In our conversations, you evade talking about anything personal." Naomi's left ankle shifted over her right knee. "Could that be because talking about feelings wasn't allowed in your family when you were growing up?"

This discussion was getting way out of my comfort zone and control. With the talk of my mother, my edginess increased. Perhaps a few push-ups on the floor would ease the tension without tranquilizers. Naomi kept telling me I didn't have feelings. I wondered, *Does one have to emote to feel?* Feelings didn't "cut mustard" in my family, so my default setting was to disregard emotions as a weakness. Only brains and playing the cello mattered.

✢✢✢

The time had come to rebuild not only my home but my life and psyche, so while floors were being sanded and refinished, I went to Minneapolis to visit Cara Mia, who had helped clear Klaus's workshop and found the boxes with his papers, letters, receipts, and bank statements. On my last day, at 5:30 a.m., my phone buzzed. I scrambled to pick it up.

"I've just come back to the kennel after spending the night at the animal hospital." It was the owner of the dogs' "spa." Her voice was hollow and laden with fatigue.

I was suddenly fully awake, all alarms activated. "Who is it? What happened?"

"Chianti. His nose started bleeding, and he's been throwing up. We're back at the kennel now, but this is not pretty."

We agreed I would drive directly from the airport to the veterinary clinic, where I met her and the dogs.

Dr. Atlas did an exam while blood oozed from Chianti's big, black button nose and ran down his stick legs. The vet's brow accordioned above his beak-like nose. He always looked worried, but now he was troubled.

"I'm afraid that I do not have the diagnostic equipment to decipher the problem," he said. "My best guess is that it is his kidneys, but you need to get him to a specialist. With all this bleeding, he has become anemic, and the black diarrhea suggests blood in his stool."

He recommended a veterinary hospital. In numb disbelief, I bundled Chianti into the car, and we drove north in evening rush-hour traffic. I had left Minneapolis early that morning and still hadn't made it home, but attending to poor Chianti was imperative.

A gorgeous, big-haired, high-heeled Puerto Rican doctor took over his case. She was both loving and authoritative. I hugged Chianti good night so she could get to work running tests for the lab to process.

Midmorning the next day, my phone rang. I braced myself upon reading the caller ID.

"Dr. Garcia?"

"Yes. The news is not good. He has Lyme's nephritis."

"What's that?" I should have known from the root of the word, since I'd spoken only months ago with Klaus's nephrologist.

"Kidney failure caused by Lyme disease. I would need to have him here for at least a week, and even then, I can't promise recovery."

The deer tick is tiny, the size of a pinhead, yet it carries a malicious virus that can cause severe neurological damage in humans. I know since I've also had it. Now it was killing my beloved pet. Long Island has an overpopulation of nearly a hundred times more deer than the environs can support. Imagine all those ticks. And Chianti was a free spirit who jumped the fence and ran into the woods whenever we went out to play. He was very sick and only five years old.

The cost of the hospital treatment was $2,500 per day. Could I afford that for a week? But more to the point, was it worth Chianti's suffering? I instructed the vet to administer the injection that would release my dog from his misery. Yet again, I was forced to make a life-and-death decision.

Chianti had been Klaus's dog. When Klaus went into the hospital, never to return home, Chianti had waited expectantly for two weeks out in the driveway, in the snow and freezing winter rain, refusing to come indoors. Now I would never fondle his floppy ears again. Even more of Klaus was slipping away and being taken from me.

I picked up his body the following morning. The hospital staff had cloaked it in a shroud of plastic Bubble Wrap. Two attendants wheeled him on a gurney through the double glass doors and over the bumpy asphalt to my car. I took my eyes off the swathed, pharaoh-like corpse of my faithful companion and glanced at the gentle face of the assistant. Tears oozed, forming little rivulets that cut through her thick, peachy foundation.

The two women eased the burden into the back of my station wagon. My eyes started to burn, but I checked the emotion. Naomi wanted me to have feelings, but I didn't deserve to feel sad. I had clearly been a bad "mother" if I could let this happen. More importantly, I hadn't cried for Klaus, so how could I cry for my dog?

I buried Chianti in my yard under a beautiful magnolia that became his tombstone and would commemorate his life each spring with a show of giant pink flowers.

✦ ✦ ✦

For my next session, I was nervous about seeing Naomi before I even got in the car. She kept pressing me to trust her. I felt so many barriers, real or imagined, that I seemed to be pushing away rather than edging closer. I felt exposed and ashamed, having trouble reconciling the facts with my decision to excuse and justify Klaus's words without weighing in his behavior.

Since I was off the tranquilizers, my adrenaline rush came one mile before her exit. The symptoms began in my knees and spread up my legs to my stomach and heart. By the time I arrived twenty minutes later, my insides were jelly. I walked in, huddled on the sofa, and told her I wanted to cut back our sessions from two times to once a week. She jumped on me in a New York second.

"Is that because you can't face your emotions and don't care about changing your life? You want to return to your previous patterns?"

She bombarded me about why I didn't cry or seem sad about Chianti's death. I drifted in and out, focusing and blanking. Her words, like ripples sent by a pebble dropped in the water of a still pond, were barely reverberating by the time they reached me.

I thought that in therapy, less was more. I wanted each meeting to be a chance to explore and experience "ah-ha" moments. My goal was to experience the maximum out of every session. I wanted practical solutions to my anxiety, reasons why

I felt an exaggerated sense of responsibility, and answers to how I could reconcile the facts with the stories I'd been told and had accepted.

Naomi indicated that she was bored with minutia—the day-to-day stuff and social interactions. With the sessions so close together, what else was I supposed to talk about? Her restrictions felt prohibitive. I didn't like being told what subjects were okay with her. I wasn't yet out of my quagmire and felt broken and unable to respond. But then maybe I was feeling so bad during and after sessions because therapy was working. So I chickened out and let Naomi bully me into staying with two sessions per week.

Three days later, we again sat in our assigned seats. Naomi loosely crossed one leg over the other. And again, she seemed to pose as if relaxing in a darkened cocktail lounge.

"I'd like you to rate your anxiety right now, with ten being the highest." She must have seen how nervous I was.

I compared my present state to how I'd felt in previous situations. Seeing Klaus on life support in the hospital, arms flailing, trying to speak while being attached to seventeen wires, tubes, and machines. Walking down my driveway, opening the mailbox, and pulling out envelopes from South Africa. When Alexandra stayed with me after Klaus's death and told me that her parents were still married and he had promised her mother half of his wealth. Answering the phone, hearing Sheryl's voice, and expecting complete annihilation, though the news often proved even more devastating. Going to court to be grilled by three attorneys hoping to ensnare me. Each of those I would rate a nine or ten. How did I feel now? I was a shrunken, shaking skeleton with a dodgy, misfiring brain.

"Let's say a four," I replied. "I'm feeling intimidated, out of control, insecure, and unsupported."

"Maybe you have a problem with trust. Do you think my job is holding your hand and handing you tissues while you weep? Are you afraid I may reveal your faults?"

I tried to look her in the eye. Couldn't do it. Of course I was afraid. That was why I was shaking.

"Perhaps your inability to trust me comes from your parents not allowing you to become independent."

"I don't understand that comment," I responded. "I supported myself from the age of twenty and lived on the other side of the world. In fact, my goal was to get further and further away from authority. I wonder, instead, if trusting someone is a corollary of having enough self-confidence to open up, show vulnerability, and be able to take the consequences of possible hurt or risk and reap the joys of intimacy."

Her next words were a whisper, a sure sign that she wanted me to listen. She was about to say something she thought was important. "You drive yourself too hard and fill every minute. You need to learn to stop and relax. Take time." She sounded like a broken record.

"I have so many responsibilities." As I murmured my response, my heart started pounding. Sweat popped out on my temples. My hands froze. My head swam. My breath quickened. Was I breathing in or out? I started hyperventilating, doubled over, lost focus, and almost fell out of the chair.

Naomi was unmoved. "What's happening?" She could work as a 911 operator.

I felt like a caged animal in that controlled environment. I was trying to keep myself together: to exercise, feed my soul with poetry, music, and art, socialize to avoid isolation, restore my house, run the concert series and my business, pay bills, survive the court case. Now the "treatment" was adding more pressure. I sat up and pretended nothing had happened.

Naomi stated, "You just had a panic attack, yet you don't want to talk about it."

She hit the bull's eye. No way was I going to talk about it. Denial was still my middle name. I changed the subject. "This weekend I took another thousand pounds of debris to the dump. I see that as a representation of all Klaus left me with."

She changed positions. More rigid. Time was up.

CHAPTER 34
VARIATIONS ON A THEME

I went to Dallas again to visit my family at Christmas and stayed with Darrel and Judy, his wife. During a pig-out at a Tex-Mex restaurant, Darrel shifted his attention from his margarita to me. "Did you know Jeff Neal opened a business just two miles from here?"

I looked up from my tortilla. "Uncle Tom's son? The last time I saw him was probably thirty-five years ago, around the time I graduated from high school. He must have been about three."

Darrel sipped his drink. "Yep. He joined the Marines, was married to a real sweetie, had a bunch of kids, then was shipped off to Iraq. After experiencing all that war, bombing, explosions, and shooting, he came home totally screwed up, couldn't cope, and left his family."

Jeff was our youngest cousin, our mother's brother's second son. "Didn't he grow up in Fort Worth? What's he doing here in Dallas?"

"He's a chiropractor and just set up a practice in a strip mall, more or less, around the block from here."

I wanted to meet him, so Darrel arranged a dinner the following evening with Jeff and his new wife, his business partner. She was a massage therapist working toward her doctorate in chiropractic therapy. We met at a little Italian hole-in-the-wall. The chat was easy and convivial, with mostly biographical information circulating between mouthfuls of lasagna, tortellini, and chianti. I expressed interest in his practice, especially his take on my anxiety issues. Jeff offered to show us his new office and give me a treatment.

The next day, we arrived as arranged, and after Jeff showed us around, he instructed me to climb onto the table. With assured expertise, he assessed the alignment of my legs, spine, and neck. Then, with his hands gently on my head, he eased my neck to the right. *CRACK*. Unexpected, violent, weird, but not unpleasant.

I steadied myself back into a sitting position and asked Jeff if he thought spinal manipulation could positively affect the health of my nervous system and help me overcome my biweekly panic attacks.

"Absolutely, but with your anxiety concerns, I'd go for acupuncture," he advised.

This recommendation was coming from a relative with no money in the game. His talk was impressive, and I listened. The idea appealed to me. Because of the way Western doctors had handled Klaus's illnesses and my own experience with psychotherapy, I was open to this "alternative" medical discipline.

Back in New York, I asked friends for a reference. I knew nothing of the science but desperately wanted help and was ready to try anything that wasn't chemical (an aversion from when I was little and my father instilled in me that illness was self-made). The owner of the local health food store described good results for his chronic back pain. I took down the number.

The appointment was set. At the agreed time, I entered a cubicle at the back of a physical therapy studio. The lights were subdued, and a low-pitched flute invoked tranquility while rain fell and crickets chirped. The inviting, relaxing atmosphere helped ease my edgy insides.

Don was a Vietnam veteran and looked to be a few years older than me. A wall of certificates attested to his expertise and training. I briefly told him my anxiety issues.

"The Chinese have been practicing acupuncture for over two thousand years." His manner was calm and unaggressive. "If it didn't work, they would have stopped a couple millennia ago."

The exam was unlike any I'd had. After taking off my socks, watch, earrings, and glasses, I climbed onto a table and lay on my back. Don lifted my left wrist. His finger probed for three distinct pulses. Then he walked around the table and checked the inside of my right wrist. He peered down at me through the bottom of his bifocals. "Stick out your tongue, please. Further. Excellent. Thank you."

This was weird. "What's that all about?"

"I look at the shape, color, and coating of the tongue as part of the diagnosis. Now, tell me if this is sensitive or hurts."

Don slightly pinched my left arm at the elbow. My right leg shot into the air like a kung fu black belt—a knee-jerk reaction. He continued probing: above each heel, the ball of each foot. I lifted my sweater, and he poked around my abdomen. Too ticklish. He then prodded points under my collarbone. His touch was gentle, yet I nearly jumped out of my skin with many of the pressure points.

"How are you sleeping?" he asked.

"I'm not," I admitted.

"Your yin, the feminine aspect—nurturing, helping, supporting—is depleted. There is an imbalance with the yang—male, hot, aggressive energy—which affects the flow of *qi*. So, your qi, the life force, is splintered. Your heart and mind are not in sync. This means your thoughts go around and around and can't connect to your heart or emotions. Emotional factors such as anger, grief, or fear can cause disease if left unchecked."

He moved to a cabinet and selected a packet of needles.

"On both sides of the body, there are meridians that connect the vital organs: liver, kidneys, heart, spleen, and lungs," he continued. "The placement of each needle sends a message to the body. Its goal is to clear the channels and open the pathway to send and balance qi where needed. The results should be a calming of your nervous system."

With alcohol-dampened cotton wool, he swabbed the insides of my wrists, elbows, and on top of my feet. Quietly and systematically, he sought a subtle pulse on each target, positioned the needle, delicately thrummed the spot with his fingers as a distraction, and tapped the needle into place. I felt nothing. Perhaps the puncture was a millimeter deep, or less. Then he sensitively twirled each needle to an exact depth. I assessed the damage. Twelve needles.

"Are you comfortable? Close your eyes and relax. I'll be back."

He angled a heat lamp on my bare feet for warmth. The flute sounded throatily as I tried to regulate my breath and cancel out darting thoughts. With so many precarious protrusions feathering my body, I was reluctant to move. I didn't want to screw it up.

Twenty-five minutes later, Don returned. "How are you doing?"

"Fine." I felt no different.

Methodically, he removed the needles.

"Now what? What happens next?" I sat up, swung my legs off the table, and reached for my socks.

"I'd like to see you again in two weeks." His response was measured. "It takes longer to show results with emotional problems rather than physical, and your condition is acute. After my time in Vietnam, I returned with multiple layers of post-traumatic stress. You show the same symptoms. I can treat you successfully, but we'll need patience."

Don had opened an avenue of hope. I knew from decades of experience that one cello lesson or practice session couldn't yield lasting results; long-term commitment was required. I booked another appointment.

✦✦✦

That January, I presented another concert on my chamber music series with my violinist and pianist colleagues Naho Parrini and Richard Pearson Thomas. After performing the first trio by twentieth-century Spanish composer Joaquin Turina and Beethoven's monumental "Archduke" Trio, we accepted congratulations and shook hands with audience members.

I was standing in a small group of regular subscribers when the subject of concentration and focus came up. Yoga as a discipline was discussed. I related the agitation I experienced holding a pose in winter on a bare floor. We discussed the benefits of meditation. Though at this point I'd been meditating twice a day for over a year, I admitted that my mind was still all over the place.

"I'd like to try tai chi. I've read that it is a moving mediation that, with practice, helps to develop balance, control, and peace of mind."

"I'm in," a friend chimed in enthusiastically. "I've read it's a miracle for relieving stress while increasing flexibility and balance."

One of our regular concert-goers, Charlie, was matter of fact. "I've been practicing and teaching tai chi for several decades."

My little group buzzed excitedly. "Let's put together a class. Will you teach us?"

The next week, three ladies and I stood expectantly on the exposed wood floor in my studio. The carpet was rolled up, table edged to the window, and violin cases moved into the living room. Charlie stood in front of us and demonstrated, much as I imagined a ballet choreographer would position himself in front of the troop. He lifted his arms chest-high with loose wrists and angled his right heel forward with bended left knee. He pivoted to the right. Four women attempted to mirror the movement.

"Slowly. No, slower," Charlie admonished. "Breathe in. Slow is strong and fluid. Now swivel to the left and swing your arms and body like so."

He was patient with our impatience. We expected results, but we were learning exotic motions, a discipline, a "martial art." I'd never studied dance and found it difficult to remember the motions and poses. There were no notes or music to read. This required pure muscle memory. If you couldn't remember what to do, how could you practice?

After several weeks of painstaking repetition, the form started to stick. Our gestures became more flowing, graceful, and less hesitant. The discipline demanded concentration, balance, and upper-leg strength, with many moves requiring us to stand on one foot with a bent leg and swaying arms. I looked forward to the lessons and drilled the steps every day. Before long, however, the little class had shrunk into a solo practitioner—me. Tai chi was on my healing list. This little bulldog was determined.

CHAPTER 35
DA CAPO

Unexpectantly, Naomi phoned me while I was judging an international violin-making competition for the Violin Society of America. The change of scenery felt good—a hotel in Cleveland.

"I'm moving," she explained. "There is a parking problem here at my home office, so we will meet next time at my new location."

I was in the process of assessing fifty-five cellos for tone, projection, playability, character, complexity, warmth, balance, and response. The work was so engaging that I didn't need this kick-in-the-gut reminder of my "real" life. My two colleagues and I chose our top three instruments after three days of playing, comparing, listening, and discussing. The violin, viola, cello, and bow winners were announced at a celebratory gala dinner at the end of the week.

I flew home and dove back into pulling together my shattered life. I had to drive an extra twenty minutes to Naomi's new premises. My first reaction was that the space was cozier. An old house with the downstairs divided into three professional suites, it was advantageously situated a half block from a Starbucks. I parked under an old, ivy-covered oak tree, ascended wooden steps in the back of the building, and entered a tiny waiting room. The carpet, furniture, and professional certificates had been transplanted from her home office, along with the white-noise machine.

In an attempt to keep the session on target—my target—I arrived bearing a typed agenda. Naomi didn't want minutia, so I furnished a list of discussion topics. She ushered me into her torture chamber, repeated the statement about the parking problem, and asked me where I'd like to sit. This time around I nixed the white leather sofa and chose a wicker armchair near the door. Naomi sat in a corner with a perfect view of the ubiquitous half dozen clocks that circumnavigated the room.

I jumped in with the first item. "My one regret is that I never spoke with Klaus about death. I was simply incapable of dealing with life without him."

"You didn't know how to talk to him." She considered my statement. "You were completely tuned out. His illness, doctors' visits, piles of pills, tests, procedures. Your coping mechanism only allowed you to provide for and run the house. For years you have been living life wearing a mask and surrounded by a screen. I want to expose the barriers that are holding you back from feeling."

This was a common refrain of hers: that I didn't feel. But she was wrong. I felt negative, numb, broken, crumpled, disillusioned, saddened, disappointed, angry, hyper, impotent, depressed, used, betrayed, and cornered. And hadn't numbness allowed me to cope?

I responded, "Most of the time, I'm dizzy and feel faint. But worst of all is the pain in my heart. It feels tight, as if it's being roasted and is shriveling into burned ash."

Naomi instantly fired back. "You take on so much responsibility that you include the actions of others as part of your purview. Overintellectualizing is a defense against getting in touch with your feelings. Because you have low self-esteem, you seek approval from others and have no inner security or strength, so you need it from the outside. You are a pleaser and don't count yourself. As far as your heart goes, go see a doctor and have it checked out."

I was doing the best I could, and my heart was perfect. I'd just had a complete physical. This was acute emotional pain. I glanced down at my agenda, but before I could change the subject, Naomi did.

"You have only talked superficially about your father. Your portrayal of him was that he was erratic and cruel."

She was correct on this score. As a child, dealing with my father was like skating on partially frozen ice. Darrel and I never knew how he would react—encouraging or disparaging, angry, negative, hostile, inattentive, and critical.

"Yes, I learned to be defensive and fight or shut down. Home life was a battleground. I often wonder how Darrel ended up so sunny and positive, while I feel wounded and brutalized."

"You escaped by running across the globe, and your brother escaped by getting high."

I averted my gaze and noticed a small fridge near the door, disguised as a table with a bowl of fake flowers.

"That may be, but I have very few memories of my childhood. We moved around a lot because our father was never happy in his work. I guess he thought somewhere else would be better."

"What was that like for you?" Naomi's voice dropped to *mezzo piano*.

Didn't I just say I can't remember? I had attended six different elementary schools. By the time I entered junior high school in Dallas, we'd moved seven times to five different states. I shoved my hands under my thighs, balancing the typed notes in my lap.

"I got good at meeting people and coping with new situations. The most important lesson I learned was discipline. We had to practice our instruments an hour before breakfast, and only then were we allowed to go to school. If we arrived late and got a detention for tardiness, we'd get into more trouble at home."

A shadow of memory invaded—cello lessons with my mother. My cellist mother had been a good teacher, but lessons were a constant source of conflict. I'd want to play for her so she would pass off that week's assignment and I'd have something new to practice, but she'd be busy. Or she was available, but I had homework. Every session turned into a war zone. As an adult, I could understand my parents' sentiment: why should they pay when she could teach me for free?

Naomi changed directions. "Is it possible that you don't remember your childhood because something so bad happened that you don't want to remember?"

"Like what?" I glanced up from my agenda. "What are you implying?"

"Your mother didn't protect you. You've told me that your father hit you and your brother for the slightest infraction."

"Yes. Darrel even had to make his own paddle in Woodshop to my father's specifications, though he stopped hitting me when I was twelve or thirteen. As I've said, we lived in a police state. He was the dictator whose favorite line was 'Assume the angle.'"

Naomi raised an eyebrow.

"That meant to bend over and grab your ankles."

"I've never heard that one before," she admitted. "How was he when you were alone with him? Was there other abuse?"

"What do you mean? Like what?"

"It sounds like an emotional hothouse." Her voice became intimate. "Maybe his need to control breached inappropriate boundaries."

I suddenly realized where she was going with this line of questioning. It was outrageous, even absurd. My shaking increased, and I struggled to breathe. She seemed to be the one crossing inappropriate boundaries. I told myself to own up and take responsibility for my feelings: *Naomi can't hurt me. Her accusations are my interpretation and perception, which she can't impose upon me.* But I was afraid of her and her criticisms.

She must have seen my unrest because she continued, "I'm going to think about how I can make you feel safe."

I finally shared my thoughts. "I wish you would. Talking with you is like jumping out of an airplane without a parachute or standing in front of a firing squad. You've said that our sessions are like a laboratory where we can assess feelings. Well, I feel like a lab rat."

I barely made it home. When I opened the front door, I found my little Berman kitty, whom Klaus and I had brought back from Texas twelve years before, lying in her own urine. Thaïs had been failing, but now she was so bony that I was afraid to lift her. We said goodbye at the vet's office. Now it was only Shiraz and me.

Then my septic system backed up. The only solution seemed to be a complete replacement. The old tank and pipes could not be salvaged. Before the new equipment could be installed, the slate deck and stone wall had to be demolished. A colossal backhoe, looking like some prehistoric monster, devoured most of the land and garden behind the house to dig two twelve-foot holes for the enormous cement tanks.

+ + +

Naomi's probing about Dad's possible unsuitable behavior toward me as a teenager left a question mark in my thoughts. That evening, after the machinery and crew had left for the day, I called Darrel and asked if he had memories of our father ever touching me inappropriately.

He was resolute. "She's barking up the wrong tree."

"That's what I thought. But do you remember in high school, when I'd have music friends over to rehearse, he was always trying to tickle them?"

"What an asshole. He was just showing off and trying to get attention, as usual."

Our mother certainly wasn't happy with his juvenile behavior either.

"His conduct didn't encourage me to bring friends home," I remembered. "We didn't get much of his attention, unless it was to mete out punishment."

Darrel's voice turned steely. "When I was sixteen and you'd gone off to college, I finally had enough. He brought out his belt, ruler, or flyswatter, whichever was the chosen weapon of the day. That was the last straw. I decided I wouldn't let him hit me one more time, ever again. I'd take him out first."

"Watching you get beat up enraged me. I felt protective, but there was nothing I could do."

"I think you are still enraged." Darrel cut me no slack, as usual. (What are siblings for?)

"Well, I went from an authoritarian, controlling father to an authoritarian, controlling husband. Naomi says that we marry one of our parents. In other words, we marry who we know and what we are used to."

The voice on the other end of the line turned from hard to adamant. "Tell Naomi to back off that sexual abuse bullshit." Darrel was defending me. "There's more than one type of abuse. How about withholding love? Has he ever said he loved you? He never said it to me."

I felt relieved that my brain hadn't wiped out something so horrible. I didn't want to see my father as a sex offender—or worse. Then I considered his question. "Now that you mention it, I can't think of a time, but I always assumed he did."

"Don't be so sure. Living with him was like walking through quicksand. We could never be sure if we'd sink down and get swallowed up."

I told him about Thaïs and the septic system.

"If I had all the responsibilities you have, I'd be shaking too. Give yourself a break and accept that you are doing everything you can."

CHAPTER 36
CON MISTERO

Through all the turmoil of Klaus's death, the revelations about Ute, the court case, and my psychotherapy, I couldn't stop trying to wrap my mind around who Klaus was. Each new fact shattered a little more of the structure of my marriage and myself. I sought a reality to hold on to.

I hoped to discover something of relevance about his father, assuming the apple didn't fall far from the tree.

Under the Freedom of Information Act, I requested records from the Federal Bureau of Investigation pertaining to Friedrich Wilhelm Freiherr von Österberg-Bauer. Several months after applying, I received a large brown envelope. The FBI's cover letter stated that nineteen out of a total twenty-four pages were released, which surprised me; Alexandra had stated she had over nine hundred pages from the FBI.

The letterhead trumpeted JOHN EDGAR HOOVER, DIRECTOR. A chilly frisson scuttled down my spine as I read in a corner box: CHARACTER OF CASE—INTERNAL SECURITY—GERMAN ALIEN ENEMY CONTROL. In the margins of the typed sheets were handwritten scribbles, date stamps, arrows, and notes of declassification.

The transcripts were from 1941 and 1942 and contained references to newspaper articles from the *New York Daily News, The New York Times*, and *Washington Times Herald*. I immediately set about trying to access copies of these articles.

Again I went to my local library for help, where Patrick, the reference librarian, submitted a requisition to the Library of Congress. Two weeks later, the microfiche cassettes arrived. But there was a snag—no way to read the film. Patrick once more came to the rescue, booking an appointment with a regional county library that had a large reference department and microfiche equipment. That afternoon, I jumped in the car and drove fifteen minutes to the library in Patchogue, where a helpful young librarian fed the film into the reader and showed me how to wind through to the pages referenced in the FBI reports and how to magnify the images.

I decided to begin with the earliest issue, published August 5, 1937, in *The New York Times*. It was a short piece naming the securities firm of Österberg & Halle as "Nazi aides" and accusing them of "illegally selling German securities." Without reading the article, I made photocopies, then searched for the next citation.

My heart almost stopped. Screaming at me in huge headlines from the *Daily News*, Tuesday, August 13, 1940, was FBI UNMASKS NY GESTAPO. I quickly scrolled through to page 28, where the article continued. There, pictured in the middle column with his name in bold italics, was Klaus's father: CENTER OF INVESTIGATION. The photo was so large and article so long that I struggled to copy both but was finally able to move on to March 14, 1941, in the *Washington Times Herald* and *The New York Times* of April 7, 1942. I whirled through, printed the relevant pages, and rewound the film.

I had it all. We carefully repackaged the cassettes, and with a handshake I thanked the young man who had assisted me. I returned to my local library and handed over the bundle to be returned to the Library of Congress.

Sitting at my dining room table in an anxious and dazed state, I started to puzzle together a picture of this man. I gathered that Friedrich (Fredrich), Klaus's father, had established a money laundering operation.

On June 20, 1940, a bomb exploded on the eighteenth floor of 17 Battery Place, New York City, one floor below the German consulate, at the door of the headquarters of the Gestapo, which Friedrich led. A G-man (FBI agent) reported that Friedrich left New York "before the FBI could question him." Seventeen were arrested on charges of plotting to overthrow the government.

On March 13, 1941, the *NY Daily News* reported,

> Probing a new bomb threat to offices under the German consulate, in lower Manhattan, police and state investigators became convinced today that Nazi Gestapo activities have been suddenly transferred to uptown Yorkville from a downtown site below the consulate. It is pointed out that the bombing last June of the Travel Agency located in the building and the exposure of its boss, Baron von Österberg, as an officer in the German Secret Police, who was recently recalled to the Reich . .
>
> . [sic]

I digested this information. It seemed Klaus had grown up in Switzerland because either Fred/Friedrich/Fredrich was fleeing the FBI, which was tracking him down as a Gestapo spy agent operating in the exchange of illegal German securities, or Hitler's regime had recalled him to the Fatherland. There had to be more. Hadn't the Nazis recorded every nuance of their structure and purges? The picture remained incomplete, but I wasn't sure how to go about researching German and Swiss historical records.

A couple of months later, serendipity played an ace card. I was on a Lufthansa flight from Frankfurt back home after once again attending the cello festival in Kronberg. The young man next to me slept until halfway to New York. Now awake, he was abuzz, excited to visit his girlfriend. The conversation turned to his family. His father was a social historian specializing in the Second World War. When I shared the little information I had about Fred/Friedrich/Fredrich, he jotted down his dad's email and suggested I connect with him.

Herr Marco Huggele became intrigued when I related the basic bones of Friedrich's bio. He had entrée to archives in Germany that would have been entirely inaccessible and impossible for me to negotiate. After running down many rabbit holes and finally hitting pay dirt through German police reports from the 1930s, Swiss documents, and information in books, he put together a compelling synopsis of the life of Friedrich Freiherr von Österberg-Bauer prior to the New York City bombs and his consequent flight to Germany/Switzerland with his family.

CHAPTER 37
BRAVURA

With Herr Huggele's information and what I had discovered, I now had plenty of facts. A portrait materialized. It began with a 1934 report from the Criminal Office of the Police in Oppeln; Friedrich had been recalled to Germany to explain to a court why he bought an aristocratic title and name.

According to the report, Friedrich was a cavalry guard in 1919 when he took part in the abduction of Rosa Luxemburg, an outspoken communist and socialist of Polish Jewish descent. She was seized in Berlin, murdered, and thrown into a canal. Because of his participation in the murder, Friedrich was repeatedly threatened and beaten by members of her communist party, Spartacus. After he was shot for a third time during an attempted coup d'état in 1920, Friedrich moved to Pomerania (now in Poland), where he lived under an assumed name, worked as a night watchman, and joined the Nazi Party.

In May 1921, Friedrich was a combatant in the third Polish uprising in Upper Silesia, a section of the German empire where over 50 percent of the population spoke Polish, not German. In an explanation of his duties, he wrote in the report: "It was also my task to shoot two traitors in our ranks. So as to leave as few clues as possible, I laid the traitors outside the demarcation line. [This was known as "frontier justice" when those perceived as traitors were summarily shot without trial.] Later this caused many difficulties for me, but I did it for the sake of my comrades."

The next year, 1922, he was jailed as the suspected assassin of Walter Rathenau, who had been the imperial armaments chief during WWI and served as finance minister in the Weimar Republic.

Though he was released after several weeks, Friedrich was still being hunted down for his crimes. He explained:

> I was blackmailed by members of my former military unit due to the executions at the front. Because of that and other political difficulties, I tried to immigrate to the USA. This was not easy because my name was known to the US Embassy in Berlin in connection with political activities, and I couldn't prove that I had acted honorably for the last five years, so I couldn't get an immigration visa under my birth name—Bauer. So, I considered adoption as a way to avoid slander, insults and false information, which I couldn't counter.

So Friedrich Bauer bought the "von Österberg" name from Freiherr Arthur von Österberg under the guise of an "adoption" in return for payments of fifty reichsmarks per month. Friedrich used the title "baron" ("Freiherr") but stressed that he only used it to "avoid the difficulties arising from the executions and to begin a new life abroad."

He ended his explanation to the German court with "I did all this for my Fatherland and bought the name for my Führer."

Though Friedrich went to Germany to explain his name change and title, my friend Jim, who was helping with the translation, and I wondered if the real reason for his return was in preparation for the *Röhm-Putsch*, also known as the Night of Long Knives, when Hitler had the SS kill the opponents of his regime. From June 30 to July 2, 1934, several thousand leaders of the Sturmabteilung (SA), the Nazi's rival organization, were massacred. Its commander, Ernst Röhm, was personally arrested by Hitler, who put a revolver in Röhm's hand and gave him ten minutes to either shoot himself or be executed. Röhm replied that Adolf should kill him himself. When no gunfire was heard after the allotted time, a soldier stormed in and shot him at point-blank range.

Over the next few years, Friedrich traveled back and forth between Germany, New York, Portugal, Switzerland, Scandinavia, Manchuria, and Japan, ostensibly as a businessman.

He met Marie Gabrielle Heinrich, Klaus's mother, in New York and married her after his second marriage dissolved. (That wife later married the Nazi envoy to Iran.) I have their marriage certificate, a document from the Court of Common Pleas, Baltimore, MD. It records the marriage of Friedrich F. Österberg-Bauer, age thirty-nine, occupation banker, single/annulled, born in Germany, with Marie G. Heinrich, age twenty-five, occupation student, single, born in Germany. It is dated March 20, 1939. Seven and a half months later, Klaus was born in New York City, an American citizen.

The FBI reported in March 1941 that "Friedrich Freiherr von Österberg-Bauer was investigated by the Bureau for espionage activities" but left the US in September 1940 for Germany and was "reported to be extremely pro-Nazi."

It seems that Friedrich was traveling between Germany and Switzerland when he died in a taxi at 3:50 a.m., April 1942, in the town of Dietikon, Switzerland (just across the German border).

Three days later, his briefcase was found in his Baden, Germany, hotel room. It was opened and the contents inventoried, as witnessed by his wife and an attorney representing a Swiss bank.

An October 1942 report from the FBI states that British sources were informed that Friedrich Bauer was probably one of the most important German agents operating in the US.

+++

How did Friedrich die? Why in a taxi at 3:50 a.m. in Switzerland? Was he transferring illicit moneys from Germany to Switzerland or back? Was he operating as a spy? Though I had plenty of "facts," I suspect the mysteries surrounding Friedrich's life will remain. Clearly, he was a murderer as well as opportunistic, self-serving, and self-aggrandizing. Did Klaus inherit those qualities?

Over the years, Klaus's stories about his father became shifting "truths." I remember him saying that his father suffered from WWI wounds, had a heart attack, or was murdered because he worked for anti-Nazi organizations. Klaus often mentioned how "kind" he was.

Friedrich's activities as a banker/money launderer for Hitler made him a wealthy man and left Marie a healthy inheritance from assets securely deposited in Swiss banks. This allowed her and young Klaus to live in relative comfort in Switzerland during the war when there was great scarcity.

Eight years later, in 1950, Marie remarried while living in Ascona. Hans Marschall was a German doctor and artist. In March 1951, husband, wife, their new baby son, and eleven-year-old Klaus flew to Windhoek, the capital city of former German Southwest Africa (now Namibia), to start a new life.

Recently, I spoke with a friend, a trustee of the Yaphank (New York) Historical Society. Their historian had assembled photos and films regarding the Nazi gatherings at Camp Siegfried, a pro-Nazi boy's summer camp that attracted hundreds of youngsters and their parents from New York and Pennsylvania in the mid to late 1930s. We met and viewed the historical footage of thousands of marchers and beer drinkers carrying swastika flags up and down streets named after Hitler and Göring.

This was sixty miles from Friedrich's NYC business, one mile from the laboratory where Klaus worked, and five miles from where we bought our home. The FBI called Friedrich the "head of the American Gestapo." Though I cannot prove it, I speculate that Friedrich had been at these rallies, which took place every weekend in Long Island during the time he lived in New York City.

CHAPTER 38
PARLANTE

Richard Pearson Thomas and I have performed together for over two decades. He is an extraordinary composer, consummate pianist, and sensitive musician. Over the years we became close friends and colleagues. He dreamed of Africa. I said that if he wanted company, I'd join him.

Escaping to the other side of the world could be healing and distracting. What did he want to see? In 2012 Egypt was out of the question because of the political situation. Maybe a safari, but so much of the continent was a war zone or dangerous. Kenya might be good, but Tanzania seemed safer. We started envisioning the wildebeest migrations in the Serengeti, Kilimanjaro, Arusha, Ngorongoro Crater, Tarangire, Lake Manyara, and the exotic spice island Zanzibar.

We were bouncing around ideas when my phone rang. I immediately recognized a South African accent. The caller, Sarah, had received my name from a cello maker in Cape Town. She lived in the Hamptons and wanted to learn the cello.

Sarah was gorgeous and sophisticated, spoke several languages, had a high-powered NYC job in international branding, and had traveled the globe—including Tanzania. I invited her and Richard for dinner to discuss travel plans and hear her suggestions.

During the evening's discussion, Sarah admitted to having bouts of anxiety. I didn't understand how such a beautiful, accomplished, successful woman could suffer as she described it. Upon probing, she revealed that her salvation had come in the form of hypnotherapy. She had been put into a trance and regressed to a very young age she no longer consciously remembered. A scene from the age of three had emerged. This memory allowed her, through the perception of an adult, to see that a toddler's response no longer served her. With this revelation, she understood her present-day reactions and could cope with situations that had previously triggered her.

When she told us of this experience, I simply thought of it as an interesting story. Then the conversation returned to her adventures traveling alone through Kenya, Tanzania, and as far south as Malawi and Mozambique.

With the help of a knowledgeable travel agent, our safari dream took on aspects of reality. My passport was valid, no visas needed, but entry into Tanzania required proof of inoculation against yellow fever. I called around and found a place nearby that offered the injection at a relatively reasonable price.

I drove to Holbrook at the appointed time, parked, and confidently strode to the wellness center's entrance, ringing the bell. A tall, dark-haired, well-dressed lady opened the door.

"I have an eleven o'clock appointment. Do you give the yellow fever injections?" I inquired.

"No, I'm the hypnotherapist." Her smile was warm and friendly. "Come on in. Go down this hall. The office is on the right."

As I rolled up my sleeve and the nurse swabbed my arm with alcohol, a little light bulb illuminated in my head, making the connection with what Sarah had said about hypnotism. I truly admired her, so I figured being put into a trance must be okay.

The needle jabbed, and the nurse swiped away a drop of blood and plastered a bandage over the puncture. We discussed malaria pills, and she handed me a certificate proving my immunity to the potentially lethal virus. After a quick thank-you and handshake, I passed in front of the main office.

On impulse, I caught the eye of the lady who had welcomed me in.

"I'm struggling with anxiety and panic attacks. Do you think you can help me?" I asked.

"Absolutely." She was confident but not pushy. "Here's my card. Check out my website. It'll give you an idea of what to expect. When you're ready, give me a call."

The card introduced her as Carol Denicker. I thanked her, went home, and did a little online research. She certainly had the qualifications. The site claimed she could help in smoking cessation, weight loss, relieving stress, improving sleep, and increasing motivation. She had a training center for healthcare professionals to learn hypnotism. I pulled the trigger and booked an appointment.

The day came. Like Pavlov's dog responding to habitual stimuli, I felt the dreaded adrenaline rush halfway to her office in anticipation of having to talk about my situation with a stranger who might judge me.

As the second hand on my watch approached the hour, I turned the doorknob and entered the little office building. Carol ushered me into her office with a nonthreatening smile and indicated a large, well-worn leather armchair. I sat and was swallowed by its size; heavier folk than I had sat here. She circled around an enormous desk. It was clear except for a recording device and headphones. Leaning to her left, she opened a drawer and took out paper and a pen.

Her eyes met mine. "Did you have a chance to fill out the intake forms? I know you mentioned anxiety. Can you tell me about it and its cause?"

My hand quivered as I handed the papers across the barrier of the desk. Instinctually, I thrust my hands under my thighs and, with a little shudder, launched into my story.

Though Carol kept her eyes trained on me, she took assiduous notes and murmured the occasional comment to show that she was engaged and following my discourse. Her demeanor seemed completely nonjudgmental and open.

"How are you feeling right now?" she asked.

"Pretty nervous," I admitted. Even thinking about Klaus gave me heart palpitations. Far worse was telling a stranger.

Carol's manicured nails dropped the pen. "Well, that's no good. Coming here should feel relaxing and comforting. Before we begin, I'd like to conduct a little experiment."

She rolled her chair alongside mine and handed me a small, teardrop-shaped stone hanging on a thin chain. It looked like a simple necklace. "Hold this as steady as possible. Now focus. Concentrate. Let's see if the pendant starts circling in a clockwise direction."

I put my right elbow on the chair's armrest, the stone dangling inertly from my fingers. As I gazed in amazement, the bobble started to gyrate, then rotated in a tiny orbit. I was definitely not influencing the motion with my hand.

"As you see, Lauri, your thoughts have great power." Carol went back to her desk and continued. "Hypnosis is an altered state of consciousness where the subconscious mind is in a state of hypersuggestibility. I'm sure you've experienced an altered state while cruising down a highway, lost in thought, or practicing your cello while in deep concentration. In a hypnotic trance, the suggestions I feed you will bypass your conscious mind and feed directly into your subconscious, which controls much of your subliminal actions and responses—especially emotions."

I took in her words and thought: *Please let this work for me.*

Carol wasn't finished. "While in trance, I can give your subconscious positive suggestions, such as that you remain calm, tranquil, and at ease. This will reprogram your response to anxiety. At all times, you will be in complete control and will never have to accept anything I say that does not comply with your values or desires."

I wanted to believe her. She was offering me hope.

"Okay. Sit back and get as comfortable as possible. Put on the headphones, and if you like, prop your feet on the footrest. I will record the session with background music. Don't worry; it doesn't go anywhere and shouldn't distract you."

I removed my glasses, then tried to follow her instructions. My back remained obstinately straight, leg muscles tight, fists clenched. The music filtered into my ears through the headphones.

"Is the volume okay? Words clearly audible? Good. Let's begin."

Her voice changed. It became extremely soothing, even caressing.

She counted down from ten to one, asking me to take several cleansing breaths and become more and more relaxed as I opened and closed my eyes with each descending number. When it became almost impossible to keep my eyes open, I was asked to visualize a peaceful place and "really be there." Then, starting with my face, I was to relax the muscles between my eyes, in my forehead, and in my jaw.

"If your face is truly relaxed, the rest of the body can relax." She systematically guided me through the process. Though my body started to feel numb, I was aware of the traffic, the front door whispering open and clicking closed, the nonmusic, and her steady, almost uninflected voice. When my breathing finally became very shallow, a reaction I knew from meditation, she began her affirmations of empowerment, wellness, calmness, confidence, and changes for the better.

"Your mind has become so sensitive and receptive to positive ideas—if in accordance with your desires—and they are becoming so embedded into your subconscious mind that nothing can erase them. Consequently, these ideas will have a greater and greater influence over how you feel, act, and think. No matter where you go, what you do, who you are with, these positive suggestions will continue to exercise a powerful influence over your thoughts and actions."

Some minutes later, her voice instructed that on the count of five, I would open my eyes and come out of the trance refreshed, confident, relaxed, and in control.

I couldn't assess how deep a trance I was in, but Carol explained that it didn't matter because she had recorded the session and wanted me to listen to it daily for the next twenty-one days. As she handed me the CD, I pictured myself listening with the backdrop of roaring lions, trumpeting elephants, and circling vultures. The scene was not far from my future reality; I would find that peaceful place only days later while lying in a hammock overlooking the African savanna, with exotic birds calling from the baobab and acacia trees.

As we wrapped up, Carol peered into my eyes and said thoughtfully, "Stop therapy. That counselor is not right for you."

Her body and hands were tranquil and motionless. She did not elaborate. She was not competing or maneuvering to steal a client; this was a fact, and it was up to me to recognize its validity.

I had heard the same sentiment from my friends for months, but I wasn't a quitter. The idea of giving up seemed like a cop-out. I thought my anxiety somehow meant therapy was working and I was making progress.

I walked out of Carol's office and climbed into the blazing heat of my car before collapsing behind the steering wheel. *Is she right? Should I stop therapy? Will she be able to help me heal?*

Had the two and a half years in analysis been for naught?

I was reminded of my sophomore year in college. My cello teacher was an abusive autocrat who had a reputation for having inappropriate sexual relations with his female students. I had been so fearful of being alone with him that I threw up before every cello lesson. The irony was that he had been my mother's teacher, which was why my father insisted I study with him.

I struggled through the year, then took the scary and bold step of transferring to a conservatory in Hartford, Connecticut, where I supported myself since I no longer had my parents' blessing. Consequently, the ensuing three years were some of the happiest of my life. I made lifelong friends and found the cello professor who became my musical inspiration and irreplaceable mentor.

When life becomes unbearable, the only choice is change. At this point, I'd read enough self-help books to understand that recognizing the problem can be the beginning of the solution.

I decided to be moderately brave. Leaving the country for several weeks would allow me to cut the cord with Naomi. However, I didn't have long to ponder the issue, since I was still going twice a week, and my next session was the following day.

As usual, I dressed carefully and professionally—a gesture of respect. I took our work seriously and wanted to look the part. Even though acupuncture was helping to relieve the anxiety, I still felt the surge of adrenaline within ten minutes of arriving at Naomi's office. Sitting in the waiting room was not an option. I stood, trying to contain my jitters. When the interior door opened, I entered the torture chamber with a confidence I didn't feel, closed the door behind us, and sat in my usual chair. I focused on closure but still hoped for some final insight.

I made a confession. "I'm writing a book. A memoir. I think the story is compelling."

"Why?" Her eyebrows lifted.

"I'm hoping the process will help me find out who Klaus was." Silence. *Approval, disapproval? Why do I care?* "I started with the scene in the hospital when he dies."

"How do you feel about that?" She was the cat pouncing on a terrified mouse.

"Neutral." This was well-covered ground. I took a breath to harden my heart and nerves.

Naomi didn't give up so easily. "Are you happy not feeling? You have no need for the highs and lows? Living your life like a machine is working for you?"

I considered her question. This didn't seem fair. I "felt" music and thought my playing was expressive. But after the course my life had taken, I was simply trying to survive. My self-esteem had been hammered so low that no matter how much professional success I earned or how much I changed my environment, there was no joy. I often wanted to melt away and dissolve into oblivion.

"I want to cut out the lows and eliminate those emotions." My sigh was jagged.

Naomi shifted her position and closed her eyes with a small breath of exasperation before she went for the jugular. "Maybe you are living at a completely rational zero and feel guilt and disgrace over Klaus because you were the 'other woman.' When you found out he was married, you didn't get out of the relationship. Instead, you accepted his promises and went along with his pretense of being divorced. You even got married without seeing the divorce papers."

Hearing this truth spoken aloud brought profound shame. This was my burden. I had been exposed. For the rest of the session, we ping-ponged through old territory until Naomi's eyes dodged over to one of the clocks—a cue for the end of the session. We both stood.

"Our work together has meant a great deal"—I fought down a shiver of panic—"but I've decided to take a break. I didn't sign up for analysis. I hoped for relief from grief and understanding of my acute pain. I never intended to stay for years."

Her gracious response astonished me. "I'm not the kind of therapist who clings to clients. I think writing is a good idea and could help your healing process. Let's make it clear, however. You said you want a break. You didn't say stop. I want you to call me in the fall, and we will discuss how to proceed."

As I walked out, I didn't feel relief or satisfaction in the closing of this chapter. The only time we had ever touched was at the first introduction when we shook hands, almost three years before. How many intimate hours ago was that? Maybe that said it all.

In a funk, I started my car, drove to Starbucks for a double macchiato, then went home to pack, surrounded by a caffeinated cloud of guilt. My shame at being a "quitter" was tinged with regret that all those hours Naomi and I had spent together had yielded so few insights and so little relief. Yet I sizzled with anticipation for the upcoming adventure.

***

The next day at JFK, I checked my tiny suitcase all the way to Tanzania via Amsterdam. Richard and I met and boarded our plane. Twenty-four hours later, we arrived dazed yet excited. Our passage through Immigration was expedited with hundred-dollar bills tucked into our passports, which we'd been told was essential to facilitate entry into the country.

A waiting jeep whisked us to our hotel at the foot of the mountain. Without a moon, the sky and landscape were one, except for a quadrant of heaven where there were no stars: the dormant volcano Kilimanjaro, Africa's highest peak at over 19,000 feet. The frogs and insects sang their contentment as our suitcases rattled through the flowering gardens to our room.

Over the following weeks, we took in sights beyond dreams. The Maasai—tall and regal with long, sure strides—herded their fortune (cattle) across arid miles in search of nourishment. Prides of lions hunted so close we could have reached out to pet them. The vast Serengeti looked like an ocean. We witnessed a fraction of the two million wildebeest crossing and recrossing a river while commingling with half a million zebra. The intensity of sound, sight, and commotion of their drive pounded through the bedrock of our bones. Elephants waded through rivers, oblivious to the surrounding crocodiles. A leopard climbed a tree trunk to nestle on an overhanging branch for a daytime snooze. And we saw bloats of hippos, clans of hyenas, parliaments of owls, sounders of warthogs, journeys of giraffes.

The intoxication of these sights—the vital richness of our animal kingdom—awakened my sense of wonder. The birds! Dozens of species ranging from sweet weavers and colorful lovebirds to the predators: kites, vultures, eagles, secretary birds, pigeon falcons, bustards. I couldn't keep up with the "bird checklist" we'd been given by our guide upon arrival.

The landscape was both empty and teeming—if you knew where to look. Our African guides' eyesight was remarkable. Over years of scanning the sky, bushes, trees, and horizon, their eyes must have been trained to see far distances. I squinted through powerful binoculars to discern what our guides Erasto and Martin could spot as they drove overland, skirting potholes through the brush. One of the men would point, and out of a tangle of branches or a clear horizon, a necking pair of giraffes or sleeping lion cubs would emerge. All the while, their walkie-talkies' Swahili communications assailed the timeless tranquility.

Crossing miles of Africa, my worries drained away. Several days into the trip, I lay in a recliner overlooking the Tanzanian bush outside our tent in Tarangire National Park and plugged into Carol's hypnosis recording. The only sounds were insects and the occasional call of unidentifiable birds. The high-altitude air left me breathless, and the sun felt golden on my northern-blanched skin. The scene was primordial in its apparent simplicity yet seethed with unseen life.

I leaned back, eyes closed, and released all the tension from my body while Carol counted down and urged me to visualize a sacred place of peace. I was there.

+++

As comfortable as our accommodations were, the trip was not an easy one. We rose early because dawn is when the animals are active. We rode in open Land Rovers under the pulverizing African sun, often swatting at swarms of tsetse flies. My poor wrists ached from my death grip on the vehicle rails. We jarred and bounced, traversing off-road across the savanna or on corrugated and pitted dirt roads, often for twelve hours at a stretch, sometimes covering over 200 kilometers a day. Occasionally, we stopped to relieve ourselves behind the vehicle. The guide thankfully kept an eye out for lions, guns ready.

We loved every minute.

Our chance to recuperate came at the end of the trip when we flew from Arusha, "the Safari capital of the world," to Zanzibar. Twenty-eight miles off the coast of Tanzania in the Indian Ocean, the island is known for spices: clove, cinnamon, black pepper, and nutmeg. Like on the mainland, the spoken language is Swahili, though its history cloaks a dark past as an outpost for the slave trade.

Richard and I waited in the shade of an acacia tree for our transport. A high-cheekboned man wearing the traditional Muslim attire of white trousers, a long white shirt, and a white fez served us fruit juice. In a cloud of dust, a twelve-seater propeller plane landed. The pilot jumped to the ground and shouted: "Who's going to Zanzibar?" That was check-in. We climbed up the four steps, ducked into the vessel, and tossed our suitcases into an open well behind the seats. There were no other passengers, so we each sat beside a window.

The little craft flew over the bush and skirted Tanzania's capital city, Dar es Salaam, which looked bleached next to the glistening turquoise-and-emerald sea. The water was so transparent that I imagined seeing the sunken ships of ruthless Arab tradesmen drowned on their way to sell the slaves.

All too soon, the wings tilted, and we swirled into our descent, effortlessly gliding onto a paved airstrip (one of the first).

Hordes of taxi drivers accosted us in the bare cement terminal. From the milieu popped a small, hand-scrawled sign with Richard's surname. After a half-hour ride through impoverished roadside villages, I started to get worried, and not just because young children were playing in gutters with rotting garbage and mangy goats. I sensed we were lost. The only Swahili we had learned up to this point was *karibu*, "welcome," and *asante sana*, "thank you very much." Communication was a challenge.

After a moderately tense adventure, we arrived at our resort on the island's north side—a secluded paradise. This brief and unexpected excursion into the Third World's reality of starvation, disease, and lack of hygiene and probably education left me feeling that my problems were infinitesimal, but this realization merely increased my mental burden.

We settled into our seafront oasis, then took a short, meandering walk to get our bearings and ogle the flowers. The ocean was intoxicating and dazzlingly brilliant. The gentle waves sparkled like stars on the white-powdered beach.

I casually turned to Richard. "There's nothing to do here."

"I rather think that's the point." Through his sunglasses, his eyes hooded by his baseball cap, he stared at me. "I'm going to wade out in the ocean and look at sea creatures. What about you?"

He turned and headed toward the beach. I'd traveled thousands of miles to find resolution and peace. But peace is in the mind, and mine was not yet cleared of the recent trespasses and residual pollution.

Our room was a private thatched-roof rondavel. The temperature was in the low eighties, and though the humidity was about the same, a cooling ocean breeze gently swept up the hill from the sea to our deck. I popped in my earbuds and heard Carol's countdown. I was in paradise. My goal was to live in this special moment and not in the past, future, or somewhere else.

✦✦✦

The trip home from Stone Town, Zanzibar, to New York was agony. I had been so careful with water and diet, but with juggling luggage, passports, schedules, flight numbers, and plane changes, I ate something dodgy at the "restaurant" in the Dar es Salaam airport, which served long-ago-fried food roasting under heat lamps (even too hot for the circling flies). I was in an intimate relationship with Montezuma when I lived in Mexico

City, where he had first taken his revenge on me, but wasn't so familiar with the scourges of East African warrior gods.

With an eight-hour layover in Nairobi, we had considered leaving the airport to explore the city, but the advice was adamant: It's not safe. Stay put.

The Jomo Kenyatta International Airport is truly international—an African hub. Flights arrive from the Middle and Far East and continue to South America and back. Tourists and business travelers from Southern Africa change planes for other African destinations and North America. The list of European cities served is a geography lesson.

Though the selection of flights was impressive, the amenities offered at the airport were not. There was no restaurant and only one dirty ladies' room. The few beverages for sale were bottled water and sugary soft drinks, like orange Shasta. We waited the entire eight hours on the folding chairs lining the long corridors.

A far worse torment was the public-address system. The arrival and departure of every flight was screamed, not only in Swahili but also in every other known and unknown language: Spanish, Afrikaans, Chinese, French, Arabic. The blast of words plucked our already frazzled nerves.

Richard was sick and completely out of it. When we eventually changed planes (yet again) in Paris, he was barely holding on. Finally, at JFK, we cleared Immigration and Customs. Richard took the subway to Manhattan, and I caught the AirTrain to Jamaica, Queens, then connected to Patchogue on the Long Island Rail Road.

My taxi pulled into the driveway. The house was empty and boiling hot since it had been in lockdown during the weeks I was away. The garden was scorched, the mail stacked sky-high, the phone blinking messages, all my clothes disgusting. My stomach churned. I desperately needed a shower and sleep. I was alone, ill, but glad to be home.

A universal law seems to be that we return from vacation nice and relaxed. We resolve to stay calm and continue delighting in the sun on our skin, laughing, and taking pleasure in simple pleasures. And then we walk through the front door: the fridge is empty, the family is hungry, the phone is ringing, and there are mountains of bills and a 9 a.m. meeting tomorrow. Former habits of stress, and our reaction to them, throw us right back where we were before the getaway.

I was determined to bypass this rule and maintain tranquility in my everyday life, even with the pressures of running a business, bookkeeping, managing chores (which had formerly been divided), and practicing a new repertoire. The goal of retaining inner calm after the trauma of Klaus's betrayal and lawsuit became my full-time job.

I made new resolutions. Sitting on the sofa where Klaus had lain for so many months brought more anxiety, so I threw it out. And no more television. Violence and disasters did not resonate with my search for serenity. I completely disconnected from the daily harangue of news broadcasts. I canceled the weekday *Times* delivery and only opened the weekend sections. If the headline shouted DEAD, SHOOTINGS, WAR, ATTACKS, CRISIS, TERRORISTS, EPIDEMICS, HOSTAGES, MELTDOWN, etc., I ruthlessly avoided even a glance. If something important happened, someone would tell me.

Without external interference, I found a profound silence of both emptiness and the promise of healing. Instinctually, I knew stillness begat peace, though reaching that equilibrium was the challenge. I followed all the recipes: exercise, meditation, journaling, communes with nature, chants of affirmations. I devoured self-help texts, took notes, and jotted down passages. I threw away and donated many of the tangible memories of my past: high school yearbooks, most of my wardrobe, photos, years of magazines, the detritus of Klaus's life, and hundreds of books.

I'd been visualizing peace for so long that I couldn't help wondering, *When will all this indoctrination kick in?* I understood I had to take responsibility for my thoughts and that tranquility lay in my perception of events, but there was still a lot of garbage bouncing around my head. I was desperate for this plague to end and go away.

As soon as I knew which time zone I was waking up in, and after the East African plague had worked through my system, I booked another hypnosis session.

A week later, I sat for a few minutes in the waiting area before Carol ushered me into her office with a welcoming gesture and questions about the trip. I reported a few cursory episodes before explaining why I was there.

"I still feel like I am to blame for what happened to me. I'm torn between thinking that this occurred because of my screwups and that Klaus was really so unfeeling and insensitive that he didn't care if I was left with this mess."

She sat behind her huge, imposing desk, pencil in hand; it had almost no point.

"Could your anxiety and guilt be the reaction of an intimidated child who couldn't stand up for herself? Family dynamics can affect children for their entire lives, and we end up with default behaviors," she explained. "Those behaviors then become responses to situations outside the family circle. Let me ask you: how do you see yourself reacting to negative stimulus such as criticism, confrontation, disrespect, anger?"

I took a moment to process the question. "Well, I shut down and stop communicating. Sometimes I bury it or simply run away." This was getting unpleasant, but I was there for help. "I take on too much responsibility to the point where I accuse myself of someone else's mistakes."

"I hear you saying that you want to please people so that they like you." Carol adjusted her reading glasses, which perfectly matched her necklace and fingernails.

Do I need to hear that again? Evidently, my habits hadn't changed, and my psyche hadn't healed.

"I don't say what I think and have been told that I don't feel. My emotions seem limited to panic attacks." I took a breath, then continued. "Is guilt an emotion? I feel that too."

She dropped the useless pencil and picked up her headphones. "You certainly are giving me plenty of material. The subconscious works without the structure of time. So, I'd like to take you back to your childhood and start to erase negative programming. There is nothing to be afraid of. I'll do all the talking. Make yourself comfortable. Do you want to put your feet up?"

I tried to settle into the recliner but still felt edgy with the process. The headphones drooped, big, floppy, and heavy.

"How's the volume?" Her voice was distant. "Can you hear me clearly? Music not too loud? One of these days I'll get it right."

I breathed and consciously released my raised shoulders. On tense thighs, I placed sweaty, rigid hands.

"Close your eyes and take a nice, slow, diaphragmatic breath. Good. And now another, even slower breath. Your imagination is the rehearsal room of your mind. You're going on a journey to your special, soothing, safe place. Perhaps it's a garden with leafy trees. You hear gurgling fountains. See the clear, sparkling water surrounded by brightly colored birds. Feel a gentle breeze caressing your face. Smell the perfumed flowers.

"It's so peaceful that it is easier and easier to relax with each breath you take. Your subconscious mind will allow you to accept this deeply relaxing state as it becomes more and more real, so that every nerve and muscle can respond to your desire to relax. Imagine that it is easier and easier to go deeper and deeper as I count from ten down to one.

"The sound of my voice, coupled with your intention to heal and find total peace, allows you to feel safe and comfortable. You are becoming more receptive and ready to make changes. Panic and anxiety are reactions of the past. As you listen to my words, you become more and more free of the limiting, biased beliefs that began with hurtful things people said or did long ago. As I talk, your subconscious mind will be doing the work of erasing programs that no longer work.

"I'm sure that there was a time in your life, a recent time, when you said to yourself: 'I wish I knew then what I know now.' In the state of hypnosis, we are able to use all levels of the mind at once, so this is possible. There is no time. These false beliefs were instilled when you were younger and didn't understand. Tell the younger you what she needs to know to grow up confident and unafraid. See yourself so young and unaware that you feel safe. Imagine you are together with that tiny little you. Tell that little girl some nice things about herself. Tell her how special she is: she is completely lovable. Talk to that sweet child and tell her what you know now. What would you tell her? Take a moment."

My legs were numb and my hands still rigid, but I saw myself as I was in a photo at age one. The baby me smiled with delight into a mirror, her white ruffled dress not quite covering chubby, splayed legs that ended in minuscule booties. Her almost translucent hair was adorned with a ridiculous flowered headband. She was so happy. There was no worry about the future—only joy. Her short little legs and tiny shoes radiated innocence. What did I know now that I wished that charming child could know and grow up with?

I told the baby me in my mind's eye: "You can express your thoughts, feelings, and opinions and still be loved and understood. Accept your parents' limitations. They were doing the best they could, given who they are. You can make your life full, rich, and extraordinary. When confronted by angry, aggressive people, stand up for yourself with confidence, integrity, and assurance. You can take care of yourself, but if you need help, don't be afraid to ask for it."

Carol had been silent, waiting for me to indicate that I was finished. I raised my forefinger, and her disembodied voice floated over the digital mist of electronic background chords.

"Now that child can grow up confident, safe, secure, and strong. All the changes that have happened to her in this moment are now occurring within you. Changing the baby you changes the adult you. All the negative programs have been removed. Only the helpful, truthful programs remain. Your subconscious mind is listening to and replacing the old information. You now know what you wish you had known then."

Her voice was soft and reassuring as she spoke throughout the half hour without hesitation, stammering, or correcting words. The input was all positive.

She was so nice to me that I became sad. Therapy had been about my mistakes and screwups. Here was kindness and support. It hadn't registered that I should be directing love toward myself.

CHAPTER 39
TREMOLO

The summer was heating up. The humidity rolled off the ocean and into my un-air-conditioned house. I taught fewer students. My motivation to practice dissolved. However, I remained fixed on my goal: peace, serenity, equilibrium, calm. Especially calm.

In conversation with a customer buying a beautiful viola for her college-bound daughter, I learned about a Chinese herbalist who had worked miracles with a friend of hers. I was open to all alternative options, took down the herbalist's name, called, and made an appointment. Her exam was similar to the acupuncturist's: tongue, pulse on wrists, pinching feet.

"Tell me about your diet." Her tone carried an edge of aggression.

"I eat really healthily."

"What does that mean?" She tapped her pen several times on the notepad.

I thought back to breakfast and lunch. "Well, fruit, salad, fish, chicken, rarely meat, and hardly ever dessert."

She cleared her throat. "How much do you weigh?"

I admitted to a scrawny ninety-five-ish pounds.

"What do your feces look like? Dry, wet, regular?"

Woah! I wasn't prepared for that question. I was used to picking up after Shiraz, but myself?

"Just as I thought." She looked over the top of her readers. "Your yin and yang are out of balance. You are massively yin [female] deficient. It is essential to change your diet. I recommend you eat only red meat, especially game. Cut out all raw vegetables and cook everything. Root vegetables, such as beets, carrots, potatoes, parsnips, and onions, have yin energy. No more coffee. No more chicken or fish. No more salad. Forget fruit. Go to bed earlier. You stay up way too late and don't get enough sleep.

"After I finish analyzing your profile, I'll order herbs from my supplier in Chinatown." Her tone was commanding—no room for discussion. "Take five pills a day with plenty of water."

I stood, and we shook hands as I left. Walking out to the car, I thought: *Is she crazy?* Lacking yin or not, no way was I going to follow that advice. I loved my predominantly plant-based diet.

The herbs arrived a week later, embalmed in horse-sized capsules. Through the transparent skin of the medication, I saw a concentrated quagmire of broken sticks, dried-out grass clippings, and brown seed pods. Yum. Unfortunately, their only impact was on my wallet. Maybe I wasn't open enough. Maybe I'd "man-upped" so often I was repressing my femininity. My path was to experiment and learn. What I had done in the past had not worked for me. I was now aware of other options and determined not to judge before I tried the alternatives.

⁂

Summer became fall. After months of indecision, I decided that rather than call, write, or blow her off, I'd say goodbye and thank Naomi face-to-face. She represented an authority figure, and I wanted to prove to myself that I had a backbone. Also, as a matter of personal ethics, I needed to conclude this relationship with integrity. After all, I had seen her twice a week for over two years. I called and booked the appointment.

At breakfast on the day of the send-off, my anxiety sparked dread. What if she accused me of being a quitter? Would I backpedal against my better judgment?

No. I could do it.

As if no time had passed, driving west past exit 59 on the Long Island Expressway sent adrenaline surging through my legs. I reprimanded myself: *Stop it right now!*

I arrived early and parked under the giant oak with time to regroup. Closing my eyes, I straightened my back, rested my palms on my thighs, and slowly breathed in through my nostrils. Very slowly.

After years of not breathing and taking "lessons" on breathing, I could now take deep, relaxing breaths. The air seemed to fill my lungs all the way down to my hips. As I exhaled, I felt and "saw" a golden cloud of peace permeating my body from my head down through my neck, shoulders, torso, hips, legs, and into my feet. I tried to clear my mind and sighed. I was still nervous as hell. *Oh well. Not there yet.* Remaining calm was as unlikely as Klaus coming back to life so I could kill him.

Naomi emerged from her lair. She looked good, trimmer than three months earlier.

"Welcome back," she said, neutrally.

We took our respective seats. The clocks were still ticking, the white noise still hissing. I tried to ease into the session with a cursory description of the African adventure. I wanted my money's worth—and to postpone the fatal blow. She didn't fall for the bait and simply sat there. I put my hands under my thighs to keep them from shaking and changed gears.

"In my rampage to cull and clear my history, I found my diary from 1987 when I had returned to the United States from

South Africa and was waiting for Klaus. He'd promised to come find me when he was divorced."

"That's gold." Her face brightened with approval.

"Yes, maybe." I wasn't sure. "The entries revolved around a main theme: if he loves me, why doesn't he understand what he is doing to me? From the tenor of the text, it is obvious that I didn't believe his excuses but was so insecure and immature that I was unable to break the cord."

Though I couldn't meet her eyes, I soldiered on with my confession. "Occasionally he threw me a bone, which I clung to with a determined urgency." I glanced up, hoping for an illuminating nugget, but as usual the analyst's face was blank, passive.

Silence. The ball was still in my court. Thankfully, I had my agenda ready, and we reviewed some of the same issues: being hard on myself, my relentless pushing, fear of confrontation, my inability to say no, empathy for others to the point of disregarding myself—the same issues I'd been addressing in hypnotherapy. *How can she stand all this repetition?*

I guess she couldn't, because she said, "We'll continue next time."

"That is why I came today," I blundered on. "I had to tell you in person that I won't be back."

I had done it. The deed was done. To my utter astonishment, Naomi tried to make me feel better by saying I shouldn't feel bad.

I left the office for the last time, feeling sick. The session was much harder than I had anticipated, maybe because she had been so nice. I felt no sense of relief. Stopping therapy was for the best, but I experienced the same frustration and sense of inadequacy as always.

··

In my home office, I opened my email. Almost buried in the electronic detritus was a message from Alexandra. Months ago, the court action had concluded, and the documents were finally signed. She expressed a desire to open the channels of communication since "this is Johannesburg, and you never know when your life may abruptly be snuffed out." She would feel bad going to her grave without at least trying to contact me.

The family had almost cleaned me out financially, which was nothing compared to the emotional strain. She had promised to deliver a painting I had commissioned from her and paid for. To me, its delivery was the only starting point for a reconciliation. I decided to disregard the email. Enough betrayal.

I gazed out the window. After three years of burning mountains of debris and hauling discarded building material to the landfill, I had finally hired a bulldozer to dig a hole and bury the last of Klaus's pile. Pim had cleared many of the trees. The entrance was taking on a clean, fresh look. I sat back and experienced a frisson of liberation.

CHAPTER 40
SOTTO VOCE

As my environment cleared, so did my head. All that reading, journaling, exercise, and hypnotherapy seemed to be paying off. The regular meditation practice soothed my nervous system bit by bit. My mind slowed down, my ego loosened its powerful grip, and some of the barbs in my personality eased. I became less demanding, aggressive, impatient, critical, and judgmental.

Instead of my habitual automatic defensiveness to anything my parents said, I found myself first thinking and assessing my words. I no longer needed to prove myself, argue, or view them so harshly. Situations and conversations became opportunities to be kinder and more accepting. Bit by bit, I climbed out of the hole I'd fallen into and even felt a spark of inspiration from my modicum of psychological success.

Staying on task had been my everyday mode of operation since my childhood, and the work with Carol was no exception. She had an arsenal of practical therapeutic techniques. Since she recorded the sessions, I could listen and work daily with the recordings.

We had tackled anxiety, which eased as I noted the triggers, but after several months, she suggested another approach: eliminating negative feelings.

"The subconscious mind communicates what it wants or needs through feelings, but feelings are like smoke: you can't get your hands around them. So, we use the imagination to apply physical properties to the emotions, giving them size, color, shape, weight, texture, temperature, and so on. You turn a problem or negative behavior into an object, which you can then expel."

For weeks, I envisaged my sadness, anger, fear of confrontation, and feelings of uselessness due to self-delusion. Then I moved on to the poison gnawing through me from Klaus's family, financial betrayal, and bigamy.

After several weeks, Carol again changed direction—to forgiving. We had been talking for some minutes when she observed, "You are loving to everyone but yourself. Perhaps you are trying too hard to find equilibrium, balance, and peace. You are fighting the natural process. It's time to treat yourself as well as you treat others."

"Yes." I wasn't sure. "But I still can't accept my part in all the drama I lived through. I must be accountable for my actions."

She was silent in a way that radiated love and kindness. Her expression was nonjudgmental. "That may be so, but you must let go of taking responsibility for Klaus's actions. It's time to forgive yourself. Are you really so bad? Can you afford to carry this weight around any longer?"

She dropped her nubby pencil. "Think of times with Klaus when you excused and rationalized his lies, kept your mouth shut, buried your feelings, and consequently felt ashamed because you thought you could have somehow brought about a different outcome. I want you to remember the times when there might have been opportunities for a turning point."

A spotlight centered on my heart. I began shakily. "Okay then. I'll try. My first mistake was not asking him if he was married. I assumed he was single because he was always alone. He didn't wear a ring, and we spent so much time together. But perhaps a bigger mistake was not calling it quits when Ute answered the door in Nature's Valley and said she was Mrs. von Österberg. The truth was apparent, yet I chose to excuse it."

I lifted my eyes from my lap, hardly believing I'd so candidly admitted my mistakes. Pretending to be invincible was my armor. I pressed my hands to my thighs, hoping the quivering wasn't too noticeable. Maybe I could take a bathroom break.

No, I can do it.

"I put up with Ute threatening to sue me, smashing my windows, and verbally assaulting me in public. I finally got fed up, quit my job, left South Africa, then stupidly waited nine months for Klaus, during which time he swore at least a hundred times that he was divorced and would be 'coming the next week.' I believed his elaborate stories about building a nuclear bomb for the Israelis and being under house arrest. When he finally came, he never showed me the divorce papers, because 'the marriage had been too painful.'"

"All right then. Let's get to work." Carol peered over her reading glasses, which were back in position, before again removing and placing them on her desk. "Are you okay? Can I get you some water?"

My heart was racing, and my breath had quickened. This felt different from a panic attack. Something inside had shattered, exposing a small, dark piece of me. Maybe it was weakness. I wasn't sure I liked it. For decades, I had swept my feelings, inadequacies, and vulnerability under a carpet. Carol had asked me to pick up an edge and peer under a corner.

"No, thank you. I'm okay." I took a breath and scraped my hands down my thighs. "There's one more point. We drove to

Virginia to get married, and he bailed, but I still didn't leave. Deep down I knew he was dishonest, but I couldn't face the prospect of starting my life over without him. I was in love."

I felt lightheaded, like the gravity in the room had weakened.

Carol said, "You are experiencing a great deal of shame, which is hugely disempowering. It's not necessary to hold on to these thoughts. They simply no longer serve you. Let's start with forgiving yourself one aspect at a time, like being a young, immature twenty-six-year-old. You must forgive yourself before it is possible to forgive anyone else."

Is that true? I wondered.

Over the next few months, we met twice a month, and she gave me exercises of release to purge my mind of built-up fear and guilt. It couldn't hurt to say nice things to myself, but try as I might, a part of me felt I was letting her down because my progress was so slow. Each time I walked through her door, she asked me if I felt better. I invariably replied, "Still working on it."

Several months later, after I had diligently envisaged forgiving myself as per Carol's instructions, we had a session that jolted me into full realization of my lack of self-acceptance. She suggested that we try age regression since I had almost no memory of my childhood. (Naomi had noted that my memory had suppressed the bad and taken out the good with it.)

Carol induced the trance, her voice smooth and creamy as vanilla ice cream. Systematically, we went back in time. The calendar and numbers passed in my mind's eye—my forties, thirties, college, high school. Then I "saw" myself in kindergarten. It was rest time, and all the children were lying on mats on the floor. My father was coming to play the violin for the class after our nap. I was so excited that I wet myself. At home, I had always been spanked for accidents. I was embarrassed and terrified of the punishment I would receive at school, and then again at home.

Carol's ice cream voice floated into my trance state.

"Now cradle that little you and tell her she is safe, cared for, and that you understand. Tell her she will grow up to be a successful, productive, and worthy woman. Tell her how good she is and that you love her. Hold and hug that sweet child."

My body started shaking violently. My thighs calcified, stubby nails dug into my palms, my throat gnarled, and sweat mushroomed. *No way! Completely impossible. I can't do it!*

"No. She is a bad girl. I can't love her. She is bad, bad, bad." I was gasping for air.

Carol counted to five, telling me that when I emerged from hypnosis, I would feel happy, relaxed, and calm. I opened my eyes. We stared at each other in stunned silence.

I knew then and there that I had serious work to do. I hadn't realized how much I disliked and could not accept myself. Was she helping me out of my self-inflicted prison of shame, or had I escaped only to run into another set of barriers: feeling unworthy?

CHAPTER 41
SUSPENSION

Because of my background as a regular contributor to the London-based magazine *The Strad*, I was contacted by an importer and distributor of string instruments, bows, and supplies. The Long Island–based company was expanding, and its marketing director asked me to do some educational writing for their website. Grace and I met professionally several times, liked each other, and became friends.

One evening over Chinese food, I told her about Klaus.

"You've got to see my psychic!" Grace almost dropped her cup of jasmine tea in her excitement.

I wiped soy sauce from my lips with my napkin. "You're kidding me, right?"

"Absolutely not. Karen is the real deal—totally intuitive. She'll tell you all about your past lives with Klaus and why that happened to you."

"And I want to do this . . . because?"

Her grin was puckish. "Obviously, you're still suffering, and she'll help you."

As Grace plied me with anecdotes, stories, and woo-woo, I recalled a fabulous travel memoir I had read by the Italian journalist Tiziano Terzani: *A Fortune-Teller Told Me*. For decades, he had reported on wars, politics, and mayhem as the Far East correspondent for the German news publication *Der Spiegel*, the US equivalent to *Time* magazine. While living in Hong Kong, a friend coerced him into visiting a fortune teller to see if it was an auspicious day for gambling in Macau (or Macao), "the Las Vegas of Asia."

This was 1976. The seer, an old Chinese man, told Terzani that for the entire year of 1993, he must never travel by air, or he would run the risk of accidental death. Impossible, ridiculous rubbish. His job required him to cover Vietnam, Laos, Thailand, Burma (now Myanmar), Malaysia, India, and China.

However, as the clock struck twelve on New Year's Day seventeen years later, he decided not to tempt fate. So, for the entire year, he only traveled by foot, bus, car, train, and ship. His account records the people and events on which he reported, his travel adventures, and the fortune tellers he encountered along the way. In every country, he made a point to have his cards, tea leaves, and palm read, his horoscope charted, and to participate in other exotic Eastern divination techniques. In fact, a helicopter he would have taken that year crashed. There were no survivors.

Grace and I cracked open our fortune cookies. Mine read: You are loved. I decided to let her advice vegetate. Several days later I thought, *Why not?*

Karen the psychic proposed that we meet at a hotel off the Long Island Expressway. I was early and self-consciously pretended to know what I was doing there. A beautiful, tan blond surged toward me, her hand extended.

"Hi! I'm Karen. Let's go sit at that table over there."

We settled across from one another. A TV mounted on the wall was silent, but the news ticker streaming along the screen's bottom was distracting. She stood and nonchalantly flicked it off. I had barely introduced myself when she turned back to me.

"As I came in, I saw bigamy. Is that you?"

What? Karen knew nothing about me; I had contacted her without Grace's knowledge. I was struck dumb as she continued.

"I see it like a movie. You are an important woman in Africa in charge of lots and lots of land and a large staff. You must be taking care of it for your father. I don't think you could have owned it as a woman. You are with a group of your staff, who all carry rifles for protection."

My hands turned icy cold. "Am I White or Black?"

"That hadn't occurred to me. You are White and have many Black attendants."

She seemed to be reading something over my left shoulder.

"There is a young White man, twenty-five or thirty years old, dressed in old, worn-out clothes, like a vagabond, who wants to help you manage the properties. His humble demeanor is attractive, but in fact he is very devious and lies as a ploy to get your sympathy. He gains your trust, but without your knowledge he is poaching and killing the wildlife and confiscating your lands, which are so vast that it is impossible for you to be everywhere at once."

Karen's eyes skittered back and forth. "Slowly you begin to realize that there are problems on the estate and become suspicious but pretend everything is okay. Your distrust becomes so palpable that even your sister says you've changed. You work out this man's con because his accent is high-class British, even though he's pretending to be poor."

I was so mesmerized that I was almost in a trance, watching her eyes dart around an unseen point. She continued, "Your love and respect for wildlife is greater than that for humans. Elephants and rhinos need protection against unscrupulous hunters. You know that this man is destroying and profiting from killing hundreds of animals on your lands.

"In a confrontation, you shoot him with your rifle. There isn't time to have him arrested, tried, and sentenced. It is a visceral response when you pull the trigger. Taking the life of one man saved scores of beautiful African creatures. But for the rest of your life, you asked yourself if you had done the right thing. You often pondered what would have happened to that man if you hadn't killed him."

Even though she was still, Karen radiated the intensity of a dervish. Sparks flew in all directions. Her brown eyes had become fireworks.

"That man was your husband in this life. He loved you but was so burdened by layers of negative pathology that he couldn't escape and break away from his past and the habits of his personality. You must understand that he was doing his best, and so were you."

She had hardly taken a breath. Neither had I. What was I to make of this? *In another life, I killed Klaus?* And supposedly in this life, I had faced and endured the consequences of actions and decisions made during another incarnation. Karma, okay, but this was way too intense—even radical—for me to assimilate. As I perched on my chair, feeling like a deer trapped in headlights, Karen gently touched my arm.

"Your husband was so insecure that he couldn't trust himself to show you, and the world, who he really was. He was so damaged in his childhood that he couldn't love himself. He had to make up stories to bolster his persona. Your response was to give more than anyone else ever would have, because of your past life together and the imprint of regret. If his early years hadn't been so lonely and barren, he could have learned to love himself and others. He was doing the best he could."

What does she mean, the best he could? The best he could do was to say how much he loved me, yet lie and steal from me? The best he could do was to abandon his family and promise he would send for them while he was living with me? His best was staying married to someone else who, after his death, sued me? His best was fraud?

But more to the point, this smart, attractive, charismatic, put-together woman was talking about reincarnation. Under hypnosis, I had done age regression with Carol, and she talked about trying past-life regression, but I had always believed dead was dead.

Karen clarified. "By best, I mean he couldn't do better because of his level of awareness. He was so burdened by layers upon layer piled on by childhood experiences and society's expectations that his true soul couldn't shine through."

At this point, my cognitive abilities jammed, like the episodes I'd had with Sheryl, my attorney, when I could no longer take in everything she was saying.

"What do you mean by aware?" I stammered.

Karen brushed the bangs from her forehead. "Your husband was unable to anticipate and comprehend the consequences of his actions, which would have allowed him to break away from the encumbrances of his upbringing. I'm referring to his level of consciousness."

I considered my decisions and behavior that had led to the last six or seven years of anguish. "You make it sound like we don't have a choice. Where does our ability to choose begin and end? I'm hearing you say that the role I played with Klaus was in some way predestined. I don't get it."

She shook her head. "We always have a choice and free will. You could have chosen at any point to walk away, but you didn't. You decided to use this relationship as an opportunity for your soul to grow."

Is she saying that betrayal was on my agenda for this life and the best I could do was stay with Klaus?

Karen continued, "We are given opportunities for awakening. If you are unable to open and integrate those discoveries, then your soul's desire for those awakenings will stay with you in subsequent lifetimes. I'm not talking about karmic debt, which for me is not valid. In this life, you were given the chance to evolve, and you took it. We are eternal beings having a physical experience here on earth. There is much more to our existence and perception than our five senses allow us to experience."

While she talked at warp speed, I analyzed the scenario. If what Klaus did to me was out of my control because of something "I" did in another life, maybe I didn't have to take on so much responsibility and could forgive myself.

Dusk settled, and the lights in the lobby began flicking on. Karen glanced at her phone. "I see endless possibilities for you. This is a period of assimilation. You didn't lose those years you view as difficult, even miserable. Time is never wasted, nor energy lost. Your soul wanted to use this opportunity to give yourself a chance to ascend to a higher level. If you are really honest in evaluating what you went through, and how you have been changed by it, I think you will find that positive results came out of your ordeal. I predict those optimistic outcomes will continue to emerge."

After the session, we walked our separate ways out of the hotel. I went to my car and unlocked the door. I was in no state to drive yet, so I sat behind the wheel and took a few calming breaths.

It didn't seem to matter whether the scene she had painted was true. Perhaps, this concept of actions in another life could release me from my pain. Perhaps, I could finally begin to let go of the self-blame and need to atone.

Karen had given me a new perspective, and I wanted to try it out.

CHAPTER 42
RUHIG

My path to happiness was a steep climb out of a deep hole. I clawed up the cliff face inch by inch with my stubby, callused fingertips. Often the trail leading away from grief, betrayal, and loss felt like the proverbial one step up and two steps down as I fell back into darkness. Maintaining a steady pace skyward proved impossible.

Rather than focus on the difficulties of the ascent, I decided to enjoy the rewards from my mountaintop, surveying the chasm below and all the lessons the journey taught me: expanding self-awareness, self-reliance, and self-assurance. The view of the future included more mountains to climb, but I knew the vistas would continue to foster my growth.

I can't imagine what direction my life would have taken if I'd never met or gotten involved with Klaus. Instead of being swallowed by the pain of the experience, I choose to align with growth and dedication to healing. Today, I have evolved far beyond what my trajectory would have been had his bigamy and financial betrayal not forced me to examine my actions and beliefs.

And like my other biggest passions—music, art, and literature—I will never reach the end of the quest. There is always more to learn, more to release, and more to heal.

I now know that forgiving liberates the forgiver, though sometimes I think there is nothing to forgive. If Klaus and I were drawn together in this lifetime to repair wounds from former incarnations and to aim for higher awareness, then I am acting out my purpose.

Twice a day for over a decade, I have continued my practice of quiet breathing, emptying my mind. One morning in meditation, while in a trance state, I heard an unbidden voice. It spoke loud and clear: *"Forgive Klaus."* I suddenly knew I no longer wanted to be rooted in the past. It was time to unbind the ties and find freedom in the present moment. My higher self was instructing me, and I listened.

I had previously learned a technique of forgiveness and in that moment used it. I imagined an altar of light (which looked a lot like my dining room table). On that altar, I envisaged Klaus. I silently spoke to his image in my head:

"I forgive you, Klaus. Though you said you loved me, what you did was not right, honest, caring, or loving. I do not condone your behavior or actions, but I let go of your negative hold on my psyche. I was mired in the fallout of your lies and deception, which was compounded by your family's attack on me.

"You were a casualty of your murdering, Nazi father and negligent mother and were not a whole human being. You were tethered by your lack of empathy and integrity and need to control. We were drawn together for the purpose of elevating one another in this life and to work through past karma. Your final words to me were, 'Here is where we call it quits.' I say the same to you and release you. I choose to move on and be free. You gave me the opportunity to advance my spirit and let go of anger. I unbind all our contracts, past and future."

With those thoughts, his image dissolved.

Next on my forgiveness list was Klaus's family, whom he had grotesquely mistreated. Since Klaus was not alive to blame, they targeted their anger, hostility, and revenge on me. They did what they felt compelled to do.

Forgiveness and compassion are close cousins. Understanding someone's history helps cultivate compassion, while angry confrontation and retaliatory action can dampen, if not obliterate, that feeling. I strive to eliminate judgment and strengthen my sense of compassion by replacing negative thoughts with uplifting ones: *Maybe this person or situation is my teacher. What can I learn? How can I grow?*

Everyone is worthy. Who am I to judge the path of another? Judgment is my ego's way of conning the mind into believing that I am "better than" and "more loveable than" another person. It is all too easy to fall into the trap of judging on appearance, ethnicity, religion, race, sexuality, the quality of others' lives, professions, income, marital status, number of children, clothes, cars, vacations, homes. And, of course, the culture and background of my upbringing have worn deep impressions in my subconscious. However, I want to treat every individual as I want to be treated.

Being kind to oneself has no downside. We've likely all been told by parents, teachers, and friends that we need to improve and must act and behave in a prescribed manner. So often criticism leads to feelings of inferiority and insignificance. My parents did the best they could, but my upbringing left scars that are my responsibility to understand and heal.

While I was in analysis and in the grip of the legal system, as an exercise I folded a piece of paper in half with headers on each side. On the right I wrote, WHAT I LIKE ABOUT MYSELF. On the left, WHAT I DON'T LIKE. The right side was completely blank. I couldn't think of one good quality. This process was revealing and very sad. I had work to do.

Thoughts beget reality. I become my outlook and materialize my goals and dreams. Everything begins with an idea. Emily Dickinson seems to agree when she penned in 1862:

A word is dead, when it is said
Some say –
I say it just begins to live
That day

From *The Dhammapada*, a collection of the Buddha's teachings, I have taken the following to heart:

Our life is shaped by our mind; we become what we think.

All that we are is the result of what we have thought.

We are made of our thoughts; we are molded by our thoughts.

I have learned that my state of being is pulled in the direction of the words reverberating in my mind. Negativity brings me down, while gratitude and appreciation uplift. I can't persuade others to act as I desire or always get my way, but I am learning to control my attitude and perspective.

Negative thoughts are a barrier to contentment and a magnet for like thoughts. When I think bad things about myself, the subconscious believes them. Pessimism creates a vicious circle. Gossip inspires gossip. Complaints fuel more complaints. Horror stories are meant to be topped.

I am no longer imprisoned in a cage of fear: fear to leave, fear of lack, fear of seeming less than in others' eyes, fear of pain and hurt. As negative thoughts recede and dissolve, pleasure grows. The practice of watching my thoughts and slowing down has (mostly) allowed me to catch my ego and recognize its insidious and destructive demands.

Several years ago, when it was time to plan a new season of my concert series, I felt overwhelmed. Planning was a massive juggling act of deciding on the programs, organizing the venue, booking the musicians, balancing budgets, designing publicity, and sending out mailings, subscriptions, and tickets, and applying for grants. Additionally, I had to practice my part, get the piano tuned, and set up the concert space. I had very little help. The whole process felt like an onerous obligation.

I went for a walk on the beach and, while gazing at the ocean, said to myself, *If you aren't enjoying playing, stop. No one is making you do it.* With that stroke of insight, I understood that I love bringing chamber music to my community, and their enthusiastic response is enormously gratifying. That realization tripped a switch. The responsibility became a pleasure.

Expressing love is the gold standard of spiritual and emotional development. I am still working on softening my heart, and I trust there is a plan bigger than mine. I am drawn to the idea of karma (cause and effect) and reincarnation, not as an excuse for my behavior but as a reminder that I have the privilege to understand the universal laws of love: honesty, integrity, creativity, kindness, empathy, compassion, generosity, gratitude, nonviolence, sympathy, and truth. Don't forget joy!

There was a purpose in my pain and suffering—to those years of uncontrollable anxiety, worry, depression, guilt, and shame. Peace and contentment were the gifts. If I can come out the other side happier and content, anything is possible.

POSTLUDE
FUNERAL

Some years ago, my "adopted" mother, Anne, whose home I had lived in before moving to South Africa, started showing disturbing signs of forgetfulness and seemed to be losing control of her bodily functions.

I first met her while still in high school, at a summer chamber music camp in Taos, New Mexico; she was one of my coaches. I was drawn to her wit, artistry, sense of fun, and razor-sharp mind. Several years later, on her suggestion, I transferred from the University of Texas to the Hartt School of Music in Connecticut, where she was a piano professor. Her mentorship evolved into a profound friendship.

Upon hearing her troubles, I drove up to Massachusetts, where she lived at the time, and met her other "adopted" daughter, Ileana, a gorgeous Cuban pianist who had studied with both Anne and her husband, Raymond Hanson. Ileana and I were "sistas."

The scene we found was not encouraging. Anne had gained thirty pounds, could hardly walk, and her speech was slurred. She had been a gourmet cook, but Ileana and I prepared dinner since she was incapable. Though the meal was seasoned and spicy, Anne poured a small Himalaya of salt on her food. Obviously, her taste was shot. Only four weeks before, she had played a two-hour solo piano recital from memory in Washington, DC. The concert was followed by a standing ovation and several encores.

All too soon, we learned the cause. A nurse rushed her to the hospital in Springfield the following morning for tests. That afternoon, Mother's Day, the results revealed glioblastoma—the most virulent and lethal form of malignant brain cancer.

The following day was Anne's birthday. During a three-hour operation, the surgeon removed a tumor the size of an orange from her brain. Unfortunately, he was unable to extract all the tentacles and smaller masses. Chemo and radiation followed, which prolonged (what seemed to me) her agony. Then my mentor and soulmate of forty-one years was gone.

Anne had been joyous, vibrant, generous, loving, and passionate about music, people, fun, travel, and knowledge. I will continue singing her song forever. My belief that we will be reunited has stanched the pain, though I miss her every day. Ileana and I often "cook" together via telephone and remark how much Anne would enjoy the meals we make.

A few months after her cremation, Anne's birth daughter, Cecile, called, and I agreed to visit her stepfather, Anne's husband. At ninety-six, Mr. Hanson was blind and confined to a wheelchair. He spent every waking minute listening to Anne's solo recordings or the two-piano works they had played together. I needed to stay in touch.

The occasion was somber yet relaxed. Anne was not with us in the flesh, but her spirit lingered everywhere. During a quiet moment away from her father, Cecile handed me a bag of light-gray powder.

"Mama would have wanted to be with you. I hope you can find a special place for her."

I took the precious bundle of ashes back home to Long Island. At my favorite nursery, a vigorous climbing rose called to me. It would look fabulous outside my dining room, where I could visually connect with my friend every day.

Buoyant clouds were scattered amid the glazed Della Robbia–blue sky. The bright-green foliage of spring was finally erasing the gray brown of March. Hope germinated the air. I felt alive and exuberant, knowing my friend was close to me. I positioned the chair on the bluestone path, then realized the soil was too soft for my cello's endpin. I went back inside for the rock stop and music stand. My gardener had dug a hole, which he was filling with water.

"Thank you. That's enough, Ronald. We don't want her to drown, and I want to talk with Anne."

I called out, my face breathing in the sun and salt of the nearby sea. "Anne, can you hear me? Are you listening, Anne? I know you're here."

I sprinkled the ashes into the dirty puddle and read Emily Dickinson's words:

> Unable are the Loved to die
> For Love is Immortality,
> Nay, it is Deity -
>
> Unable they that love - to die
> For Love reforms Vitality
>
> Into Divinity.

"Ronald, you can plant that rose while I play." I looked up from the poem and opened the score of the Bach Cello Suites. "Anne, do you want a happy or a sad one?"

Ronald still held the hose over the hole. He was laughing.

"Stop laughing, Ronald. And turn off the water. This is serious. Anne says she wants a happy one."

I played the sunny Suite no. 3 in C major, all the while thinking: *Wow, I sound pretty good. I bet Anne is enjoying this.* Seven movements later, I put down my bow and turned the page to the next suite. The E-flat major is much more difficult and wasn't really in my fingers.

"Anne, how about another one? Maybe the fourth?"

Gosh—so many fumbles, and I was horribly out of tune and missing notes. Now I was playing like a pig.

"Sorry, Anne! I sound really bad."

Fun, joy, and hope were in the air and in my heart.

ACKNOWLEDGMENTS

Where can I begin when I have so many to whom I am grateful for helping me realize the sharing of this story? I'll start with the most recent players—those who facilitated turning my beginner efforts into the polished product you are now reading. Three freelance editors reeled me in, then squeezed a more expansive yet contained version out of me. Nancy Mendez-Booth inspired my first efforts, Alexandra Shelley took me through the equivalent of an MFA, and Ronit Wagman forced me to feel the pain and write it down.

After the guidance of these sensitive and gifted women, my dear friend Jennifer Vorbach connected me with Barbara Donsky, who twisted the arm of Nancy Rosenfeld. Nancy became my trusted and dogged agent. Through Nancy's expertise, connections, and insights into the labyrinthine workings of the publishing world, I garnered a contract with Köehler Books. The Köehler team: John Köehler, publisher; Catherine Herold, graphic designer; and Hannah Woodlan, editor, have held my hand every step of the way—and I needed it. Thank you all!

I must thank those whose generosity of contacts and open sharing of ideas prodded me through myriad troughs: Trish Hall, Tricia Foley, Andrea Lippke, and Kate Bernstein.

My support team has included emotional, physical, and spiritual healers. I credit Carol Denicker for "saving my life."

She opened a world of limitless potential, which included the tireless support of Karen Garvey, Raymond Henriques, Gloria Karpinski, Don Carey-Shaw, Anne-Marie Dobek-Lantiqua, Elizabeth Karlson, April Lindevald, Lynn Eastman, and Sandra Couts. I must have some good karma to have found them.

My writing process was looong and arduous. Thankfully, I was able to call on Carol A. Hess, Steven McCloskey, Jim Bonomo, Anita Comtois, Jennifer Vorbach, and Sarah Cristobal. Their expertise and enthusiasm were invaluable.

Long-suffering friends! Thank you for listening to my woes and still putting up with me. Much gratitude to Ada Hasloecher, Marilyn Lehman, Deborah Birnbaum, Pim Broere, John Kocay, John De Stefano, Francisco Costa, Cara Mia Antonello, Selma Gokcen, Marcus Henkel, Peter Kingan, Wolfgang Lehner, Grace Newman, Irit and David Oshry, Naho and Alberto Parrini, Joanna Pieters, Sheryl Randazzo, Jonathan Reed, Naomi Sadler, Ileana and David Shaner, Richard Pearson Thomas, and Mark van Wagner.

A special thanks and hugs to my goddesses: Angela Marschall, Beverly Allan Starke, Tonja Pulfer, and Alissa Fishbane.

Christopher Gallagher deserves a Purple Heart for patience as he step-by-step taught me social media. I wish everyone could work with such a talented and calm mentor.

My final, most profound, and deepest appreciation goes to my mother, Nelta; my brother, Darrel; my sister-in-law, Judy; and my niece, Chelsea. Words cannot express my gratitude. Hopefully, my love can.

www.ingramcontent.com/pod-product-compliance
Lightning Source LLC
LaVergne TN
LVHW041743060526
838201LV00046B/896